JUDAISM

Rabbi Dr Isidore Epstein was educated at Jews' College in London – the Jewish theological seminary of the British Commonwealth – and the University of London where he obtained the B.A. Hons. Degree in Semitics (First Class) and the Doctorates of Philosophy and of Literature. After serving for some years as Rabbi of the Middlesbrough Hebrew Congregation, he was appointed in 1928 Lecturer in Semitic Language at Jews' College and became its Principal in 1945. A prolific author, he edited the thirty-six volumes of the Soncino edition of *The Babylonian Talmud in English*, and has written monographs on Jewish medieval scholars, as well as significant works on Jewish religion and ethics of which *Judaism*, in the Epworth Press Great Religions of the East series, is among the earliest, and *The Faith of Judaism* and *Step by Step in the Jewish Religion*, a book for young readers, are the latest. His other writings include contributions to the 1950 edition of *Chambers' Encyclopaedia*, of which he was the Advisory Editor for the Jewish sections, and to the *Encyclopaedia Britannica* (1958 Edition). Dr Epstein died in 1962.

JUDAISM

A HISTORICAL PRESENTATION

Isidore Epstein

PENGUIN BOOKS

PENGUIN BOOKS

Published by the Penguin Group
27 Wrights Lane, London W8 5TZ, England
Viking Penguin Inc., 40 West 23rd Street, New York, New York 10010, USA
Penguin Books Australia Ltd, Ringwood, Victoria, Australia
Penguin Books Canada Ltd, 2801 John Street, Markham, Ontario, Canada L3R 1B4
Penguin Books (NZ) Ltd, 182–190 Wairau Road, Auckland 10, New Zealand

Penguin Books Ltd, Registered Offices: Harmondsworth, Middlesex, England

First published 1959
17 19 20 18

Copyright © Isidore Epstein, 1959
All rights reserved

Set, printed and bound in Great Britain by
Cox & Wyman Ltd, Reading
Set in Monotype Imprint

CONTENTS

PREFACE

THIS book is by no means a history of the Jews; neither is it an account of the contributions of the Jewish people to human civilization and progress. It is essentially concerned with Judaism as a religious and a distinctive way of life which it seeks to present against a background of 4,000 years of Jewish history from Bible times to the establishment of the modern State of Israel in our own days. Beginning with the migration of Abraham, the founder of the Jewish nation, from Ur of the Chaldees, the book proceeds to trace the origin, growth and steady development of Judaism – its beliefs, its doctrines – ethical and religious – its hopes, aspirations, and ideals. It also discusses the spiritual movements and influences which have helped to shape the Jewish religion in its varied manifestations, and describes the contributions made in turn by a succession of prophets, legislators, priests, psalmists, sages, rabbis, philosophers, and mystics, whereby Judaism came to be the dynamic religious force it is today.

The book makes no pretensions to being exhaustive either in scope or treatment. Considerations of space have crowded out episodes and names which would otherwise have figured in the account; but even within these limitations it is hoped that the reader will gain a glimpse into the unique panorama of Judaism, with its vast treasure-house of thought and action, which has succeeded in registering itself in the religion, law, and morals of more than one civilization.

The author is only too conscious that not all his assertions and assessments of the various events, situations, and personages that pass under review in these pages will command the assent of all readers. The traditional standpoint, which he frankly avows, determined in particular his interpretation of the biblical period as well as his appraisal of the Jewish movements, ancient, medieval and modern, of which he treats in this work. At the same time he has sought to set down accurately the facts which he saw fit to select for the purposes of this work, and to be objective as far as possible in his presentation of them.

The footnotes at the end of each chapter give the references as well as additional information relevant to the context, and occasionally advance arguments in support of a view adopted in the body of the text. Yet these notes have been kept down to a minimum in order to avoid wearying the reader. A selected bibliography has also been included for the benefit of those who by reading the book may be stimulated to further study. The scriptural passages are cited according to the numeration of the Hebrew Bible, that of the Revised Version being placed within square brackets. References to tractates of the Babylonian Talmud are prefixed by the abbreviation T., and those of the Jerusalem Talmud by T.J.

I.E.

CHAPTER I

THE BEGINNINGS

HALF-WAY between Baghdad and the head of the Persian Gulf, some ten miles west of the present course of the Euphrates, where today stands the Mound of Bitumen, called by the Arabs Al-Mukayyar, lay the ancient city of Ur. With a population ranging from 250,000 to 500,000 engaged in agriculture, manufacture, and commerce, the city was the capital of the Sumerian Empire, which during the middle of the third millennium B.C., extended from Assur and Arbela to the Persian Gulf, and from the Lebanon to Susa. British excavations at Ur, directed by Sir Leonard Woolley between 1922 and 1934, have revealed to the world the high level of civilization and material culture the city enjoyed during the heyday of its existence. But this glory was not destined to last. Elamite hordes sweeping down from their mountain fastness across the Persian Gulf attacked Sumeria, and in 1960 B.C. Ur went down in disaster and shame.

A Sumerian lamentation over the fall of Ur, discovered at Nippur in 1900, describes 'the all-annihilating destruction' wrought by the invaders. The city's walls were razed to the ground, its buildings reduced to ashes, and its very gates filled with the bodies of the slain. Both weak and strong perished by famine or were overtaken in their houses by fire; whilst those who managed to survive were scattered far and wide. Families were broken up. Parents abandoned their children, and husbands their wives.[1]

Among those who escaped the cataclysm was an Aramean nomadic family, whose original home had been at Haran,[2] in north-west Mesopotamia, on the Belikhi, a tributary of the Euphrates, but who for some time, probably attracted by the prosperity of Ur, had taken up residence in that capital city. At the head of this refugee family was Terah, and back to Haran did Terah with his sons and kinsmen make his way. But he did not intend Haran to serve him for more than a mere temporary halting-place. This was a period in which the whole region was in a state of turmoil and general unsettlement. While the Elamites were reducing Sumeria from the south-east, the Amorites were overrunning it from the west, and Haran lay on the route of this westerly incursion. Faced with such conditions, Terah might well have felt the impulse to remove himself and his household as far as possible from this centre of unrest; and certainly no better refuge could be found than the secluded hill-country of central and southern Canaan. Terah, however, died in Haran, and the succession to the head-ship of the family fell naturally to Abram, his eldest son. But Abram had different ideas from his father. Terah, sharing the normal religion of his time, was a polytheist; Abram a mono-theist. Terah worshipped a congeries of idols which in all prob-ability included the moon-god, Sin, the chief deity at both Ur and Haran; Abram broke with idolatry and turned to the ser-vice of the one and only God whom he recognized as the Creator of heaven and earth.

Monotheistic beliefs and tendencies existed before Abram arrived on the scene. But these had little in common with Abram's monotheism. Unlike the deities of other religions, as for example, the Sumerian high-god Anu and the Babylonian universal-god Shamash, Abram's God was not a Nature god – a sky- or sun-god – subservient to Nature; nor was he a terri-torial god restricted to a particular locality or country. As the Creator of Heaven and earth and all that is therein, the God of Abram was independent of Nature and of any geographical limitations. Furthermore, unlike other deities, Abram's God was essentially an ethical God to whom the doing of justice and righteousness was of supreme concern.

How Abram first arrived at this conception of God – a con-ception which had been appropriately described as 'ethical monotheism' to distinguish it from all other forms of mono-theism – we are not told. Perhaps he reached it by way of speculative reason, as others have come by their own particular monotheistic conceptions, and his own innate nobility of character, as evidenced by the Biblical story, may have led him to attribute to the Deity he worshipped those very moral qualities which he strove to realize in his own life. Or, possibly the whole of his religious faith might have come to him by means of some inner illumination, a mystical experience, a revelation. In any event, his deliverance from Ur proved a turning-point in his spiritual progress. Sensitive to the Divine, he felt his escape was providential, and soon the conviction grew upon him that he had been preserved to the end that he might become the founder of a new nation – a nation which was to bring the knowledge of God to the world, and the blessing which flows from such a knowledge to all the families of the earth.

With this conviction fixed in his mind, Abram detached himself with his wife and household from the heathen environment of Haran,[3] and resumed the family trek towards Canaan interrupted by his father's death. But over and above the material motives which had determined his father's choice of that land, Canaan had a special spiritual appeal for Abram in that it was eminently suitable for the fulfilment of the destiny to which he believed himself to have been appointed. Whilst the secluded nature of the hill-country would make it possible for him to serve his God in comparative peace, the position of Canaan on the crossroads through which passed all-important trade routes of the ancient world made it a unique centre for the spreading of his new faith to a multitude of peoples.

Proceeding south along the eastern bank of the Jordan, Abram and his family crossed the river into Canaan and reached Shechem (the modern Balatah, some twenty-seven miles north of Jerusalem), where he learned in a revelation that the land he had entered and chosen as his new home was the very land which had been predetermined in the counsels of God to be given to him and his descendants.[4] Thence he moved further south through the hill-country towards the Negev, making on his way converts to his new faith. This was, indeed, something revolutionary, as the idea of converting people from evil-doing to faith in God and righteous living was entirely unknown before Abram.

Coming from the other side of the Euphrates, Abram and his family became known in their new surroundings as Hebrews, a term usually derived from a root meaning 'the other side', although the identification of this term with the roaming Habiru (or Khabiru), who made their appearance in Western Asia between *c.* 2000 and the eleventh century B.C., is not at all improbable.

After a temporary sojourn in Egypt owing to a famine in Canaan, Abram returned to the Negev and finally settled in the plain of Mamre in the neighbourhood of what later became known as Hebron. There he experienced a revelation confirming what he had divined from the very beginning that his deliverance from Ur was a special act of providence, directed towards a definite purpose: 'I am YHWH⁸ (the Lord) that brought thee out of Ur of the Chaldees to give to thee this land to inherit it' (Gen. 15. 7). This promise was ratified subsequently by a divine covenant with Abram by virtue of which he was to become the founder of a new nation, chosen by God – chosen for the sake not of domination, but of universal service. This twofold significance of the covenant – national and universal – was further enforced by the rite of circumcision which accompanied and sealed it. Primarily intended as a national mark of consecration to the service of God, the rite provided for the inclusion within its scope of all strangers who were willing to join the Abramic nation in this communion of service (Gen. 17). Furthermore, in order to emphasize the universal element in this national rite, the Patriarch's name, Abram, was changed on his circumcision to Abraham. Literally meaning 'the father of a multitude [of nations]', this new name signified that the promises under the covenant went far beyond those who were the Patriarch's physical descendants, and embraced all the families of the earth, who were to be blessed in him and in his seed.

Abraham's work for God was carried on after him by his son Isaac, and after Isaac by Jacob, with both of whom God renewed the covenant with all the promises it entailed. Jacob, after a mysterious experience of wrestling with an angel, was renamed Israel, a term denoting 'the champion of God'; and this name, essentially religious in connotation, was ultimately to replace the name Hebrew by which the descendants of the Abrahamic family were known.

Jacob had twelve sons who became the progenitors of the Twelve Tribes, who for some time constituted the people of Israel. With Joseph, one of Jacob's younger sons, the destiny of the Abrahamic family entered the arena of history. Through a combination of events and circumstances Joseph rose from slavery to become Viceroy of Egypt at the time when Egypt was under the domination of the Hyksos (Foreign Chiefs), who had made themselves masters of the country since *c.* 1730 B.C. Of north-west Semitic stock, they were closely akin to the Hebrews, and this made it possible for a Hebrew like Joseph to rise to power in the Egyptian court. Urged by famine in Canaan, his family joined him and was assigned as a place of settlement the district of Goshen near Avaris (later, Tanis), the capital of the Hyksos. The expulsion of the Hyksos invaders by Ahmose about 1580 B.C. brought about a change in the fortunes of the Hebrews who, because of their racial affinities, were suspected of Hyksos sympathies, and before long the former Viceroy's kinsmen, who in the meantime had greatly increased in number, were reduced to a slavery, which as time went on became increasingly inhuman and degrading.

The worst phase of the oppression was inaugurated by the great conqueror Thothmes III (1485–1450), who as a result of a series of brilliant campaigns extended his empire to the upper reaches of the Euphrates, and whose reign was marked by cruel forced building operations. The revolt of the Egyptian semitic subject-states which followed his death, involving the whole of Syria and Palestine, led his son and successor Amenophis II (1450–1421) to institute the most ruthless measures against the Hebrew slaves, whom their oppressors had now every reason to fear more than ever; and nothing seemed at that time to stand between them and their complete destruction.

It was at this critical moment in the history of the children of Israel that there arose for them a national liberator in the person of Moses. The adopted son of an Egyptian princess, identified by some with Hatshepsut, the sister of Thothmes III, Moses was brought up in the royal court, and thus spared the experience of slavery. But his own good fortune did not make him indifferent to the plight of his kinsmen. On the contrary, it only served to make him feel the more keenly their miseries and to embolden him to take their part against their task-masters. Soon he had to flee the country for the grazing lands of Midian where he became a shepherd. One day as he was feeding his flock in the Sinaitic wilderness he came to Mount Horeb, and there, from the wondrous spectacle of a flaming but unconsumed desert bush, he heard the voice of God bidding him go back to Egypt in order to deliver his brethren from their bondage and lead them towards the Land of Promise.

In this first divine call to Moses, God named Himself as 'the God of the Fathers, the God of Abraham, Isaac, and Jacob'. But Moses was not satisfied. He desired that God should communicate to him a name he could carry to the oppressed slaves as an assurance that He was also *their* God. The reply came (Ex. 3. 14): 'EHYeH ASHeR EHYeH' (I AM THAT I AM). This was the form of the divine name YHWH (HE IS THAT HE IS) when used by God himself, which involves the thought of God as He who is ever-present with His people, with the children as with the fathers, through all the unfolding of their history, past, present, and future.

It was this message that Moses brought to his enslaved brethren on his return to Egypt in 1448, shortly after the accession of Amenophis II. The people soon recognized the message and accepted it as authentic. It was, after all, no strange God, unknown to them, who they were now assured was about to guide history on their behalf, but the God YHWH, the covenant-God of the patriarchs. The ruling Pharaoh, however, still needed to be convinced, and after a series of divine visitations – connected with natural phenomena in Egypt and known as the ten plagues – which broke down his hardness of heart and obduracy, the Hebrew tribes on a spring day in the year 1447 – according to Biblical reckoning[6] – made a hasty departure from Egypt accompanied by a 'mixed multitude' of non-Hebrew inmates of the slave camps that abounded in the 'Land of Bondage'.

From Egypt Moses led the people towards the Sinaitic wilderness by way of the Red Sea, which they crossed somewhere near Suez, while the Egyptian hosts in hot pursuit after them sank into its depths. The effect of this succession of stupendous events on the spiritual life of the people was overwhelming. It made them particularly sensitive to things divine, and inspired in them a faith stronger than ever in the God of their fathers who had interposed to save them from the House of Bondage and the hands of their enemies. The song of Moses, sung by him and the Children of Israel, takes us to the heart of this faith:

> I will sing unto YHWH, for He is highly exalted:
> The horse and his rider hath he thrown into the sea.
>> (Ex. 15. 1)

> Who is like unto Thee, O YHWH, among the mighty?
> Who is like unto Thee, glorious in holiness,
>> Fearful in praises, doing wonders?
>>> (Ex. 15. 11)

It was in this state of spiritual exaltation that the people followed Moses in the wilderness of Sinai where they were to learn the end for which they had been redeemed, and the nature of the destiny which was awaiting them.

NOTES

1. See James B. Pritchard, *Ancient Near Eastern Texts relating to the Old Testament* (Princeton University Press, 1950), pp. 455 ff.; and H. Frankfort and Others, *Before Philosophy* (Pelican, 1950) pp. 154 ff.
2. Haran was the birthplace of Abram, as is evident from Gen. 24, 4 and 40. See next note.
3. 'Thy land and thy birthplace' in Gen. 12. 1 must be understood as referring respectively to Mesopotamia and Haran, and *not* to Babylon and Ur.
4. Gen. 12. 7. It is only at this stage that God is said to have appeared to Abraham, imparting thereby to what had hitherto been a subjective feeling of the mind the objective reality of a revelation.
5. The pronunciation of the Tetragrammaton is unknown, and this divine name is therefore best left unvocalized.

6. Several other dates for the Exodus have been suggested, ranging from 1584 B.C. to 1144 B.C., but the Biblical date has been adopted, with minor modifications, by one acknowledged scholar after another. See S. L. Caiger, *Bible and Spade* (Oxford University Press, 1935) Appendix 1, pp. 192–3.

CHAPTER 2

ISRAEL'S SELECTION

In the third month of their departure from the land of Egypt the Israelites arrived at Sinai, which, in the judgement of many scholars, is located just east of the Gulf of Aqaba. This burning desert, with its beetling cliffs and volcanic mountains, was the scene of the ever-memorable Covenant which made YHWH the God of Israel, and Israel the people of YHWH. The Sinaitic Covenant had its roots in God's covenant with Abraham, which in turn had its antecedents in the divine covenant with Noah. This Noachic covenant, as will be seen later, forms an important moment in the process of universal history as unfolded in the opening chapters of the Bible; and it is within the framework of this universal history that the significance of the Sinaitic Covenant is to be found.

The story begins with the creation of the world by God and the formation of man in His image. But this creative process did not cease when the world and man had been made, for that which had been created had to be developed and fostered. This task God entrusted to man. Made in the image of God, man must conform to the character of God, and because God creates, man must also create. He must work and cooperate with God in maintaining and developing the work He had committed to man's care.

The basis of this creative cooperation is obedience to the Creator, which must express itself in obedience to the moral law. This moral law falls into two classes: (1) Justice, which is concerned with recognition of human rights; (2) Righteousness, which stresses acceptance of duties.

The first precept of the law of Justice was communicated to mankind through Noah when, after the Deluge, God entered into a covenant with him, wherein He enjoined respect for the sanctity of human life. Furthermore, in order to enforce this respect, He forbade, on the one hand, the consumption of animal blood, blood being the symbol of life and as such to be treated as sacred, and, on the other, prescribed the death penalty for the wilful shedding of human blood.

These Noachic precepts were obviously offered as a *modus vivendi* to a society which had to be re-created, after having broken down badly, in consequence of 'violence' (Gen. 6. 11), and were by no means intended to constitute the whole content of the law of Justice. But Justice, however widened in scope, inasmuch as it seeks merely to safeguard human rights, is but the negative aspect of the moral law. Justice, therefore, is only regulative, not creative. Creativeness alike in man and the Divine enters into full activity only when prompted by Righteousness. This is a truth which was first perceived and acted upon by Abraham. God in consequence entered into a covenant with him claiming him and his descendants as instruments for making known to mankind 'the way of the Lord to do Righteousness and Justice' (Gen. 18. 19), and thereby performing the universal service for which he and his seed had been chosen.

It was in ratification of the Covenant with Abraham, in all its implications, that God's Covenant with Israel at Sinai was made. Fundamental to this Covenant was the divine exhortation 'And ye shall be unto me a kingdom of priests, and a holy nation' (Ex. 19. 6). The charge thus conveyed was both national and universal. As a 'kingdom of priests' Israel were to render service to the universality of mankind, whilst as a 'holy nation' they were to follow a particular way of life – a life of holiness – which was to mark them off as a distinct people among the nations of the world.

The scope and substance of Israel's universal priestly mission was indicated in the inaugural revelation on Mount Sinai with the giving of the Ten Commandments. The psychological experience involved in this Sinaitic revelation, like all other disclosures of the Divine, cannot be determined, but it is unique in its claim to have been shared by a whole nation. This collective national experience of Israel served to authenticate for the people the revelational claims of the individual Patriarchs as well as those of Moses. Hitherto they had accepted these at best merely as a matter of tradition and faith, and at worst they ignored them. The Sinaitic revelation left no room for doubt as to either the Patriarchs' claims or the divine character of Moses's mission.

Conforming to the pattern of God's Covenant with the Patriarchs, the Decalogue is introduced by the Declaration: 'I am YHWH thy God who brought thee out of the land of Egypt. . . .' (Ex. 20. 2), making God's redeeming acts on behalf of Israel the ground of His special claims upon the people to His universal service, in the same way as Abraham's deliverance from Ur, as we have seen, was the ground of the divine claim upon the Patriarch.

The Decalogue possesses a unique universality which makes its application most relevant to Israel's universal priestly mission. The rules of conduct it prescribes are sufficiently comprehensive to constitute the primary requirements – religious and moral – for all peoples and all times. It forbids the deification of Nature, as well as the making of graven images, enjoins Sabbath observance, extending the blessings of the day of rest to the non-Israelite labouring servant, and even to brute creation; the honour of parents; respect for property, life, and woman's honour; and the eschewing of any word or thought potentially inimical to one's fellow-men. Several of these commands have their parallel in some ancient Egyptian or Babylonian texts, but nowhere else is piety enjoined as an obligation, and moral conduct as a duty. Nor is there to be found in any other code anything corresponding to the prohibition of lust and covetous desires.

And what is true of the practical prescriptions of the Decalogue is equally true of its doctrinal affirmations which provide the warrant for these prescriptions. They are all charged with a universal significance which bring them within the scope of the service of Israel's priestly mission.

The opening declaration in stressing the redemptive acts of the Exodus expresses the fundamental religious truth of God's activity in history. The prohibition of worshipping Nature, and of its correlative, the making of 'graven images' establish the distinctive character of Israel's monotheism, which marks it off with sharp definition from all other forms of god-belief –

whether polytheistic or monotheistic. The gods of all other nations were identified with Nature, and like finite Nature could be given form; the God of Israel transcends every phenomenon, and any plastic or pictorial representation of Him is but a lie and an offence.

The Sabbath Law proclaims God as the sole Creator, contrary to the notion that fixes the creative principle in the regenerative power of some natural element from which the Deity itself is said to have emerged. And, finally, the Decalogue contains clauses affirming the doctrine of retribution – reward for obedience and punishment for disobedience.

Whilst the Decalogue indicated the substance and scope of Israel's 'priestly mission', it did not provide for the specific duties and obligations that devolved upon the people as a 'holy nation'. These were developed in the series of revelations to Moses which he transmitted to the people and which, incorporating the Decalogue, finally became the Torah, commonly known as the Law, of which the Pentateuch is the written record.

CHAPTER 3

THE TORAH

THE Torah, which denotes 'the teaching' *par excellence*, includes doctrine and practice, religion, and morals. The Torah, as already stated, is the direct consequence of the Sinaitic Covenant in its twofold implications – universal and national. While the Ten Commandments indicated the substance and the scope of Israel's universal 'priestly mission', the other Commandments were designed to train Israel for the holiness which they were to follow as a nation called upon to become 'holy unto God'.

The significance of this holiness is indicated in the meaning of its Hebrew equivalent, *kadósh*, which, whatever its etymology, expresses a quality consisting negatively in 'separation *from*' and positively in 'dedication *to*'. Applied to the charge laid upon Israel, holiness entails negatively a separation from all that is opposed to the will of God, and positively a dedication to His service.

This holiness was to be carried into the domain of religion and morality. In religion, holiness demanded *negatively* the abhorrence of idolatry with its debasing and degrading practices, such as human sacrifice, sacred prostitution, divination, and magic; and *positively* the adoption of a cult and ritual that were both ennobling and elevating.

In morals, holiness *negatively* demanded resistance to every urge of nature which made self-serving the essence of human life; and *positively*, submission to an ethic which placed service to others at the centre of its system.

It was to meet these demands of holiness that the Torah was given to Israel. With this end in view the Torah prescribes two sets of laws, religious and moral. Each set of laws is in turn divided into two classes, negative and positive, corresponding to the two aspects of Holiness. With holiness as their common motive the difference between religious and moral laws disappears. They are no longer disparate and unconnected, but

23

are correlated with one another, both combining to constitute the scheme of training in Holiness provided by the Torah.

This close connexion of the religious and moral laws is not merely incidental, but is derived from the moral elements in the religious laws. For what is not actually moral law is law helping thereto, or a means educating thereto, although the connexion may not be evident in every case.

This is true of the negative religious precepts no less than of the positive ones. Both sets of laws have one common aim – Holiness. While the positive precepts have been ordained for the cultivation of virtue and for the promotion of those finer qualities which distinguish the truly religious and ethical being, the negative precepts are designed to combat vice and suppress other evil tendencies and instincts that stand athwart man's striving towards holiness.

Thus conceived, the religious laws are charged with a moral dynamism capable of transforming the individual and, through the individual, the society of which he forms a unit. The disregard of a religious law is accordingly no longer a private affair: in so far as it lowers man's moral fibre and his power of resistance to evil, every religious offence is in a sense a social offence. Likewise the observance of religious law is no longer a mere isolated act: in so far as it contributes to the individual's moral stability, with effects upon his general conduct, it is a social act.

The educative character of the positive religious laws is introduced and maintained by a system of symbols under the technical name of 'signs' and 'remembrances' which serve to impress holiness on the mind of the devotee. Among these mention may be made of the frontlets, *tefillin*, falsely translated phylacteries, from a Greek word meaning 'amulets'. Nowhere are the *tefillin* described as protecting charms, but as 'signs' and 'remembrances' (Ex. 13. 9). So are the *tzitzith*, the fringed garments, 'remembrances'; as is distinctly written with reference to them, 'In order that ye may remember and do all my commandments and be holy unto your God' (Num. 15. 40).

The negative religious laws are likewise assigned educational aims and purposes. Foremost among these is the prohibition of eating the flesh of certain animals classed as 'unclean'. This law has nothing totemic (animal-worship) about it. It is expressly associated in scripture (e.g. Lev. 11. 45) with the ideal of holiness. Its real object is to train the Israelite in self-control as the indispensable first step for the attainment of holiness.

And even the sacrificial system, which was instituted while Israel still sojourned under the shadow of Sinai, is charged with a moral content. Whatever the origin of sacrifices, these, unlike in all other contemporary religions, were never regarded in the Torah as sacraments identifying the worshipper with the deity. Sacrificial offerings were a special means of moral training which was to be achieved through the holiness enveloping the sacrifice. Everything pertaining to the sacrificial worship – the sanctuary, the priests, the vessels, and the sacrifice itself – was designated as holy. But this holiness was not intrinsic to the system itself, but symbolic of the holiness which was to influence individual and corporate life.

As a constant reminder of the moral content of the sacrificial cult it was ordained that the two stone tablets recording the Ten Commandments should be kept in the Ark which was housed in the Sanctuary. The fact that the sacred shrine contained nothing besides the Ten Commandments was to impress upon the mind of the people the fundamental moral significance of the sacrificial institutions they were enjoined to observe.

In conformity with its moral content the sacrificial system of the Torah is characterized by two features unique to it. First, sacrifices were ordained exclusively for ritual or religious sins, but not for social sins. Second, no sacrifice could be offered in expiation of a deliberate sin, ritual or religious, but only for such offences as had been committed in error. These two reservations, which are without parallel, affect the whole quality of the sacrifices of the Torah. It is not the needs of God which the sacrifices are intended to satisfy, but the needs of man. They are not conceived as gifts to an offended deity in appeasement of its anger or in reparation of a wrong done to one's fellow man. Their aim is essentially man's holiness, with all it implies of religious and moral regeneration and perfection. They are designed in all their parts to foster in the mind of the devotee a sense of the awfulness of a religious offence in that it creates an estrangement alike between man and God and between man and man.

Holiness is also the keynote of the 'Appointed Seasons' of the Torah. Foremost among these is the weekly Sabbath. The Babylonians too had their day of rest, called *Shappatu*. But whereas the Babylonian *Shappatu* was a day of danger (*dies nefas*), the quality of holiness ascribed to the Hebrew Sabbath makes it into a day of moral and spiritual regeneration, and thereby into a day 'blessed of the Lord' (Ex. 20. 11).

The same is true of the three harvest festivals: the Feast of Unleavened Bread, Pentecost, and Tabernacles, celebrating respectively the barley harvest, the wheat harvest, and the vintage. They are all described as 'holy convocations', in contrast to the harvest festivals of the Canaanites which were marked by obscene fertility rites and orgiastic scenes. The New Year festival (Num. 30. 1), with which the Day of Atonement is closely connected,[1] is also described as a 'holy convocation' to mark it sharply off from the Canaanite New Year in which the Tammuz ritual of a dying god formed the central feature of the celebrations.

Holiness lay also at the root of the moral law. Unmistakable in this connexion are the words 'Ye shall be holy' which form the introduction to that compendium of moral laws comprised in Lev. 19.

Fundamental to the moral law of Holiness are the two principles which, as we have seen, lie at the basis of man's creative cooperation with God – Justice and Righteousness, Justice being the negative aspect of Holiness; Righteousness, its positive aspect. In the common life, Justice meant the recognition of six fundamental rights. These were the right to live, the right of possession, the right to work, the right to clothing, the right to shelter, and finally the right of the person, which includes the right to leisure and the right to liberty, as well as prohibitions to hate, avenge, or bear a grudge.

Righteousness was to manifest itself in the acceptance of

duties, especially in the concern for the poor, the weak, and the helpless, whether friend or foe. It was also to show itself in the conception of earthly goods, the possession of which was to be regarded not as a natural right but as a divine trust. When a neighbour was in difficulty, a loan was to be made to him for which no interest was to be charged (Ex. 22. 24). If he was obliged to sell his ancestral land through poverty, it was to revert to him in the Jubilee (Lev. 25). The difficulties of a man's neighbour were not to be used to increase his own income. Economic life in the Torah was thus to mean essentially services to one's fellow man; and behind this ethic stood the law of love as formulated in the golden rule 'Thou shalt love thy fellow² as thyself' (Lev. 19. 18), which is expressly stated (v. 34) to include the non-Israelite stranger.

Righteousness was also to express itself in the humane treatment of dumb animals. An ox fallen by the way had to be raised with the same solicitude as if it were a human being (Deut. 22. 4). The animal employed in labour, as for example the ox treading corn, was not to be muzzled (Deut. 25. 4). Nor might animals of different species, differing in character and strength, be yoked together (Deut. 22. 10); and the blessing of the Sabbath was not to be denied to the brute creation.

Allied to the moral law of the Torah is its civil or judicial law. The aim throughout is to give practical effect to the doctrine of holiness, which conceives Justice and Righteousness as regulative principles of all human relations. In marked contrast to the other ancient codes, such as those of Hammurabi and of the Hittites where the motive is the protection of property, in the Torah the motive is the protection of personality.

The restrictions which the Torah places on the powerful show how strongly this passion for rights of the person was to be felt. The employer was forbidden to exploit his workmen or to withhold the payment of their wages when due (Lev. 19. 13). The creditor was not allowed to affront the dignity of the person of the debtor by entering his house to take a pledge (Deut. 24. 10–11), much less was he permitted to deal violently with him as was sanctioned by other systems of law. Even the slave had the rights of the person and was never recognized as an absolute possession. The smallest injury to his body gave him his freedom (Ex. 21. 26–27); and if he ran away, it was forbidden to deliver him back to his master (Deut. 23. 16–17), in marked contrast with the Hammurabi code which imposed the penalty of death on those who aided runaway slaves.

The judicial law of the Torah also repudiated all that caricature of human justice found in other codes, which included such monstrosities as imposing the death penalty for theft and putting a son to death for the crime committed by his father. The Torah further refused to admit any distinction, other than those of social function, between king and noble, commoner and slave, native and stranger, all being equal in the eyes of the law, and all enjoying the same sovereign human rights.

Finally, holiness was to express itself in personal morality and family purity, in abstention from all incestuous relationships, as well as bestiality and sodomy; in the control of lust and sensuousness; and in the practice of chastity in deed, word, and thought.

The command to Holiness is grounded on the Holiness of God. 'Ye shall be holy, for I YHWH your God am holy' (Lev. 19. 2). Divine Holiness is thus the ideal pattern for man to emulate in all his strivings after holiness.

Like the holiness to which man has been summoned, divine Holiness has a twofold connotation,[3] negative and positive. Negatively, as applied to God, holiness denotes His separation from all that is natural and physical; hence, His transcendence and independence of all besides Himself. Positively, it denotes His free and unfettered activity in conformity with His moral character.

The fullest disclosure of the moral attributes of God was made to Moses in a special theophany in which God revealed Himself as a merciful being, gracious, slow to anger, abundant in loving-kindness and truth, keeping loving-kindness to a thousand generations, forgiving iniquity, transgression, and sin, but who will by no means clear the impenitent guilty (Ex. 34. 6–7).

These characteristics, generally known as the Thirteen Attributes, constitute the Holiness of God. None of them, it will be noted, bear any relation to God's essence. They are all specifically related to His dealings and actions with man.

These attributes resolve themselves into two principal groups, Justice and Righteousness. In the organization of these attributes, justice expresses itself in God's intolerance of evil and His punishment of sin. The Torah accordingly provides for a system of penalties varying in accordance with the gravity of the offence and the intent with which it has been committed. Promises of reward, primarily temporal and national, are also made for obedience, as part of divine justice which is to distribute to each according to his deserts. No specific mention is made of reward and punishment after death. There is, however, clear indication that the penalty of *kareth* (cutting off) threatened in connexion with some religious offences, connotes a 'cutting off' from the presence of God in the hereafter (see Lev. 20. 2–3) – an idea which by implication carries with it the idea of reward for obedience. Scripture, nevertheless, found it necessary to cast a veil over the whole question of survival beyond the grave, in order to wean people away from the idolatrous cult of the dead with which this belief was at that time associated.

Divine Righteousness fulfils itself in the quality of mercy, which includes among its derivatives 'abundant in loving-kindness', bestowing on the good man more than he deserves, and in the judgement of the sinner tempering justice with mercy, and, moreover, holding back punishment in the expectation of his penitence.

The love of God is held up as a pattern for man's love. This is exemplified in the command to love the stranger, which is significantly grounded in God's love for the stranger. 'God loveth the stranger . . . love ye therefore the stranger' (Deut. 10. 18, 19). In this law of the stranger is revealed the universal love of God. True, God has chosen Israel, but that does not limit or damage His love for the human race. Israel has but the distinction of being the peculiar people through whom has been revealed God's love for all.

While the attribute of divine Justice is held up as a motive for man's fear of God, God's love is made a basis for His claim upon the love of man. In this command of the love of man for God, no appeal is made to the senses as in the polytheistic cults. In every case the call to love God is followed by the injunction to observe His commandments and to seek His righteousness through a life of service and duty (*e.g.* Ex. 20. 6; Deut. 6. 4, 8).

The Torah constitutes the ultimate uniqueness of the religion of Israel. Many other faiths are shot through with moral motivation, but none possesses a system with a power to train in the holiness of life comparable to Israel's Torah.

The distinct approach of the Torah to the problem of human conduct is by way of the heart. While speaking to the mind in communicating to it a body of facts concerning man's duties, the Torah applies itself to the perversities of the human heart – its vices, evil propensities, and dispositions – that are a bar to obedience, while also at the same time impelling by its inspiriting ideals to an eager performance of duty.

As for its scope, the Torah embraces the whole of life with its activities. All the common ways of life, all human interests, come under its rule. Thus, the Torah becomes a means for strengthening the supremacy of the divine holy will as the measure of all strivings of the human heart, and for bringing all the details of life, individual and corporate, into relation with the service of God.

The separation which, we have seen, is the negative aspect of holiness, included for Israel a separation from all contaminating contacts with the idolatrous civilizations and cultures of the surrounding nations. But the destiny of the priestly mission entrusted to Israel was the world as it was. It was to be carried out by men who, after centuries of Egyptian bondage, had escaped from an environment of sophisticated vice at the top and brute degradation at the bottom. And, finally, the torch was to be carried not to an isolated few but to the many, not to abnormal visionaries and super-normal saints, but to the masses of the common people, from common man to common man, even from nation to nation.

Israel had thus to be apart *from* the world and yet remain *of* the world. Whilst keeping distinct from the surrounding nations, they had to throw the whole of their effort into the midst of current civilizations, seeking to raise human life to higher levels of existence. This was no easy task; yet they were to perform it because the Holy God who had chosen them was to be served in Holiness, and because their life could achieve its meaning only in the universal service to which they were summoned.

Such was the significance of the Covenant promulgated at Sinai and of the Torah which was given to enforce it; and as the curtain rings down on that most momentous event in history, Israel is seen starting off on its national career, pledged in consecration to the service of God and humanity.

NOTES

1. The context makes it clear that the ritual of the blowing of the (Ram's) horn on the first day of the seventh month is prescribed in preparation for the Day of Atonement which follows.
2. This is the precise meaning of the Hebrew term *rea*; the usual rendering 'neighbour' is misleading.
3. See p. 23.

ISRAEL'S DEFECTION

FROM Sinai the Israelites journeyed on, and within a short time reached the southern borders of Canaan. But neither were the people ready for the land, nor was the land ready for the people. The Exodus and Sinai had truly impressed them, but their slave-mind still possessed them. Largely undisciplined and spiritually enervated, the people were incapable of feeling and acting as one, even where their own material interests were concerned. Much less could they rise to the loftiness of their mission for the fulfilment of which the land was promised to them as an inheritance.

Nor was the land yet ripe to receive the people. At that time Egyptian rule was maintained unchallenged in Canaan by a system of loyal vassal kings who, bound together, could offer effective resistance to an invading host. Forty years had therefore to elapse before the Israelites could enter upon their long-promised inheritance. These were the years of Israel's wanderings in the wilderness. During that period, amid the hardships and privations of desert life, Moses was able to weld this heterogeneous mass of newly emancipated slaves into one united and well-disciplined nation, and impress upon them those spiritual and ethical qualities on which their destiny was to be founded.

The precise route taken by the Israelites under the leadership of Moses in the wilderness cannot be traced. None of the places named in the Bible can be identified with certainty. But what is clear is that, after following a circuitous route, the people moved past Edom and Moab into Transjordania, where, after defeating the Amorites who occupied that land, they established themselves securely before proceeding to invade Canaan. It was there that Moses, the servant of God, the greatest of the prophets, died, at the height of his powers, with eye undimmed and natural force unabated.

By that time, the Egyptian empire under the rule of Amenhotep III showed signs of decline, and Canaan itself, as the

Tell el-Amarna tablets (*c.* 1400–1360) inform us, was in an extreme state of turmoil, with several of its vassal kings in treacherous communication with invaders from the north and east. This was the opportune moment for the new, desert-born, hard-trained, militant Israel, under the leadership of Joshua, to enter on the possession of their Land of Promise.

Crossing the Jordan, near the Dead Sea, they penetrated Canaan and, after reducing Jericho, soon occupied south-central Palestine, next southern Palestine, and finally northern Palestine. There was no need for them to conquer north-central Palestine, as this part of the country had already been occupied by Hebrew clans, probably as a result of the wars of the sons of Jacob (Gen. 34. 25ff.; 48. 22; and 1 Chron. 5. 20ff.), even before the Israelite invasion under Joshua.

The conquest of the land, however, was far from complete. There was still a number of fortified cities, distributed through-out the country and separating groups of tribes one from another, which Joshua had failed to subdue. But, on the whole, the conquest had been successful enough to enable Joshua to begin to undertake the organization of the political and relig-ious life of the people. He partitioned the conquered districts among the tribes, allotting to each a share according to its num-bers, and set up at Shiloh a central sanctuary containing the Ark, which now served as a strong cohesive force unifying the tribes religiously and politically.

But this federal organization of the tribes was too loosely knit to survive the days of Joshua, and his death was followed by a period of anarchy during which 'every man did what was right in his own eyes' (Jud. 17. 6). Disunited, the tribes could not combine even when faced with the danger of the yet unsub-dued enemy. They therefore had to resort to peaceful pene-tration and this, in turn, led to their fatal imitation of the religion of their neighbours, with its sensuous fertility cults and other extremely degrading practices. Some deserted YHWH for the local Baals and Astartes, to whom they came to ascribe the yield of the soil and the increase of cattle. Others served YHWH and Baal, YHWH being the custodian deity of the nation, while Baal was the territorial God, the giver of the harvest and vintage. Others again practised a syncretism by transferring to YHWH all the titles and attributes and modes of worship of the local gods.

Brave leaders called 'Judges', some twelve in number, set their faces against these soul-sapping idolatries; and, appearing on the scene as liberators from enemy pressure, they succeeded in recalling the people to the pure worship of YHWH. But most of these 'Judges' were not national figures; they were more or less tribal heroes and their influence did not outlast the crises which brought them to the forefront as leaders. Yet their efforts were not in vain; so that by the time of Samuel, the last of the 'Judges', the worship of YHWH was firmly established in the North, with the Shiloh sanctuary serving as the central shrine. There families would repair annually for worship and sacrifice, taking the little children with them as soon as they could walk. A special cell for worship was assigned to the guests, and the sacrificial meal, which was partaken of in the holy place, was divided among the members of the family by the father. Normally, the religious life of the people centred mainly round the local shrines, 'High Places', consisting of a stone altar, on which offerings were made, and sometimes also of a hall for the sacrificial feasts. Often these 'High Places' were equipped like the Canaanite shrines with pillars, and sacred poles; but these appurtenances, whatever their symbolic significance in pagan cults, were merely conventional adaptations in Israel and did not affect the purity of the people's worship.

By the time Samuel was born, practically all the surrounding Canaanites had been subdued; but a new enemy arose to trouble Israel – the Philistines who, moving forward from the narrow Southern coastal belt which they inhabited, invaded the highlands of Ephraim and inflicted upon Israel a signal defeat, which was marked by the destruction of many Israelite towns, including Shiloh, and the capture of the Ark. This overwhelming disaster enabled Samuel, who had by then emerged as 'Judge', to bring about a reform leading to the abolition of Baal worship in Israel. On the other hand, the Philistine danger worked in favour of centralization of secular authority. Thus arose the clamour for a king, not so much to fight their battles as to judge them (I Samuel, 8. 5), that is to say, a king invested with supreme power over their lives. Samuel, fearing that such a king might become a tyrant, at first opposed the demand, and yielded only after having had a constitution accepted which strictly defined and limited the royal rights and powers. This 'Magna Carta' he embodied in 'a book' which he placed before YHWH for the guidance of future kings of Israel (I Sam. 10. 25). Thus Samuel's is the credit for 'one of the greatest contributions ever made to the political thought of man – the truly democratic theory of the relation between the governor and the governed'.[1]

The man to be chosen as the first king of Israel, and, indeed, chosen by common consent, was Saul (c. 1025), who may also be regarded as the first constitutional king in history.

Saul did not fulfil the high hopes placed in him; yet by his patriotism and courage he freed the Israelites from the Philistine yoke, and brought about a large measure of unity among the rival Hebrew tribes. With David (c. 1012–972), his successor, began Israel's golden era. He quickly rallied the tribes about him, and by a series of brilliant military victories he extended the kingdom of Israel from Phoenicia in the west to the Arabian Desert in the east, and from the River Orontes in the north to the head of the Gulf of Aqaba in the south. Most far-reaching in its consequences was his capture of the last of the Canaanite strongholds in the land, the impregnable Jerusalem. In this citadel city he established the national capital and set up a national sanctuary to house the Ark. Lying midway between the tribes of north and south, Jerusalem attracted to itself the loyalty and devotion of all Israel, and soon became the focal centre – national and religious – of a united people.

The worship of YHWH was now well established throughout the land. David next turned to the ritual of the sanctuary. With the cooperation of the priests and Levites, whom he organized in courses, he adorned the service by the introduction of an elaborate musical orchestration, and he himself contributed to the religious enthusiasm of the worshippers by some of his masterpieces in psalm and sacred song. Conscious of his

own failings, and serving at the same time as a moral example
to others, he attached to his royal court 'mentors', in the
persons of the leading prophets, Gad and Nathan, who did not
hesitate, whenever the occasion demanded, to rebuke him for
his sins and constrain him to right action.

David's policy of political and religious centralization was
carried on and developed by his son and successor Solomon
(c. 971–931), who, in order to centralize the cult, built in Jerusalem a superb Temple which was to serve as the only shrine,
superseding all other shrines in the land, which since the destruction of Shiloh had been considered legitimate places of
worship, but which because of their idolatrous associations
were henceforth to be forbidden. In building the Temple,
Solomon employed Tyrian artisans. But whatever the native
designs they may have introduced, these in no way influenced
the Israelites' idea of God, who remained enthroned invisible
in the Holy of Holies as the sole ruler of the entire Universe.
The centralizing influences of the Temple, however, could not
counteract the influx of pagan ideas that came in the wake of
the increased prosperity and opulence which marked Solomon's reign. This was a period of unparalleled peace for
Israel. Its weaker neighbours had long been subdued by David,
whilst its powerful neighbours, Egypt and Assyria, were at that
time in an enfeebled state. Secured against foreign interference,
Solomon embarked on extensive commercial operations on an
international scale. His merchant fleet based on the port of
Ezion-geber (at the head of the Gulf of Aqaba), with its copper
mines and refineries, recently discovered, ploughed the seas
for distant lands and brought to Israel the wealth of the
nations. Parallel with this economic and material progress of
the country went its cultural progress. The wisdom and fairy
lore of the East found their way into Israel, together with its
gold, silver, sandalwood, and peacocks, extending immensely
the intellectual horizon of the people. The arts and sciences
flourished, Solomon himself contributing by his wisdom, wit,
brilliance, and consummate literary gifts, to their growth. But
Israel's close contacts – commercial and cultural – with the outside world brought with them a tendency towards assimilation

of heathen ideas. Solomon's marriages to foreign princesses, for whom he built idolatrous shrines, only served to hasten the process of assimilation, which profoundly affected the purity of Israel's religion. The God of Israel was no longer the one and only God, but a mere national God. This was not without effect upon personal religion, as it was not part of the national God to concern himself directly with the individual to whom He was linked with ties of the most precarious character. Thus was the way open for the intrusion of all kinds of petty cults, for example, magic and necromancy, for the satisfaction of individual desires, side by side with the worship of YHWH, as well as for the accommodation to strange gods of all sorts, as political expediency, foreign alliances, marriages, and economic relations dictated.

The inevitable course of all this was the disruption of religious unity, which in turn was followed by the disruption of national unity. Conscript labour and forced exactions only served to aggravate the situation. Rumbling noises of the coming storm could be heard even before Solomon's death, and when he died, after a rule of thirty-eight years, there was nothing to prevent the storm from breaking and to save his kingdom from disintegration.

The disintegrating blow to the Solomonic Kingdom was delivered by Jeroboam (c. 931–910) of the tribe of Ephraim, who headed a rebellion which ended in the establishment of the kingdom of Israel, or Ephraim, comprising ten of the original twelve tribes, with himself as its first king. Only the tribes of Judah and Benjamin remained loyal to the house of David and together constituted henceforth the kingdom of Judah.

NOTE

1 T. H. Robinson, *Palestine in General History* (Schweich Lecture, 1929), p. 44

CHAPTER 5

NATIONAL AND RELIGIOUS DISRUPTION: THE TRAGIC KINGDOM OF ISRAEL

THE kingdom of Israel occupied the whole of the northern and central region of Palestine, whilst the kingdom of Judah occupied the south, including the city of Jerusalem. An astute politician, Jeroboam, in order to make the break between the two kingdoms complete, took steps to detach the tribes under his rule from all those religious institutions which made for national unity. To achieve this end he did not hesitate to compromise with heathenism. He decentralized the worship, forbade pilgrimages to Jerusalem, and, as a counter-attraction to the imageless worship in the Temple, he made of gold two young bulls (derisively described[1] in the diminutive as 'calves') setting up one in the extreme south and another in the extreme north of its kingdom. Prompted by the same schismatic considerations, he created a fresh priesthood, which, unlike the hereditary priesthood of the Levites, owed its position to the favour of the king and was dependent on the continued separation of the two kingdoms for the maintenance of its priestly status. He also transferred the festival of Tabernacles, with its popular religious harvest celebrations, from the prescribed seventh month to the eighth. In his choice of cult, Jeroboam was influenced by the mode of worship common among the agricultural Semites, who looked upon the bull with religious reverence. His 'calves', however, were set up not as deities, but as mere images of the one invisible YHWH. Nevertheless, the pagan associations of the bull opened the way for the eventual restoration of Baalism after it had been absent from the land since the days of Samuel.[2]

Meanwhile, the immediate effects of Jeroboam's policy was not only to create an irremediable breach between the north and the south, but also to deprive the loosely connected tribes over whom he ruled of a unifying force, and thus to lay the seeds of the anarchy that broke out in the kingdom after his death, and grew worse with the successive kings who immediately followed him.

With the accession of Omri (*c.* 886–874), order was restored to the land. He united the rival factions within his kingdom, and won over Judah to permanent and almost unbroken friendship, and under his strong rule Israel entered upon a period of prosperity and military strength and increasing prestige among the states of Western Asia. In order to meet the aggression of the Arameans (Syria), and the westward drive of the new power, Assyria, he entered into an alliance with Phoenicia and married his eldest son Ahab to Jezebel, the daughter of the King of Tyre.

Omri was succeeded by his son Ahab (*c.* 874–853). Pursuing the policy of his father, Ahab sought to strengthen his position by marrying his daughter Athaliah to Jehoram, the son of Jehoshaphat, King of Judah. The overall result of Ahab's policy was to bring to the Northern Kingdom a large measure of material strength, prosperity, and splendour, despite the disasters – crop failure, famine, and drought – that marked his reign. But religiously and morally his rule was calamitous. Under the influence of his dominating wife, Jezebel, he restored Baalism and enforced it in its lewd, Tyrian form, with its fertility ritual and human sacrifices, as the state-religion of the Northern region, in rivalry to YHWH, who hitherto had been recognized, at least nominally, as the only God in Israel.

Ruthlessly pressed, this attempt to enforce Baalism upon the people would have succeeded but for the courageous stand of one man – the prophet Elijah. Consumed by his zeal for God, he rushed through the country like a whirlwind, preaching, denouncing, threatening, and ascribing to the sins of the people and the rulers every disaster that had happened. Most daring was his single-handed encounter with all the prophets of Baal at Mount Carmel, where he defiantly flung out to them the taunt: 'How long will you halt between two opinions? If YHWH be God, follow Him, but if Baal be god, then follow him'. For Elijah, YHWH was all or nothing, and this dilemma left no place for the worship of any other god along with YHWH, much less for the denial of His supremacy.

Stirred by what they had witnessed, the people present proclaimed in no uncertain accents 'YHWH, He is the God' and, at the command of Elijah, rose against the prophets of Baal and executed judgement of death upon them. But notwithstanding the revival at Carmel, Baalism still remained in the ascendant. Jezebel was still Queen; and infuriated with Elijah, she vowed to kill him. In despair for his life, Elijah fled to Horeb, the Mount which was the scene of God's covenant with Israel about six centuries earlier. Standing on the craggy summit of this sacred mount, he sounded the very depths of depression. The scene recalled to him Israel's pledged loyalty to God and His Covenant, and contrasting it with the national apostasy about him, he could not but feel that all his work on behalf of YHWH had been in vain. But his despair soon gave way to hope. In a wondrous vision that burst upon his view, he learnt that the revelation of God was not always to be found in the storm, earthquake, and consuming fire; these were but messengers of His judgement. The presence of God was often revealed in the 'still small voice' in the heart of man. This meant that the final decision in the struggle against Baalism did not depend on the effectiveness of God's judgement on the nation's apostasy from him. There would always be the 'still small voice' which, exercising its influence gently and imperceptibly, would ensure the ultimate triumph of God's cause. This indeed was a most encouraging message. There were still in Israel, so Elijah was assured, 7,000 who, responsive to the 'still small voice', did not bow the knee to Baal, and they formed a 'remnant' from which a fulness of religious life would yet one day flower and grow.

Elijah's mission was well-nigh completed, but before quitting the scene, with almost the same sudden abruptness as he entered upon it, he figured as a fearless champion of the rights of the individual against the tyranny of kings. With merciless severity, he denounced Ahab and his queen for their judicial murder of Naboth, whose vineyard they had coveted and appropriated, and predicted the extermination of their dynasty in punishment of the bloody crime they had committed. By this act, Elijah gave practical affirmation to the doctrine that YHWH was a God of Righteousness, whose demands stood above everything, even above the interests of the state.

Another important doctrine to which Elijah gave practical demonstration, before his disappearance, was that YHWH was not only the God of Israel but also the God of all nations. He commissioned his disciple, Elisha, to anoint, in the name of God, Hazael as king of Aram, so that he might scourge Israel for its sins. Hazael was a non-Israelite and no worshipper of YHWH at all, but nevertheless the God of Israel could appoint him as His tool against His sinful people.

In emphasizing these two doctrines, Elijah prepared the way for the unique achievements of the Hebrew prophets who were to come after him.

The stern prediction of Elijah was not slow in coming to fulfilment. Ahab himself, shortly after his confrontation by Elijah, fell in battle against the Arameans (853). His eldest son and successor, Ahaziah, died in the second year of his reign, as the result of a serious accident; whilst his second son, Jehoram, who followed next on the throne, was assassinated in a mutiny of a section of his own army (c. 842). The leader of this mutiny was Jehu, whom Elisha had anointed as king for the specific purpose of extirpating Baalism from Israel.

The assassination of Jehoram was but the prelude to a revolution which swept away in torrents of blood the whole House of Ahab, from Jezebel down, as well as all the captured priests, prophets, and votaries of Baal. But Jehu's revolutionary ardour was fed more by personal ambitions and political motives than by his zeal for YHWH. Anxious to secure his throne, he slaughtered all the friends, supporters, and officers of the overthrown dynasty, as well as Jehoram's Judean kinsmen – Ahaziah, King of Judah and his brothers – who happened at the time to be in the territory of Northern Israel.

The insincerity of Jehu's motives became more than transparent when instead of establishing in Israel the worship of YHWH in its purity, he reintroduced Jeroboam's calf-cult, with its idolatrous associations and abuses. Thus, what began as a religious upheaval degenerated into a senseless political

butchery, the horror of which lingered in Israel's memory for
very long (Hosea 1. 4). Politically, Jehu's mass slaughter was as
disastrous as it was indefensible. It deprived him of Israel's
former allies, Judah and Phoenicia. Thrown back on his own
resources, he was unable to meet the attack of Hazael of
Aram, who hurled himself, as foretold by Elisha, with all
savagery on Israel, annexed the whole of Transjordania (c. 838),
and carried his depredations as far south as the country of the
Philistines. With Jehoahaz, his son and successor, (c. 814–798),
Israel reached the nadir of its humiliation and was reduced to a
mere dependency of Aram.

Under the rule, however, of Jehoash, Jehoahaz's son and
successor (c. 798–783), Israel's fortunes began to revive. Taking advantage of Assyria's pressure on Damascus, Jehoash
recovered territory previously lost to Aram. The sudden collapse of Aram as a result of civil war, coupled with the retire-
ment of the Assyrians, relieved Israel from its greatest external
dangers. Free from outside interference, Israel rapidly increased, and under Jehoash's son and successor, Jeroboam II
(c. 783–743), the old limits of the Davidic Kingdom were
almost reached, with Damascus as tributary, and the country
rose to a height of power and prosperity without precedent.

The power and prosperity of Israel under Jeroboam II was
accompanied by a religious revival. A spirit of devotion seems
to have prevailed everywhere. The sanctuaries were thronged,
offerings poured in, and the festivals were scrupulously observed. But all these external manifestations of religion were
tainted with idolatry. They were not directed to the pure
worship of YHWH, but to the syncretic worship of the
'golden calves'. Parallel with this religious degeneracy went a
moral depravity. The rulers and nobles were cruel and oppres-
sive; the judges were venal and corrupt; the rich callous and
luxurious. Drunkenness and debauchery abounded in the land,
invading the very sanctuaries. Yet the Israelites believed that
they were God's chosen people. They had seen their national
God moving history on their behalf; and their good fortune
was evidence of divine favour.

At this juncture there arose Amos, the first in line of the

Hebrew literary prophets whose mighty oracles still remain the wonder and admiration of the world.

Coming up from the rival Southern kingdom, Amos, the Judean, with supreme tact and prudence, studiously avoided any denunciation of the schism, and only lightly assailed the calf-cult, which was closely bound up politically with the schism. He concentrated his attacks on the moral perversion of a people enervated by luxury. In unsparing terms he condemned their persistent wickedness, which was rendered all the more inexcusable by virtue of their claim that they stood in a unique relationship to God.

They were deluding themselves when they imagined that they were God's favourites. YHWH had no greater regard for them than for other nations. He was not the God of Israel only; He was a universal God of universal morality, and His special relation to Israel demanded that they should make the divine standards their own. Israel's deflection from the required standards could not fail to provoke divine punishment. They had already experienced a series of disasters – pestilence, earthquake, famine, and locust – but none of these seemed to have roused them from their false sense of security. God, however, had a far greater calamity in store for them: 'a besieger and adversary' – Assyria – whom He had appointed as His instrument with which to chastise impenitent Israel. Yet their doom was far from sealed. 'Return and live', cried Amos, 'Let justice well up as waters, and righteousness as a mighty stream' – and all will be well.

The warnings and exhortations of Amos fell upon deaf ears. Israel continued to tread the path of doom, which the death of Jeroboam II in 743 rendered all the more precipitous. The removal of his strong rule brought about a radical change in the religious and political conditions of the Northern kingdom. The profligate Baal cults, which had been suppressed since the time of Jehu, began to flourish again in the land, sapping further the mental, physical, and moral vigour of the people, whilst the country itself became easy prey for regicides, adventurers, and usurpers. The internal crisis was aggravated by the renewed westward drive of Assyria. By 738 the armies of the all-conquering Tiglath-Pileser III had reached the borders of the northern kingdom, and it was only by prompt submission and payment of tribute that the ruling usurper Menahem saved the country from total devastation.

The Assyrian exactions were too onerous to be borne. The result was the formation of an anti-Assyrian party, headed by Pekah, who, seizing the throne in c. 736, formed with Rezin of Damascus a coalition against Assyria, into which they both sought to draw Judah. He also negotiated an alliance with Egypt, which likewise feared for its own Empire at the hands of Assyria. This was the beginning of the end. As a tiny buffer state between two great rival powers, Israel needed above all a strong commanding religious faith to bind the rulers and people alike in a community of interest and purpose, and to guide the nation through its present and future perils. This Israel lacked; and its prophet, Hosea, whose main activity fell during these closing years of the nation, had none but the sternest message to deliver. Israel had sinned grievously. Corruption – religious and moral – had done its work deeply. Evil-doing had become second nature with the people. Return to God and to righteous life was no longer possible. There was nothing left for Israel but to suffer the severest of retributions – defeat and exile – for her sins and follies. But with this message of doom came also a message of hope and love. Despite all its failings and backslidings, Israel was still the special object of God's love. God still loved Israel with the love of a husband for his wife and of a father for his child; and His mighty and inextinguishable love for His people will not rest satisfied until He has restored all Israel unto Himself.

The end came quickly. Apprised of Pekah's intrigues, Tiglath-Pileser III invaded the country and at one wrench took and depopulated more than half of its territory. All he left to Israel was the little province of Samaria, over which he appointed a certain intriguer, Hoshea, as vassal king. For six years Hoshea paid tribute to Assyria, then at the instigation of Egypt he rebelled. Forthwith, Shalmaneser laid siege to Samaria, the capital. For three years the city resisted desperately, falling at last in the first three months of 721 to Sargon II, who deported the population to the remotest parts of his great Empire, and replaced it by flooding the country with foreign colonists, who eventually absorbed the last remnants of the Israelites to form a semi-idolatrous people known as Samaritans.

Thus did the kingdom of Israel pass out of history.

Thereafter the name Israel ceases to bear its restricted significance as referring to the northern kingdom, and is used of all the descendants of the Patriarch wherever they may be.

NOTES

1. 1 Kings, 12. 28 *et passim*.
2. See p. 34.

CHAPTER 6

THE KINGDOM OF JUDAH:

ITS RISE AND FALL

IN striking contrast to the troubled career of the kingdom of Israel, the internal history of the kingdom of Judah ran at least during the first century of its existence on peaceful lines. The dynasty founded by David continued on the throne, undisturbed by assassinations or revolutions.

The long reign of Asa (c. 913–873), Rehoboam's second successor, and of Jehoshaphat (c. 873–849), both monarchs of high character, contributed powerfully to the consolidation of the dynasty. Religiously, the Temple and the Torah exercised a conservative influence on the people's lives. Instances of apostasy did occur, but these were largely due to the machinations of the foreign wives of the Judean princes, and to their influence which, however, rarely extended beyond the court and the nobility. The people as a whole remained loyal to God. If, notwithstanding the centralization of the worship, they still sacrificed at the old-established high-places, which were equipped in Canaanite fashion with pillars and sacred poles, they did so by mere force of habit, but without any idolatrous intent. It was this loyalty of the masses that enabled Asa, on coming of age, to remove, without resorting to bloodshed, the foreign cults and their votaries patronized by his father, and the Canaanite fertility goddess, Asherah, worshipped by the Queen Mother. He also initiated a campaign against the high places, but this mode of worship had for so long formed an integral part of the people's religious life that it was impossible to do away with it. Jehoshaphat continued the struggle against the worship in high places, but with little more success than his father. He also reorganized the whole judicial system of the country, appointing judges in all the cities to administer the law as required by the law of Deuteronomy (16. 18ff.). Far-reaching in his judicial reform was his separation of the administration of the strictly religious law from that of the civil law, placing over the former the High Priest and over the latter his own personal representative, while he himself, unlike the kings who preceded him, withdrew increasingly from the actual administration of justice to a place from where he could see that it was carried out properly (II Chron. 19. 5ff.). He also instituted measures for the spread of the knowledge of 'the book of the Law of the Lord' among the people in all the cities of Judah (II Chron. 17. 9).

Jehoshaphat's devotion to God and to the Torah did not prevent him from marrying his son Jehoram to Athaliah, the daughter of Ahab. This marriage alliance was dictated by the growing menace of the Arameans and the Assyrians, but it was destined to have grave consequences for the south. It led to the introduction for the first time into Judea of Baalism and murder as instruments of state policy. Athaliah was a true daughter of her mother, Jezebel, and under her influence Jehoram not only embraced the Tyrian Baalism, but also resolved to establish it as the official religion of the country. In order to remove opposition to his intended paganizing policy, he murdered his six brothers, as well as other members of the nobility. He died after a reign of eight years, leaving his country weakened by internecine strife, and impoverished by the loss of Edom, with its caravan traffic, Red Sea trade, and ore mines, which had played an important part in the economy of the attenuated Judean state.

Jehu's murder of her son Ahaziah (already noted)[1] gave Athaliah her chance. She immediately usurped the throne, and in order to ensure her tenure as well as her freedom of action she killed all the seed-royal; and crowned her infamy by instituting the worship of the Tyrian Baal as state cult. Fortunately, her year-old grandchild, Jehoash, escaped the massacre and, after having been concealed in the Temple for six years, the young prince was proclaimed king by the High Priest Jehoiada, who put Athaliah to death and led the people to pledge themselves by covenant in loyalty to God.

Jehoiada's religious influence alike on king and people lasted throughout the remaining days of his life, but his death was followed by a revival of Baalism, fostered by the nobility and

the king. Soon afterwards, Hazael threatened Judah, and
Jehoash bought him off with the contents of the Temple
treasury. Growing disaffection engendered by his apostasy and
sacrilege led to his assassination. He was succeeded by his son
Amaziah, who put his father's murderers to death, but, in conformity with the Deuteronomic law (Deut. 24. 16) spared their
children. Having reconquered Edom, Amaziah rashly engaged
in war with Joash, king of Israel, only however to suffer an
ignominious defeat (c. 790). The decline of Israel, however,
after the death of Jeroboam II enabled Judah to recover from
this humiliating defeat, and under the long reign of Uzziah
(c. 783–742) and the shorter one of his son Jotham (c. 742–735)
it reached the summit of its power and prosperity.

With the accession of Ahaz (c. 735–727) the son of Jotham,
the era of Assyria's interference in Judah began. For some time
Syria and Israel had been bringing pressure upon Judah to join
them in an anti-Assyrian coalition. Meeting with resistance,
they proceeded to invade Judah and were now threatening
Jerusalem itself.

A prominent figure in the reaction of Judah to this Syro-
Israelite invasion was the prophet Isaiah. He saw clearly that
the real issue was between Egypt and Assyria and that Judah's
only hope lay in a consistent neutrality. He accordingly urged
upon the king and the people to steer clear from all entangling
alliances and political alinements but put their trust firmly in
God who would protect His city. He furthermore foretold the
destruction both of Damascus and the northern kingdom of
Assyria. Ahaz, however, refused to pay heed to Isaiah's admonitions and assurances, but instead called in the aid of Assyria.
The approach of the Assyrians led inevitably to the collapse of
the Syro-Israelite attack against Judah. Judah was saved from
devastation, but at the price of its independence.

Ahaz was compelled to meet Tiglath-Pileser and offer
homage to him in person at Damascus. Ascribing the might
and splendour of his overlords to their gods, Ahaz came under
the spell of their religion. He ordered the erection in the
Temple of Jerusalem of an altar after the model of the one
he saw at Damascus, and also introduced into Judah the cult of

child sacrifice which was practised by the Assyrians, and even offered his own son to the devouring fires of Moloch.

Hezekiah (c. 727–698), Ahaz's son and successor, continued the submissive policy of his father, but broke with his apostasy. Immediately on his accession, he abolished all idolatrous practices, including the cult of YHWH in the high places, against which the preceding reforming kings of Judah had battled in vain. He also reorganized the Temple services, and initiated a religious revival which was marked by the celebration of a great Passover festival in which the Israelites from the north were invited to participate. He also inspired among the people a literary activity which included the collection of the writings of Solomon.

In all his work Hezekiah was greatly helped by the prophets Isaiah and Micah. Taking up the same burden as their predecessors, Amos and Hosea, they directed it also against the moral corruptions and enervating luxuries that were floating in upon Judah's tide of material prosperity. But in condemning the religious decay of Judah, they both struck a new note. What they condemned there was not the cult itself, which, as a matter of fact, had nothing of the idolatrous about it, but the way it was practised by the people – the divorcement of inner piety and integrity of conduct from their worship: their Temple, sacrifices, Sabbaths, festivals, and prayers. They both insisted that sacrifices, however meticulously offered, were no substitute for justice and righteousness. The God of Israel, cried Isaiah, was a Holy God who could not tolerate even unethical speech (Isa. 6. 5), much less unethical conduct. Whilst Micah formulated for all time the quintessence of true religion in his famous utterance: 'He hath shewed thee, O man, what is good, and what the Lord require of thee, but to do justly and to love mercy, and to walk humbly with thy God' (6. 8). And both Isaiah and Micah threatened Jerusalem with the fate of Samaria, unless the people repented and amended their way of living.

Isaiah had been called to the prophetic office by a vision in the Temple in the year King Uzziah died, so that by the time Hezekiah ascended the throne, Isaiah's reputation as prophet and statesman stood very high. His predictions had been fulfilled to the letter, and under his influence Hezekiah turned a deaf ear to the blandishments of Egypt designed to draw him into her anti-Assyrian policy. But the death of Sargon in 705 was the signal of a widespread revolt among the Assyrian vassal states, and in this revolt Hezekiah, disregarding the counsel of Isaiah, played a conspicuous part. The result was the invasion of Judah by Sennacherib. Forty-five cities were captured, and many of its inhabitants deported. Jerusalem itself was closely invested. Sennacherib demanded the surrender of the city, but Hezekiah, fortified by Isaiah's assurances that God would protect His city, returned a defiant answer. Here again Isaiah proved a true prophet. A sudden pestilence broke out and decimated the whole of the Assyrian host. Sennacherib was obliged to retire. Jerusalem was saved (701).

The miraculous deliverance of Jerusalem gave rise to those great prophecies of Isaiah and Micah with which have become intertwined mankind's highest hopes and aspirations. Before the eyes of the prophets' vision there arose a new Jerusalem which was to be the centre of a universal kingdom, to which all peoples of the earth would turn for light and leading. Over this kingdom was to rule a king who would excel all other kings in true godliness and goodness. In this kingdom, righteousness and peace shall reign supreme. Gone will then be all social sins that end in pauperism and all political sins that end in war. The blessedness of this kingdom will be reflected in the world of Nature as in human society. 'They shall not hurt nor destroy in all my holy mountain: for the earth shall be full of the knowledge of the Lord as the waters cover the sea' (Isa. 11. 9). All that is sorrowful, unlovely, and sinful will pass away and man will enter upon a new life in a world renovated and transformed.

Interlocked with these Messianic prophecies is the doctrine of the remnant of Israel which, rehabilitated in Zion, will form the nucleus of the universal kingdom of righteousness, around which all nations of the world would be gathered.

The withdrawal of Sennacherib from Jerusalem meant no cessation of Assyrian suzerainty in Judah. This continued sub-

jection to Assyria was to prove, under the long reign of
Menasseh (c. 696–641), Hezekiah's son and successor, of the
gravest consequences for the religious life of the people. A
degenerate both in religion and morals, Menasseh, like his
grandfather Ahaz, and for the same reasons, adopted the idolatrous cults of his overlords, including their astral-worship and
sacrifice of children. Thus was the stage set for the worst and
fiercest heathen reaction in the history of Judah. What was
most astonishing at this stage of Israel's development was that
these monstrosities were committed by people who professed
to be worshippers of YHWH, believing that by acting thus
they were meriting His favour.

Menasseh's son and successor, Amon, was no better than his
father. His life, however, was cut short in the second year of his
reign by a conspiracy in his household, and he was succeeded
in c. 640 by his eight-year-old son, Josiah, who proved to be
one of the best kings of Judah. His coming-of-age coincided
roughly with the death of Assurbanipal, when the power of the
Assyrian Empire was beginning to crumble. Attacked by the
Babylonians from the south and west, and by the Scythians and
Medes from the north and east, Assyria was unable to maintain
its hold on its outlying dependencies. This gave Josiah the
opportunity of asserting his independence and of instituting
(c. 621) a reform – religious and moral – which proved more
thorough than that of Hezekiah, and which he was able to
extend, without fear of Assyrian interference, into Northern
Israel.

The reformation of Josiah derived considerable drive from
the discovery among the debris of the Temple of a copy of the
'Book of the Law'. A public reading from the Book was held,
consisting of portions of Deuteronomy which describe in harrowing detail the punishments that would overtake an apostate
Israel. Deeply moved by what they had heard read, the king
and people entered into a solemn covenant before God to obey
the teachings of His Law.

The reformation of Josiah practically put an end once and
for all to state idolatry in Israel. As such, it marks an important
stage in Israel's religious growth and progress. But the battle

for true religion was far from won. Even under the strong rule of Josiah, whilst idolatry was not tolerated in public, it was still practised in private. Besides, there was still the need of combatting the current idolatrous notions that sacrifices mattered more to God than right conduct, and that the Ark and Temple were endowed with magical properties which so assured the people of protection that no amount of moral wickedness could encompass their destruction. In these erroneous views the people were encouraged by the false priests for whom sacrifices proved a lucrative source of income, as well as by the false prophets who found it profitable to prophesy soothing words to lull the people into a false sense of security.

A courageous stand against these perversions of religion was taken by the priest-prophet Jeremiah. He thundered away at the people. All their sacrifices, he told them, were so much 'smoke'. God did not want *their* sacrifices. What He demanded was justice and righteousness. Nor was their confidence in the Temple and Ark at all warranted. God hated wickedness; and would punish their wrongdoing without regard to the holiness of the place where it was committed.

But world-shaking events were taking place which militated against the effectiveness of Jeremiah's fulminations and also destroyed the hopes raised by Josiah's reformation. In 609, the Assyrian Empire, which had for some time been the prey of rival nations, came to a sudden end. Soon Babylon and Egypt became engaged in a mighty struggle to take the place left vacant by Assyria in the control of Western Asia. Josiah, instead of pursuing the policy of non-intervention, sided with Babylon, and in 608 sought to bar at Megiddo Pass the advance of the Egyptians against the Babylonians. He suffered a crushing defeat and met his death on the battlefield.

The national catastrophe, coming so soon after Josiah's reforms, had a shattering effect on the religious life of the people. Blind to their own moral turpitude, many were impugning the justice of God who had brought upon them suffering for sins which not they but their ancestors had committed, whilst others surrendered to a blank scepticism (Zeph. 1. 12). In vain did Jeremiah seek to impress upon the people the stark fact of their own sinfulness as well as the recognition of the responsibility they each bore for the misfortunes that had overtaken them (Jer. 31. 28–9). A rapid religious and moral decline had set in, and under Jehoahaz, Josiah's son and successor, foreign cults of all sorts – Assyrian, Egyptian, and even old Canaanite ones – came flooding back into the country.

Politically, the disastrous intervention of Josiah was no less shattering. It put an end to Judah's independence. No longer was it possible for her to maintain her neutrality. Henceforth, she was compelled to choose her side, either with Egypt against Babylon, or *vice versa*, inevitably incurring in any event the hostility of the one or the other.

For the moment, Judah was at the mercy of Egypt. Jehoahaz had scarcely reigned three months before Pharaoh Necho, suspecting his loyalty, banished him to Egypt and appointed his brother Jehoakim in his place.

With the defeat of the Egyptian forces at Carchemish (605) by Nebuchadrezzar, Egyptian rule in Judah was superseded by that of Babylon. Jehoakim's rebellion not long afterwards, at the instigation of Egypt, brought swift retribution. He died, however, before Nebuchadrezzar managed to lay siege to Jerusalem. His young son Jehoiachin had to bear the brunt of the Babylonian assault, resulting in the capture of the city on Adar 2 (16 March) 597,[2] when he and the flower of Judah's inhabitants were taken in captivity.

Zedekiah (c. 597–586), an uncle of Jehoiachin, was then appointed king of the enfeebled state, under an oath of allegiance to Nebuchadrezzar. But, deluded by Egyptian promises and encouraged by the false prophets, Zedekiah rebelled. Jeremiah warned the king and people against the catastrophic consequences of their policy and counselled submission to Babylon whose mastery had, for the time, been determined by the will of God. He was, however, denounced as a traitor, imprisoned, and even threatened with death. The end could not be long delayed. After a desperate siege of two years, Nebuchadrezzar stormed Jerusalem and razed it to the ground (August 586). Judah ceased as a sovereign state, and was reduced to the status of a colony. Many of its inhabitants were deported, only a remnant of 'vinedressers and husbandmen' being left behind. Gedaliah, the former *major-domo* of the royal palace, was appointed governor of the Judean colony. His murder by discontented survivors of the Davidic dynasty led to a further depopulation of the country by the Babylonians, whilst a large number fled for refuge to Egypt.

Thus did Judah share the fate of the Ten Tribes – captivity. But whilst the other tribes vanished and merged with their conquerors, Judah alone survived. But that is not all. Out of the crucible of exile and affliction, Judah emerged, purged and purified, into a new people – the Jews. Spreading quickly throughout the earth, the Jews carried wherever they settled a new message – Judaism.

Shaped and nurtured by a faith which was impervious to change of circumstance and environment, Judaism in captivity not only survived, but also developed a dynamic which in turn was destined to captivate the world.

NOTES

1. See p. 41.
2. The exact date of the Fall of Jerusalem is furnished by an inscription in cuneiform contained in a tablet in the possession of the British Museum and deciphered in 1956. This is the first extra-biblical source specifically mentioning the capture of Jerusalem (called 'the city of Judah'); the removal of its king (Jehoiachin) and the enthronement of a new king (Zedekiah) by the conqueror's 'own choice' See D. J. Wiseman, *Chronicles of the Chaldean Kings* 626–556 B.C. (British Museum, 1956), pp. 72–3.

CHAPTER 7

THE PROPHETS

THE faith to which Judaism owes its survival and dynamic is founded upon the Torah (Law) and the Prophets. The Torah, as it has been seen, communicates not only the ways of right conduct – religious and moral – but also the knowledge of God and of His Will. Fastening upon this knowledge, the prophets interpreted it with great force and freshness, leading thereby the religion of Israel into new paths through which it became the common inspiration of mankind. With them, as has been well remarked, developed a new interpretation of God, a new interpretation of man, and a new interpretation of religion. Thanks to their mighty strivings, monolatry blossomed into monotheism, nationalism into universalism, and religion became a matter of righteous living rather than mere ritual practice.[1]

This gift of interpreting the mind of God granted to the prophets was something other than that of occult knowledge claimed by secluded spirits. They were essentially men of the world, practical men, concerned with facts of daily life, but they saw these facts in relation to the Will of God.

As a result of their clear vision they became, so to speak, the conscience of their generation. They rebuked, they counselled, they guided their people and conceived it their duty to intervene in all matters of moral conduct, political, social, national, or individual.

Basic to prophecy is the inseparableness of religion and morality. This conception signified a forward leap in the religious consciousness and moral conscience of mankind. One has only to recall the abominable practices associated with ancient religious cults, and the difficulties Paul had with his converts who thought that because they were saved they could have the time of their lives, to appreciate the importance of the contribution of the prophets to the forces of moral culture and progress.

The unity of morality and religion was, it is true, not of their

creation. This idea suffuses, as we have seen, the whole Pentateuch and underlies the whole of the Mosaic legislation where
religious and moral laws appear side by side. But it was the
prophets who were the first to trace their close relationship and
to carry it to its logical conclusion, with most momentous consequences alike for religion and morality.

This unity of morality and religion proclaimed by the
prophets is the inescapable corollary of the Hebrew conception
of God. The passage from polytheism to Hebrew monotheism,
it has often been remarked, is an irreversible step which affects
the whole quality of the religion. The constant and relentless
struggle between polytheism and monotheism which the early
history of Israel reveals did not resolve itself merely into a
question of numbers – the one God against the many gods.
There came also the necessity of supplying a new conception
of the Divine character, radically different from that of polytheism. Polytheism, being deeply rooted in the variety of
nature's appearances and powers, has essentially no moral, no
spiritual quality. There is no moral attribute attachable say, to
a thunder-clap, a tree, the sea, the sun, the sky and its con-
stellations, which were the objects of polytheistic cults, since
all moral attributes are necessarily connected with personality.
Worlds asunder is Hebrew monotheism. It emphasizes the
unique spiritual and moral character of God no less than His
absolute unity – in a mathematical sense. And it was the intense
realization of the personal, and consequently the moral character
of God that aroused the passionate anger of the prophets of
Israel against all forms of idolatry no less than their, in fact,
morally degrading cults and associations. Confronting a world
dominated by the sensual, alike in its cults and morals, the
prophets were tireless in their insistence on the moral character
of God and His moral claims on the sons of man.

Chief among the fundamental moral principles the prophets
enunciated was Righteousness. Righteousness they considered
to be the supreme law of the universe, and one of the essential
attributes of God Himself. 'God the Holy one is sanctified in
righteousness' (Isa. 5. 16). In polytheism the gods give favours
or are angry according to their whims. Consequently, in poly-

theism there is no righteousness. The living God of the Universe, proclaimed by the prophets, on the other hand, is righteous and His rule is founded on righteousness.

Again, in polytheism the gods have their own rights and their own exclusive virtues. There is thus in polytheism no uniform distinction between right and wrong, good and evil. As against this, divine righteousness, according to the teaching of the prophets, is founded on the uniform acceptance of such distinctions. Right is right everywhere; wrong is wrong everywhere. The universal character of divine righteousness implied a uniform relation of God to man, and man to man. This in turn inspired the idea of the unity of men, and any violation of that unity was an injury to divine righteousness. All these ideas had been proclaimed before; but it was the prophets who developed them with much originality and freshness and who gave them the loftiest expression by applying them with detail and precision to the practical problems of their days.

Conceiving God as inseparable from the moral order, the prophets set themselves the task of promoting the rule of God and His righteousness among the sons of men. Their condemnations were thus directed not only against idolatry, but also against the moral and social evils which sprang from idolatry. Thus they became practical moralists, politicians, and jurists, resolved to do all they could to uproot social evil, and destroy its disruptive power.

The Hebrew prophets were not satisfied merely to denounce injustice and oppression. They set themselves the task of arousing among the people a feeling against social suffering – a feeling which was not to rest in knowledge, but to become full of action: 'Seek justice, relieve the oppressed, judge the fatherless, plead for the widow' (Isa. 1. 17); 'Deliver the spoiled not of the hand of the oppressor' (Jer. 21. 12). The indifference to all kind of suffering, including social suffering, which the Stoics advocated, was repugnant to the prophets. Although the individual might well overlook his own woe, he must not overlook the woes of others. Social suffering could not be compared, in the prophetic view, to that of individual suffering; because the latter is individual and subjective and can be overcome by will-power, whereas social suffering is not only the suffering of the masses, but is evidence of the jungle-law of a culture which refuses to recognize the rule of God.

The greatest of social evils the prophets found in poverty. The social distinctions for which poverty was responsible were regarded by them as the greatest hindrances to mental and moral development in the direction of human unity, and to the establishment of the rule of God.

The Hebrew prophets rose above the credulity which blindly accepted a direct correspondence between individual goodness and prosperity, and individual wickedness and misery. While recognizing individual guilt as a factor responsible for weal and woe, they would not allow it to interfere with their treatment of the problem of poverty. They did not neglect the question of the sin of the individual, but this did not paralyse their political actions and strivings for social reform. It was not God, but the wealthy and the noble who crushed the weak and ground the face of the poor. It was they who had in their house the 'spoil of the poor' (called [Isa. 3. 15] 'My People', – the people of God), and by doing so set themselves against the rule of God.

The prophets were of course troubled by the apparent injustice of divine government which social suffering represents, the opposite of fairness seeming often to prevail. With the just it goes badly, with the wicked well. Moreover, the whole of human history would seem to show that God prefers one person before another. There are differences of mind, body, and aesthetics. One man appears to be favoured more than his fellow. But they nevertheless held that no man had the right to set himself up as judge in this respect, and that differences in material wealth, like differences in intellectual and physical powers, far from preventing the doing of justice, should be rather stimulants to it. Superiority is on no account to be interpreted as involving divine favouritism. Higher attainment means higher responsibility; and material gifts should only mean greater opportunity for the exercise of righteousness and justice. 'Let not the wise man glory in his wisdom, neither let the mighty man glory in his might, neither let the rich man glory in his riches. But let him that glorieth glory in this, that he understandeth and knoweth Me, that I am the Lord who exercise mercy, justice, and righteousness in the earth' (Jer. 9. 22-3 [23-4]).

The justice and righteousness of God as exercised on earth is, according to prophetic teaching, made manifest in the process of history. History was not for them a mere succession of events without a goal and purpose. Affirming the existence of a divine Sovereign behind the scheme of things, the prophets of Israel discerned in the happenings of the day the unfolding of a divine process directed towards an ideal future.

It is this idea of the appearance of God in the events and associations of history that distinguishes the prophets and the spirits akin to them from other saints and great men of religion. Characteristic of all saints is their claim to have sought and found God and entered into close communion with Him. But other great saints of religion have sought and experienced God by fleeing from history into timeless intercourse with God. The prophets communicate with God in history. They hear His voice in the happenings of the day. They discern His will in all the vicissitudes of fortune in the lives of nations and individuals. History thus gains unsuspected significance. All that happens therein is of fundamental importance. All is living tangible drama, unfolding itself and moving amid manifestations of divine judgement, goodness, and grace towards the fulfilment of an eternal purpose.

And not for Israel alone was this future foreseen. While the prophets held fast to their national consciousness, their conception of history was that of world-history. Greek philosophy may have enriched by its speculations the conception of the soul of the individual man, but it gave no thought to the individuality of peoples other than the Greeks. The barbarians, the name whereby they designated all foreign peoples, did not enter the horizon of Greek philosophy. The prophets of Israel, on the other hand, rose above the boundaries of their own nation to a vision of a unified humanity, and made the conception of mankind a content of religion. They had a vision of a world unity and harmony in which all men and peoples acknowledge and reverence God, the Lord of all the earth.

Analogies to this conception of divine purpose in history can be found elsewhere, but they are foreign to the heart of these thoughts. In primitive ages of awakening culture there is the notion of the destruction of the world – a destruction which indeed contains in itself the idea of world-renewal. The Hebrew prophets took over this idea, which, among the people, was associated with the 'Day of the Lord'. Some of the prophets revel in pictures of storm, earthquake, floods, fires, ruins, valleys splitting and mountains crumbling, pests, famine, and war. Such are the judgements of God that fall upon the peoples of the earth, and no less over Israel. Out of this idea, however, comes a higher idea – the idea of the purification and of the guidance and moral training of the world by God, a guidance that involves step-by-step development. Thus the 'Day of the Lord' becomes the symbol of Messianism with the rule of universal righteousness on earth. In Joel there is the promise of the outpouring of the spirit of the Lord on all flesh, without excepting the manservant and maidservant (Joel 3. 1–2 [2. 28–9]). The prophets thus became the originators of the conception of world history, marching to the transcendental reality of an earthly future, 'when the earth shall be full of the knowledge of the Lord as the waters cover the sea' (Isa. 11. 9).

This consummation would not spell in prophetic teaching the end of Israel's national distinctiveness. No prophet had laid greater emphasis on the universality of religion than Jeremiah. He believed in the conversion of all peoples to the worship of the one and only true God, a self-conversion to be affected through the knowledge of the worthlessness of their idols (Jer. 16. 19). At the same time, he insisted that Israel would not lose its independent unity. For him it was ever the historic Israel which will build anew the chosen state for the extension of the true divine worship among all the peoples of the earth (Jer. 3. 14–17).

The key to this universal conversion is the knowledge of the Lord. The knowledge of the Lord draws its universal significance from the fact that it is not theoretical. It refers neither to God's existence nor to His Laws. The knowledge of God spoken of is not an acquisition of new facts, but an impression of old facts – an impression which masters man's thoughts, heart, mind, and feelings, making him willing and disposed to do and obey the divine demands made upon him. It is a knowledge which, by experiencing the divine presence, enables man to be possessed of a real understanding of, and a spiritual insight into, the character of God and of His delight in the workings of righteousness and justice (Jer. 9. 23 [24]). Such a knowledge, unlike theoretical knowledge, is possible for all men. Given the experience, it can go out to all peoples of every class and distinction.

This essential experience would come to Israel, so Jeremiah announced, as a result of a new covenant which was to enforce the covenant made with Israel at Sinai with the giving of the Torah.

But whilst the Torah had indeed served to make them mindful of their duties, their conduct had shown that mere 'remembrances'[2] were not enough to break down their deceitfulness and stubbornness of heart and to make the knowledge of God a reality in their lives. It was this lack which the new Covenant was designed to fill. In contrast with the old covenant, the new Covenant was not to be grounded on the mighty acts which God did on behalf of Israel in the far-off days of the past, but in His deeds of salvation in their everyday life. By force of this new Covenant, the Torah of Sinai would be engraved in the very heart of the people and operate with a power of instinctive and instantaneous response to the demands of God, and to His righteous and holy Will. Thus shall the knowledge of God become the common possession of all Israel and through Israel of all the nations of the world.

Jeremiah's vision of Israel's world-wide mission receives powerful expression in Isaiah, Chapters 40 onwards, and in the 'Servant of YHWH' chapters, where in a series of passages of unequalled force the prophet passes from the unique monotheistic teaching of Israel's God to the uniqueness of His people, Israel. The prophet depicts a scene of universal salvation in the midst of which stands the Suffering Servant – Israel – whom the nations had hitherto thought to have been forsaken by God for his sins. Now, however, they had come to realize that the sorrows he had endured were but the work of their own wickedness and misdeeds. It was *they* who had sinned in crushing him; it was *they* who had committed violence in oppressing the innocent servant of the Lord. While he, by a martyrdom endured without flinching, had been able to set an example in faith, loyalty, and hope, and thereby to fulfil his divinely imposed duty, culminating in the salvation that they were all now sharing in common.

Associated with this universal salvation of mankind is the Messianic ideal. For the prophets the political restoration of Israel ever remains the pre-condition of Messianism. The Messiah himself is an offspring of David who would set up again the Davidic throne. But this national calling of Israel is not an end in itself. It subserves an all-human calling for the conversion of all peoples and for their united worship and service of God. Messianism thus becomes a certain form of development which is advanced through historical relations with the highest ideal of religious life, and the Messiah is conceived preferentially as symbolizing Israel's task as the Servant of YHWH, rather than a mere person of royal lineage with national antipathies and political ambitions.

This spiritualization of the Messianic ideal does not make it over-earthly and eschatological, concerned with the 'end of all things'. The Messianic references, throughout Hebrew prophecy, are essentially to an earthly future. And not in the interests of religion (in the narrower sense) alone was this blissful future foreseen. It is the reign of 'the Lord our Righteousness' (Jer. 23. 6) that is pictured. The end and aim of Messianism is to replace the present dominated by the senses – lust, greed, violence, and passion – by a social order which through righteousness in knowledge and action creates a new earth and a new heaven. 'They shall not hurt nor destroy in all my holy mountain, for the earth shall be full of the knowledge of the Lord as the waters cover the sea' (Isa. 11. 9).

But towards this universal salvation of mankind the highest contribution must come from the individual. This was the doctrine enunciated by the prophet Ezekiel. With the earlier prophets salvation that comes from deliverance from evil was a political and social force; and what was contemplated was the salvation not only of Israel but of humanity. The salvation of the individual would be a necessary consequence – a salvation to be achieved through the universal triumph of justice. But in this universalization the individual as individual does not really count. To Ezekiel, on the other hand, the freeing of the individual from sin is all-important. His chief concern is not the reconciliation of the whole people or of humanity with God but the reconciling of the individual – the making him into a just man. This in turn demanded a recognition of individual guilt. Jeremiah, as we have seen, had sought in vain to combat the popular notion concerning the transference of punishment from ancestors to descendants and from the guilty to the innocent, and to arouse the people individually to a sense of their own sinfulness.[3] At the same time, he had announced the coming of days 'when they shall say no more. The fathers have eaten sour grapes and the children's teeth are set on edge. But every one shall die for his own iniquity' (Jer. 31. 28–9 [29–30]). These were to be the days of the exile which, precisely as Jeremiah had anticipated, brought with it a new perception of individual guilt. Taking advantage of the situation, the prophet Ezekiel sought to enforce the teaching of his predecessor and to educate the people in the faithful consciousness of personal accountability for sin (Ezek. 18).

But Ezekiel was not a prophet of doom: he was essentially the prophet of hope. Merely to arouse the people to a deeper sense of sin, without at the same time holding out to them the prospect of release from its burden, would have only served to drive them to despair. His task therefore was to proclaim to them a divine promise of individual deliverance from sin, and to bring to all sin-conscious individual souls a message of divine reconciliation through an inward renewal wrought by the power of God. 'From all guilt there may be a release and new life', is the burden of his message. The initiative, however, he insisted, must come from the individual himself. 'Cast away from you all your transgressions wherein ye have transgressed; and make you a new heart and a new spirit' (18. 31). The individual must will to be delivered from sin and make for himself, through penitence and confession, a new spirit. Having done his share, he is reconciled with God who in His loving-kindness recreates him in spirit and life. 'A new heart also will I give you, and a new spirit will I put within you' (36. 26).

Here, the idea of the personal relation of the individual with God, which pervades the whole of the Pentateuch teaching and legislation, comes to full ripeness. The individual man is no longer subject to fate. He no longer bears the guilt of his forbears, he is no longer dependent on other men or the tyranny of things. He is spiritually independent, because he is reconciled with God and belongs to God.

This new perception of the reality of personal relationship with God was of tremendous significance for the exiled people. It meant that city, Temple, and sacrifices were no longer indispensable, and that the people in exile could individually as well as corporately be both loyal to their new home and worshippers of God who would be with them wherever they might be.

NOTES

1. See Th. J. Meek, *Hebrew Origins* (revised ed., New York, 1950), p. 228.
2. See p. 24.
3. See p. 53.

PRIESTS AND PSALMISTS

THE zeal of the Prophets for righteousness was not for the sake of righteousness as a moral principle, but because it was the revealed will of God. Apart from God and His will as revealed in the Torah, the Prophets neither knew of righteousness, nor recognized moral law. It is because they believed that the Will of God was righteous that they felt impelled instinctively to do what they could to uproot evil, to banish social injustice, and to bring about righteousness on earth.

This supreme concern of the prophets for the revealed will of God made them akin in spirit to the priests with whom they are often contrasted. The prophets, it is contended, were the exponents of an exalted religion and all they demanded was inward reality, character, and disposition, whereas the priests represented a lower view of religion with its insistence on ritual and ceremonial. As a matter of fact, however, the priests were more than mere Temple functionaries whose interests would be limited to the sacrificial cult and externalities of religion. They were also teachers of Torah – in all its aspects – religious and moral – (e.g. Lev. 10. 10; Deut. 17. 9; Deut. 33. 10; Micah 3. 11; Jer. 18. 18); and in the Southern Kingdom they had a large measure in the administration of justice.[1] Fundamentally, therefore, taking equally their stand on the Torah, both priest and prophet shared common ideals, which each of them, in his own particular way, sought to promote and foster, the prophet by enunciating moral and religious principles, and the priest by attending to the ceremonial of devotion and worship. They thus complemented each other, the prophet unveiling the ideal which the ritual enshrined, whilst the priest tended the ritual enshrining the ideal. It was the divorcement of inner piety and moral integrity from external observance that aroused the prophets' scathing rebuke and indignation; even as the true and genuine priest – for there were false priests as there were false prophets – refused to countenance the notion that anyone could shelter himself behind the carcass of a sacrifice from the judgement of God upon his moral turpitude and waywardness of conduct.

Closely associated with the Priests were the Psalmists, whose hymns and songs, petitions and praises, were used by the officiating priests in the Temple as well as by congregations of Israelites assembled in worship. These compositions, each of which is the product of a vivid personal experience of God, are gathered in the Book of Psalms, in which Israel's genius for religion finds its highest expression. Here we have the soul's confession in accents, at once passionate and lyrical, of all the great fundamental truths of religion – the awareness of God, man's spiritual kinship with the Divine, his responsibility to Him, and his destiny.

Significantly enough, the Book of Psalms begins with the theme of human happiness: 'Happy is the man ...' And who is the happy man? He who, by eschewing evil and all its corrosive influences and associations, frees his heart and mind for possession by God. This tremendous fact, affirmed by the introductory psalm, supplies the keynote to the whole Book.

Happiness of a life with God is, to the Psalmist, not merely expressive of an action or emotion. It is an essential quality of the soul, a spiritual endowment which enriches the whole content of life, transforming human character, personality, and existence. It inspires the most sublime trust and faith in God that burns undimmed at all times, in adversity as in prosperity; and it spells a joy and gladness of heart, body, and mind compared with which material blessings count as nothing. Moreover, it carries with it the triumphant assurance of divine salvation even in face of death itself. 'Yea, though I walk through the valley of the shadow of death, I fear no evil, for Thou art with me' (23. 4).

The Psalmist's happiness stems from his apprehension of God. To the Psalmist, God is more than the Supreme Being, the Creator of infinite power, wisdom, and majesty, who maintains the world and orders its course. He is man's great and constant Companion, upholding and sustaining his spirit in its loneliness and isolation.

When, to all appearances, all human resource fails man, there is ever God's close inward presence to guide and support him: 'Whither shall I go from Thy Spirit or whither shall I flee from Thy presence? If I ascend up into heaven, Thou art there. If I make my bed in the nether world, behold, Thou art there. If I take the wings of the morning and dwell in the uttermost parts of the sea; even there shall Thy hand lead me, and Thy right hand shall hold me' (139. 7-10).

Divine companionship with man is rooted in the close personal relation of every individual to God. This relationship has been variously apprehended in the Psalms as that of a people to its king, a slave to his master, a child to his father. But all these conceptions derive from the fundamental relation of that of a creature to its creator: 'For Thou hast formed my reins. Thou hast knit me together in my mother's womb. . . . My frame was not hidden from Thee when I was made in secret' (139. 13-15). As God's special creation, man has his very being grounded in God, and the whole marvel of what he is goes back to God, his Maker. His life, thoughts, and purposes are all laid bare before God, and through this all-searching knowledge, God enters with power into man's life – physical and moral – determining, under every variation of condition and circumstance, his fate and destiny. Furthermore, as His handiwork, God has a plan for every individual. The process of fulfilment may be arduous and painful; it may involve hard discipline and severe trials; but, whatever its character, if man lays open his heart and mind to the influence of divine scrutiny and guidance, God will lead him into the joy and peace of His presence and life everlasting (139. 23-4).

God's plan for the individual man is but part of his larger plan for His creation. For the Psalmist the universe is more than the mere instrument of divine government. It has been willed by God to be the scene of a divine order, with ramifications in every department of life.

The most fundamental feature of the order which God has appointed for his universe is righteousness. God has made righteousness the main support of his divine governance (97. 2). Sin against righteousness is therefore sin against God, even as sin against God is sin against righteousness. Unrighteousness must consequently provoke His judgement. It is because the mighty ones of the nations have failed to establish justice and mercy in the world that divine judgement is over and over again pronounced against them (82.).

Divine judgement of a sinful humanity is a manifestation of the divine holiness which makes God intolerant of evil (99. 8). The prosperity of the wicked hardly appears to be in consonance with the conception of a holy God, intolerant of evil doing. Moreover, the success of the forces of evil and wickedness, spreading about them terror and destruction, leads not a few to say: 'The Lord seeth not and the God of Jacob observeth not' (94. 7). But to the Psalmist such an attitude is brutish, an attitude that is dominated by animal life and fails to recognize the superiority of the spiritual – a superiority which ensures its victory over the material (92. 7).

The ground of this, the Psalmist's conviction, is his belief in the omnipotence and eternity of God whose righteous will must inevitably prevail (92. 9). Divine omnipotence was first made manifest in creation and continues to reveal itself in the constant renewal of the Universe which God upholds and maintains to the smallest detail; and it will be made manifest in the end in the utter destruction of the wicked who mar God's fair creation (104. 35).

The administration of divine judgement is not an act of vengeance but has for its purpose the establishment of universal righteousness which will come to pass with the establishment of the kingdom of God. Towards this consummation in which the divine order will find its fulfilment (104. 35) the whole of human history is moving. Wars, pestilences, drought, and famine and all the other visitations of Nature that afflict mankind are all directed by the beneficent Providence towards the realization of his plan in the universe. Even wars are to the Psalmist's mind the works of God (46, 9 [8]) in that they tend to the higher end – the enthronement of the divine among the sons of men (46. 11 [10]). When God shall proclaim Himself as King, the whole of nature will proclaim the righteousness of his government (50. 6); and the righteous who have served the divine end in helping to bring it forward 'will rejoice with gladness' in its consummation (68. 4 [3]).

The strength of His kingdom will consist not in things material but in the ascendancy of the spiritual over the material under the rule of the good and true on earth. Characteristic of this kingdom will be the cooperative action of all moral qualities and virtues: 'Mercy and truth meet together, righteousness and peace kiss each other' (85. 11 [10]) – evidence of the harmony of the individual and the human race, and expressive of the unity of human consciousness that will animate the citizens of the Kingdom of God.

To the righteous, however, the joy of God's kingdom is not something belonging to the far distant future. He experiences it here and now (33. 1). In sorrow as well as in joy, he discerns the righteousness of God's government and His tender love (*chesed*) which fills the earth (33. 5).

A special mark of God's tender love is His forgiveness of sin (51. 3 [2]). It is this divine tender love which recreates the penitent and confessing sinner in heart and spirit, making him into a new creature with all his sinful past blotted out and forgotten, and filling him with the joy of God's salvation (51. 12–14 [10–12]).

The Kingdom of God is the end, in the conviction of the Psalmist, for which God has appointed all Israel. Born into freedom at the Exodus, Israel became a people chosen to serve God's realm (114. 1–2). Not for themselves were Israel chosen, but for God and His realm. This God-given liberty was not to be the licence of the desert, but the prelude to a higher servitude to which the people willingly and gladly submitted at the mountain of the Law (Sinai). In and through the Law was Israel to fulfil the divine purpose.

In Psalm 119 we have a grand hymn to the Law. In it the Law appears under a number of synonyms, each connoting a different aspect of the Law. In addition to the comprehensive term Torah (teaching), the Law is also described as 'way', 'testimony', 'word', 'precept', 'command', 'ordinance', 'judgement', 'saying' – expressive of the fullness of the content and significance of the Law.

The Law is both 'precept' and 'command', law and duty. Here is expressed the correlation of God and man, which is the fundamental characteristic of the Law. The Law comes from God, duty from man, but law is duty and duty is Law. The Israelite must accept the yoke of the Law, but at the same time he accepts the yoke of God's Kingdom. It is for him only one yoke; there is no other kingdom than the Kingdom of God.

The Law is a 'testimony'. It testifies the will of God to Israel, without the need of a priest or diviner to act as intermediary. In the Law God Himself reveals His will to His elect people.

The Law of God is to the moral world what the laws of Nature are to the physical world. Like the latter it is an 'ordinance', a statute, unchangeable and immutable, fixed as the ordinances of heaven and earth.

The Law embraces the whole life with its actions. It not only regulates as 'judgement', social relations for the stability and well-being of society, but it demands the subjection of all the faculties and powers of common life to active service and devotion. This absolute claim of the Law is indicated by the term a 'way'. A way is a course of conduct; and the Law is 'the Way', wherein man should consistently walk and never desert throughout life.

The real inspiring force of the Law lies in the fact that it is the 'Word' of God spoken to man. It is this which makes the Law, irrespective of its moral content, a channel of communion leading man near to God.

Finally, the Law is a 'saying'. It comprises many hidden mysteries which have their source in God and which, though not having been 'spoken' – that is, not directly communicated by God to man – can be discovered by those who diligently ponder over the spoken word.

Conformity to the Law is for the Psalmist not a mere external act of obedience to external command. It springs from a deeply seated love of God which engenders in him a passionate yearning after God, a yearning which permeates body and soul. It is in response to this love and yearning that Israel's genius has dedicated the book of the Psalms. Many moods and minds

– spanning centuries from the times of David and even earlier to post-exilic times – have gone into the making of the Psalter – the lyrical, the plaintive, the triumphant, the despairing; but they all melt into one glorious song of praise to God offered in unison by souls possessed and satiated with the joy, harmony, and peace of His all-enveloping Presence.

NOTE

1. See p. 47

CHAPTER 9

THE 'WISE MEN'

SIDE by side with the Prophets were the *Hakamim*, Wise Men or Sages, whose writings comprise the Books of Proverbs, Job, and Ecclesiastes, which belong to Israel's wisdom literature. These Wise Men seem to have been recognized as a definite group or guild whose functions it was, as we learn from Jeremiah (18. 18), to give 'counsel'. The tasks they had set themselves are clearly contained in the opening verses of Proverbs (1. 2–4):

> To know wisdom and instruction;
> To comprehend the words of understanding;
> To receive the discipline of wisdom,
> Justice, and right and equity
> To give prudence to the simple,
> To the young man knowledge and discretion.

In short, the Sages were concerned to impart information and wisdom to the ignorant in order that they might live wisely and uprightly, and to develop in the young and inexperienced discretion and prudence.

The aim of these Sages was thus practical and moral. With their activities going back to the earliest days of the ancient Hebrew state, they were with the prophets the great moralists of Israel. Together with the prophets they laboured for the moralization of the Jewish people and strove to foster among them a life of righteousness. With the prophets they were the advocates of the rights of man and upheld the personal virtues of Justice and Equity against the injustice and tyranny of the powerful and the strong; and with the prophets they proclaimed the worth of man as man, and sought to mitigate the burdens which lay upon the oppressed and downtrodden members of society. It was this cooperation of prophet and sage over centuries which gave birth to that deep spirituality and high moral tone which constitutes the quintessence of the national spirit of the Jewish people.

This communion of interests shared by Prophet and Sage was derived from the common spiritual background that inspired them in their strivings. Both prophet and sage started with the same religious presuppositions. They based their theory of life on the same exalted conception of God and His relation to man. What distinguished sage from prophet was the method of approach peculiar to each. The prophet spoke for God, the sage for humanity. The prophet appealed to Divine righteousness; the sage to human reason. The prophet was mastered by an overwhelming sense of Divine presence and command; the sage was impelled by a deep concern for society. This difference of source that inspired their efforts gave colour to their respective utterances.

The prophet is full of fire, zeal, and passion; the sage was dispassionate, calm, and cool. The prophet is full of idealism; the sage is the realist who looks at life in a somewhat utilitarian way. The words of the prophet are those of the eloquent Preacher; the counsel of the sage that of the wise Teacher.

The difference of approach by prophet and sage to common moral and social problems determined alike their functions and spheres of activity. The prophet's task was to make known the knowledge of the Lord; the sage's to show how this knowledge was to be applied in terms of daily life and conduct. The prophet attacked the moral problem from the top: his attention was directed to the conduct of rulers and leaders. The sage attacked the problem from below: his interest was in the man-of-the-street, whom he recognized as the source of all ethical development.

The Hebrews were not the only people who could boast of a wisdom literature. The Canaanites, the Egyptians, and Babylonians, too, had a wisdom literature, even ante-dating that of the Hebrews; so had the Persians; later, the Greeks, too, had their *Sophia*. But there was something distinctive in the Hebrew wisdom that set it as a class apart from that of the other nations.

The fundamental note of the Hebrew wisdom literature is that God's world is built on moral foundations. With a consistency that is ideal it affirms the existence of a moral order in which virtue and evil meet their due and inevitable deserts.

This note is particularly dominant in Proverbs where the young man, who is addressed throughout the Book, is warned of the awful consequences – moral, physical, and spiritual – of evil courses. The moral appeal thus made has in it an element of utilitarian prudence. Wisdom and righteous conduct are recommended as the proper ways of life for a man to choose, because they pay best. Yet with all this appeal to self-interest, there breathes from Proverbs a sound morality that is far above the lightness characteristic of utilitarian ethics. This moral quality is inspired by the religious motive that is in Proverbs the driving power behind the duty of the right ordering of life. The morality and virtue it enforces are placed on the basis of religion, and the moral judgements it pronounces are grounded on the very religious teachings of the prophets and psalmists – the affirmations of God's existence, His omniscience, His eternity, and Righteousness.

Special appeal throughout the Book of Proverbs is made to the Fear of God. It is indeed of striking significance that while this motive suffuses the whole of the Book – it.is repeated seventeen times – there is a singularly strange absence of any reference to the love of God. The silence on what Jewish teaching, from the Pentateuch onwards, has always regarded as the highest motive for religious and moral duty is not without intent. It is in accord with the Biblical view that for training purposes no motive can be more effective than that of the Fear of God and all it implies of responsibility to Him for individual conduct.

The love motive is a sufficiently all-impelling and all-inspiring force for elect and aristocratic souls who have learnt to fear God and to master all the passions and weaknesses of the human heart that interfere with man's moral strivings and aspirations. The great majority, however, with their petty vanities and foibles, evil dispositions and propensities, such as envy, greed, and lust, who are mere children in matters of morals, are not likely to be influenced in their conduct by any motive other than the wholesome sense of the Fear of God.

Faith in God's moral governance of the universe forms, in the last analysis, the background of that intensely personal book of Ecclesiastes, with all its reflections and tergiversations. It is this faith, which enables the author (either Solomon himself or one representing his many and varied experiences) to triumph over the scepticism and pessimism that now and then assail his soul. The twin facts of death and evil tend to make the world a burial ground of all human labours and hopes, with 'vanity of vanities' writ large across it; but faith in divine governance forbids despair. On the contrary, it bids to view the world as the creation of God and as the medium for the revelation of His goodness, wisdom, and righteousness. Let, therefore, man enjoy life and all its pleasures, whilst being mindful all the time also of his duties and obligations. Let him by all means amass knowledge, wisdom, and riches, but ever remember 'to fear God and observe His commandments' through which alone true manhood can be achieved (12. 13).

Whilst Ecclesiastes seeks to save man from the sense of frustration and despair in the face of the evils besetting his existence, Job is concerned with the very character of God called in question by the sorrows of innocent life. The problem of undeserved human suffering has engaged the thought of all serious-minded men of all ages and peoples. It is a problem which, as we learn from recently discovered texts,[1] exercised the minds of wise men in Egypt and Babylon; and it was a theme often presented with gloom and horror by the tragedians of ancient Greece. Yet there was something peculiar in the reaction of the Hebraic mind to this problem, which gave to it a poignancy all its own. Here the problem went far deeper than that of mere personal suffering. It was not simply a question of pain, however hard in its external form it is to bear, but one which involved the character of God. Nursed and nurtured on a faith which spoke of a just and righteous God, giving to each according to his deserts, the Hebrew mind could not but feel wounded to death by the irreconcilable discrepancies it seemed to discover between its necessary thoughts of God and its experience of Him in His government of the world. It is this divine aspect of the problem that is given prominence in the Book of Job and that imparts its tremendous force to the moving drama it represents.

Job is not a philosophic work. No attempt is here made to give an intellectual answer to the questionings of the human spirit by God's apparent misgovernment of the world. The three friends of Job may well argue at length and brilliantly that his sufferings are the direct consequence of his sins. But to all their arguments Job opposes the conviction of his integrity and freedom from serious offences that would justify the harsh treatment he had received. In these, his protestations of his innocence, he is supported by God Himself. When God appears to Job out of the whirlwind and overwhelms him by His majestic power, He declares Job to have spoken well after all, while his more pious-seeming friends spoke ill. Yet, strange to say, the voice of God speaking to him had a transforming effect upon his mind. He appears satisfied merely by having wrung an answer from God.

Herein lies the profundity and originality of the Book of Job which distinguishes it from its foreign precursors and parallels. It was not what God said that worked such a marvellous change in Job, but the very fact that God had spoken to him.

All that was said Job knew before. The glories of the creation and wonders of the universe were not new to him. Nor did he at any time, for all his sufferings, lose his confidence in God. He never doubted that God, who had so wonderfully created his flesh, would not fail ultimately to justify him in the spirit. Even before being challenged to declare whether the gates of death had been revealed to him, or whether he had seen the gates of the shadow of death (38. 17), he had beheld a brighter prospect beyond the grave, when God would arise to befriend him and to champion his cause against his friends who had assailed his integrity:

> But as for me, I know that my Redeemer liveth.
> And that He shall stand up over my dust at the last
> Yea, after my skin has been destroyed,
> Then without my flesh shall I see God.
>
> (19. 25-6)

True, his mind had not been enriched intellectually. But he had a vision of God that lit up the dark recesses of his soul and that made him humble and repentant:

> I heard of Thee by the hearing of the ear,
> But now mine eye seeth Thee;
> Wherefore I abhor my words and repent,
> Seeing that I am dust and ashes.
>
> (42. 5–6)

It was the vision of the One, Omnipotent and All-Wise, who had revealed Himself to his soul, and whom, though he could not understand, he could absolutely trust. This new experience was productive of a deeper conviction of God's close inward presence and goodness. Because of this conviction, he felt secure. His life through God's hold upon it was, amid all the sorrows and sufferings, an object of divine care – a care that transcended all his rebellious questionings.

If Proverbs, Ecclesiastes, and Job stress the fear of God, the Song of Songs, which is also reckoned among the books of the Hebrew Wisdom literature, extols the love for God. This is at least how this 'gem of literature', whatever the origin of its imagery and literary structure, had impressed itself from the earliest times upon the Hebrew national consciousness. It is a difficult book; in fact, one of the most difficult books of the Bible; but the theme in its main outlines is clear. It glorifies perfect love that remains constant and steadfast amid all allurements and seductive influences; and it is because the Hebrew religious genius saw in its poesy a veritable thesaurus of word, thought, and expression, for depicting the soul's yearning and love for God, as typified in the Shulamite's attachment to her Beloved, that it has been preserved as a national literary treasure and finally became included in Israel's sacred literature.

The imagery in the Song of Songs is admittedly bold and sensuous and hardly compatible with the sublime and pure conception of God in Hebrew monotheism, but the absence in the book of any reference to the Deity serves to cast a veil over the intimate loving relationship between man and God which it purports to portray. The human soul yearns and goes out for God, and God responds; but God Himself remains ineffable and invisible.

Another fundamental feature of the Hebrew Wisdom literature is its universalism. The writers draw from life wherever found, and admit that other nations too possess the knowledge of God. The wisdom it teaches is not essentially based on the Torah – though the Torah embodies the highest wisdom – but has its source in human reason and is derived from general experience and observation of life. It thus transcends all that is local and temporary. Its precepts are of universal application and relevance. Nor can they ever become obsolete, but will endure as the days of the heavens over the earth.

Universalism is also the recurring note in the other Books, which, together with the Books of the Wisdom literature, and the Psalms, have been gathered to form that collection known as the Hagiographa, or 'Holy Writings'. This universalism reaches its highest point in the Book of Ruth. Primarily historical in aim and concerned to trace the ancestry of David, the book also seeks to teach that true religion is not confined to the bounds of one people, but is supra-national, and that the principle of divine reward for good deeds is not dependent on race but is equally valid for all sons of men.

NOTE

1. An English translation of the Egyptian *Dialogue of the World-Weary Man with His Soul*, and of the Babylonian Hymn to Marduk, *I Will Praise The Lord of Wisdom*, both of which are the nearest ancient parallels to the Book of Job, can be read in Pritchard, op. cit., the former on pp. 405 ff., and the latter (sometimes called 'The Babylonian Job') on pp. 434 ff

CHAPTER 10

THE JUDEAN THEOCRATIC STATE

FOR generations the prophets, supported by priests, psalmists, and sages, sought to inculcate the sublime teachings of the Torah and to win the people's allegiance to its commands. But in vain. Attracted to the ways of the nations, with their sensuous cults and self-centred ethics, Israel remained refractory and turned a deaf ear to all exhortations and warnings. Then came the Babylonian exile. Almost instantaneously the whole of their religious life and outlook underwent a radical change. As they brooded over their tragic experiences which they recognized as the righteous judgement of God for their apostasy from Him, they gradually learnt to realize that their future depended on their obedience to God and entire submission to His will as communicated in the Torah.

It was in this chastened and penitent mood that the people surrendered themselves to the ministrations and guidance of the prophet-priest Ezekiel who not only stimulated and encouraged them with assurances of spiritual blessings and promises of restoration, but also sought to impress upon them the importance of the Torah for their individual and national well-being.

Ezekiel was followed by a long line of teachers known as *soferim* (scribes), under whom the Torah came to occupy a central place in the religious life of the people. The school took the place of the Temple, the teacher, or scribe, that of the sacrificing priest, the religious observances – particularly the Sabbath, prayer, and fasting – that of the sacrificial rites. At that time, too, were laid the foundations of the Synagogue, which with its regular meetings for congregational worship and instruction met the needs of the exiles.

Such then were the influences that trained and strengthened the exiles in the worship of the one and only God in purity and holiness, in spite of the intense pressure of their idolatrous environment with its orgiastic star-worship, rich temples, powerful priesthood, and bewitching ritual. With the result that by the close of the exile the people was radically cured of all idolatrous taints and tendencies, and the monotheistic faith irrevocably established in Israel.

The Babylonian captivity came virtually to an end in 538 B.C. with the fall of Babylon to Cyrus of Persia. Anxious that the key-road that ran through Palestine should be held by a people bound to his interests by gratitude, Cyrus issued a decree authorizing the return. Immediately, a band of 42,000 devout souls shouldered their goods and, under the Davidic Zerubabel and Joshua, the priest, trekked back to their ancestral land.

It was an attenuated, impoverished, and devastated fatherland to which the exiles returned. The northern hill country had for some time been attached to the province of Samaria, while the southern hill country was occupied by the Edomites. All that was left was a small stretch of territory of about 1,000 square miles in the environs of Jerusalem, of which a good part was desert land.

The returned exiles had more than enough to do to reorganize and recreate their lives and redeem their fatherland from the decay into which it had fallen. Yet amid all their many preoccupations and pressing problems they forthwith set up an altar on the site of the great brazen altar in Solomon's Temple, and started to make preparations for the restoration of the House of God, to bear witness to the monotheistic faith that at last they had made their own.

But no sooner had the first flush of enthusiasm died away than discordant voices could be heard. The moralization of the conception of God that had now found common acceptance in Judea led many to disparage the value of the Temple and its ritual, and to question in general the whole validity of the religious observances. As against this critical attitude the prophets of that period, Haggai and Zechariah insisted on the need of a rallying centre such as the Temple alone could supply for the religious and social life of the people. They held that however much religion might be moralized there was still need for some outward expression of communion with God and consecration to His service, to enable man to overcome the evil impulses and influences within and about him, and that the Temple with its well-ordered ritual possessed the power to release certain spiritual energies which, if directed aright, were capable of enhancing the whole social and moral order of the community.

Other discordant voices raised in the land presented a moral problem. The total disappearance of idolatry from Israel with all its abominable iniquities, such as bloodshed and debauchery, meant for many the fulfilment of the moral law with no further claims upon them. This was a problem which the prophet Zechariah made his own. He too attached importance to the Temple and insisted that it must be built. But for all his attention to bricks and mortar, he was principally concerned with the rebuilding of human character. He thus strove not only to see the Temple rebuilt and dedicated to God but also urged upon the builders those moral and spiritual truths without which the Temple and its worship would be but a hollow mockery. 'These are the things that ye shall do: speak ye every man the truth with his neighbour; execute the judgement of truth and peace in your gates; and let none of you devise evil in your heart against your neighbour, and love no false oath, for all these I hate, saith the Lord' (Zech. 8. 16–17).

Under the spur of these prophets, the construction of the Temple began to take shape, and in 516 B.C., exactly seventy years after the 'Destruction', a new temple was seen rising majestically on the ruins of the old.

In the meantime, under circumstances altogether unknown, Zerubabel, who was Governor of Judea under Persian tutelage when the rebuilding of the temple began, disappeared from the scene. His political prerogatives were now turned over by the Persian authorities to Joshua, who had become High Priest in the rebuilt Temple and who, by virtue of his new position, had vested in him the supreme authority – religious and civil (including political) – held hitherto by the Judean kings.

Malachi, whose prophetic activity began after the Temple had already been in existence for some years, in the spirit of his predecessors, showed equal zeal for the minutiae of the Temple and for ethical conduct. At the same time, he conceived the Temple as a symbol of the universal worship of God in the days to come, when His name shall be great among the nations 'from the rising of the sun unto the setting of the same' (Mal. 1. 11). But the fulfilment of this universal vision, he insisted, depended on Israel's loyalty to Torah, through which alone she could make her witness to God and His righteousness effective. So he concluded his prophecy with the exhortation to Israel 'Remember the Torah of Moses, My servant, its statutes and judgements (religious commands and ethical precepts)' (Mal. 3. 22 [4. 4]). With this message Hebrew prophecy took leave of Israel and the rest of mankind. It had by now fulfilled its divinely appointed role of communicating to Israel, and through Israel to the world, the principles by which nations and individuals must live in fulfilment of their destiny.

Loyalty to the Torah for which Malachi pleaded demanded, however, knowledge of its contents. This, in turn, involved instruction and study. But, strange as it may appear, there were in Judea at that time no competent teachers of Torah. The only people capable of engaging in this teaching work were the priests and levites, but their services were required for the proper ministrations of Temple worship, to which their psalmodies, songs, and music contributed the most distinctive features. This absence of Torah teaching meant that the religion of the people degenerated into a mere matter of routine practice, with little relevance to the baffling problems that were besetting their existence. Economic difficulties, bad harvests, enemy raids – Samaritan and Edomite – had indeed rendered the lot of the Judean community very hard and bitter. A general feeling of despair, a sense of frustration, became everywhere prevalent. This was not without effect upon the religious loyalty of the people. 'It is vain,' they cried, 'to serve God; and what profit is it that we have kept His charge and that we have walked mournfully before the Lord of Hosts?' (Mal. 3. 14). And although there was no return to idolatry, the resultant effect was a religious drift that did not stop short of intermarriage with the heathen neighbours – an evil that became so widespread as to imperil not only the purity of the Jewish religion, but also the very existence of this small Judean community.

Whilst religious conditions in Judea were on the decline, the Jews in Babylon were developing a vigorous religious life. Being without a temple and without a country, they saw themselves faced with imminent extinction as a people through absorption by the heathen, among whom they found themselves. But their unconquerable will to live drove them to achievement. They turned more and more to the Torah and their other sacred writings, and around these spiritual possessions they built up a new polity, stripped of all territorial limitations and political loyalties and founded upon piety and learning, religion and study.

The Babylonian authorities, on their part, perceived from the first the value of allowing the Jews to practise their own religion and develop their own institutions and of affording them opportunities for their material advancement. The bulk of the Jews rose in status in consequence. Many of them achieved positions of wealth and influence; and one of them, Daniel, became, like Joseph of Egypt, the sage of the court.

The same favourable conditions were enjoyed by the Babylonian Jews when they came under the rule of the Persians. Before long they entered fully into the business and commercial life of the Empire and some of their leaders also partook of the political activities at the royal court at Susa. Under King Ahasuerus, best identified with Xerxes (486–465), the prosperity and success of the Jews was so conspicuous as to arouse the jealousy of the king's grand vizier, Haman; and it was but by a providential concatenation of events, as described in the Book of Esther, that the Jews in the Persian Empire were saved from the destruction which Haman had contrived for them.

It was out of the ranks of this Babylonian Jewry that Ezra, the 'scribe', who was of priestly descent, came to infuse new life and new consciousness into the Judean community. Armed with a royal warrant which he obtained from the Persian King, Artaxerxes I Longimanus (464–424), granting him extensive powers to reform religious conditions in Judea, he arrived in

Jerusalem – according to Biblical chronology – in 458 B.C.,[1] accompanied by priests and levites and lay exiles. He immediately began to wage a relentless war against mixed marriages and at the same time to disseminate among the people the knowledge of the 'statutes and judgements (religious and ethical precepts)' of the Torah (Ezra 7. 10). Twelve years later he was joined by Nehemiah, the cup-bearer of Artaxerxes at Susa, who had been appointed by his royal master autonomous governor of the Judean province. Although his royal assignment lay principally in the domain of political action, the reorganization and administration – civic and economic – of the new state, and its defence against hostile neighbours, he shared Ezra's zeal for religious reforms – and for the Torah.

A decisive move in their common exertions on behalf of the Torah was made about 444 B.C., on the Hebrew New Year's Day, when Ezra, in the presence of Nehemiah, read from the Book of the Law of Moses before a large gathering who had assembled in the Temple Court in celebration of the Festival. On either side of Ezra stood professional expounders (*Mebinim*) who explained what was being read. The reading was followed by a solemn compact entered into by Nehemiah and the representatives of the people, pledging themselves to obey the ordinances of Torah, and to refrain, among other things, from foreign marriages and trading on the Sabbath day.

This public reading of the Torah was no innovation in Israel. There is evidence of such readings having been held generations before Ezra's time (cf. Deut. 31. 10–13). What was novel was the exposition that accompanied the reading. Ezra's aim was to put the Torah in the position of supreme authority and to win the people as never before to the recognition and acceptance of its rule. But if this aim was to be achieved a mere reading of the Torah would not suffice. What was read had to be explained, so that it might be understood and acted upon. Furthermore, conditions had so fundamentally changed since the time the Torah was given to Israel that the written text could no longer be deemed capable of serving as an absolute guide. If, therefore, the Torah was to occupy the position which Ezra had intended to secure for it, its contents had not only to be explained literally, but also interpreted in a way which did not ignore the changes in the situation. Such were the requirements which the exposition which accompanied Ezra's reading was designed to satisfy. It was an exposition which meant more than simply an explanation of the written text. It also involved an interpretation flexible enough to cover new aspects and conditions of life not provided for in the text itself, and to include such enactments as the exigencies of the time demanded. Nor was this method of interpretation an innovation of Ezra. It was but an application to his own times of the oral tradition which, going back to the earliest times, had been transmitted from generation to generation as oral Torah (*Torah she-be-al-peh*), in part interpreting, in part supplementing the written Torah (*Torah she-bi-ketab*), and in its total effect transforming scripture from being only a written document liable to become obsolete, into a continuous revelation keeping pace with the ages.

As a result of Ezra's efforts the Torah, instead of being the exclusive monopoly of a class, became accessible to all who desired to know it and in time was established sovereign in the state. Slowly but surely the Torah became the final source of every Jewish norm and practice, rule and custom, in all departments of life – religious, moral, political, social, economic, and domestic. This enthronement of the Torah in the mind and heart of the people was of far-reaching effect on the religion and history of the Jewish people. It saved Judaism from becoming a mere priestly religion, concerned only with matters of ritual and religious practice, and made it one embracing all life and action. And at the same time it provided a safeguard against that heathen accommodation, which had brought about the disappearance of the ten tribes and the destruction of the first Hebrew State, and thus ensured the purity of the national religion and the survival of Judaism.

Thus originated the Judean theocratic state – a state ruled by Torah – which, though politically and economically insignificant, was destined not only to give a definite direction to Jewish history, but also to prove a factor of the greatest consequence in the history of mankind.

Outside Judea in the places of dispersion, with their main centres in Babylon and Egypt, the Jewish communities in close relation with the Judean community in Jerusalem developed a spiritual unity, founded on the Torah and a common body of traditions, ideals, hopes, and aspirations. A factor contributory to the welding of this spiritual unity was the influence of Ezra and Nehemiah at the Persian Court, which enabled them to impose on all the Jewries throughout the Persian Empire a uniform pattern of Jewish faith and practice.

Illustrative of this influence is the military order of the year 419 B.C., discovered at Elephantine, given by Darius to the local Jewish military garrison to observe the Passover in accordance with the requirements of their religion. This unity remained unimpaired even after the breaking-up of the unity of the political world of which the Jews were a part, with the destruction of the empire of Alexander the Great about 300 B.C.

The peaceful existence enjoyed by the Jews under their Persian rulers enabled them to maintain and develop without any outside interferences the work begun by Ezra. A succession of teachers known as *Soferim* (Scribes), generally identified with the Men of the Great Assembly, arose with the resolve to make the Torah the common possession of the people. With this aim in view they taught the Torah in Synagogue and school. They interpreted the biblical ordinances – civil, domestic, economic, and social – formulating their underlying principles, classifying their details, fixing their norms, regulating their usages, and adapted the laws to changes in conditions and circumstances. In their interpretation of the Holy Writ they were guided by the light of reason and the principles of righteousness, justice, and equity which were for them equally part of revealed Torah. They accordingly sought to mitigate the apparent severity of the law, bringing it more into harmony with life, and with the fundamental human wants. Among many examples of their methods that could be adduced, may be mentioned their substitution of compensation for the Biblical law of retaliation in case of assault; and their lenient application of the Sabbath laws in comparison with the rigorism of certain sects who, guided by the strict letter of the law, abstained completely from all physical activities on the Day of Rest.

Another example is their relaxation of the law of evidence to establish a husband's death, the testimony of one single witness, even based on mere hearsay, being declared sufficient to enable the wife to re-marry.

On the other hand, in order to safeguard the Torah against any possible infringement, they enacted cautionary rules, known as 'fences' which are designed, so to speak, to prevent any precipitate violation of the sacred enclosure of the Torah itself.[2] This work of teaching, interpretation, adaptation, and modification represented only part of the exertions of the *Soferim*. Their purpose was to enthrone the Torah in the mind and heart of the people and enhance its power as the sanctifying source of all life and action. For this, too, they relied principally on instruction. They held regular public expositions of the Pentateuch, and the prophets, as well as of the Hagiographa (Holy Writings), and by means of illustration, story, legend, and parable sought to inspire among their hearers a deep love for God and His Torah. In addition they instituted many practices which were designed to foster piety and devotion. They organized daily worship, which included the rich expression of prayer and praise in the Psalms, and prescribed the principal benedictions, as well as most of the rites which constitute to the present day the extra-Biblical observances of the devout Jew.

All these prescriptions that emanated from the Soferic school, no less than the adaptations and modifications of the Biblical laws, became embodied in the unwritten Torah and in so far as they were brought in direct relation with the written Torah, they became part of the divine law which God had revealed to Moses on Sinai.

Persian rule came to an end in Judea in 333 B.C. when the all-conquering Macedonian, Alexander the Great, burst with ease into Asia and took possession of Palestine. Alexander was no ordinary world conqueror, bent merely on the gaining of power. His was a higher aim; it was to scatter the seeds of

Greek culture and to disseminate its gifts – its arts and philosophies, its delicacies and graces – throughout the world. But whereas all other peoples succumbed to the dazzling brilliance of the new culture that came to them from the Mediterranean world, under the name of Hellenism (from *Hellas*, meaning Greece), the Jews alone remained unaffected. Schooled by the Torah, they had developed a high sense of their mission and destiny and refused to have any dealings with a culture which was essentially pagan in character and which, with all its undoubted wisdom, refinement, and seductive charm, was at bottom cynical and as such could offer at best nothing but despair.

Alexander, however, did not believe in imposing Greek culture by coercion. Considering himself the legitimate heir of the Persian kings, he accepted and confirmed the peoples he conquered in the statutes and privileges granted to them by his Iranian predecessors. The Jews under his rule were thus able, without any outside interference, to follow their own mode of life, to practise their own faith, and to maintain and develop their own institutions.

The same favourable conditions were enjoyed by the Jews under the Ptolemies who, after the death of Alexander in 323 B.C. and the consequent division of his empire among his warring generals, became masters of Egypt and finally also of Palestine. The Ptolemies, on the whole, were not interested in the spreading of Hellenism among their subjects. Yet, in Egypt, where thousands of Jews had settled, having come there either as voluntary emigrants, attracted by the humanity of the Ptolemies, or as mercenaries or war captives, the process of Hellenization was inevitable and rapid. Before long the Hebrew language was barely understood, and by about 280 B.C. the Jewish community in Alexandria – the most important in Egyptian Jewry – found it necessary to provide the Greek-speaking Jews with a Greek version of the Hebrew scriptures. First the Pentateuch was translated, and the translation of the rest of the Bible soon followed. This Greek version of the Bible known as the Septuagint (from the Greek, 'seventy'), in memory of the seventy elders who are said to have participated in the work, is the oldest version of the Bible in any foreign tongue, and whilst primarily intended for the use of the Hellenized Jews, it at the same time served to carry the message of Judaism to the heathen world, attracting in the process numerous converts from among the higher classes, no less than the masses.

The favourable conditions enjoyed by the Judean community, under the Ptolemies, came to an end about 275 B.C. when the Greek Seleucids, having taken possession, on the dissolution of Alexander's Empire, of Babylon (312), Syria (301), and Asia Minor (281), began to make attempts at conquering Palestine. For over a century Palestine was a tramping ground of the rival warring armies.

One of the effects of the turmoil of war was the decline and final disappearance of the *Soferim* as a collective body, with the consequent practical disintegration of the corporate religious life.

With the defeat of Scopas, the Egyptian general, by Antiochus III (223-187) at Panias in 198, the country definitely passed under the sway of the Seleucids. Conditions immediately began to improve. Antiochus III, the first Syrian ruler of Judea, was well disposed towards his Jewish subjects. He gave the Jews a large measure of freedom and autonomy, and confirmed them in the rights and privileges they enjoyed under Egyptian domination. Nor were the Jews slow to take advantage of the changes in the situation.

One of the most pressing needs of the time was to revive in some form what the *Soferim* had for so long provided. A governing senate, or *gerousia*, was established to assume the general administration, political, judicial, social, of the affairs of the community, as well as to teach and interpret the Law and give authoritative and needful religious guidance, as the occasion demanded.

At the head of this governing body, which later became known as the Sanhedrin, stood 'pairs' of teachers named *Zuggoth*, one of whom was the *Nasi* (Prince) and the other *Ab Beth Din* (Chief of the Court). This dual appointment appears to have been an adaptation to changed conditions of the system introduced by King Jehoshaphat whereby the administration of the strict religious law and that of the civil law were separated from each other,³ the *Nasi*, now, being the leading authority in civil (including political), and the *Ab Beth Din* in religious matters. In the last resort, however, the supreme authority still remained vested in the High Priest, who continued to enjoy under the Seleucids the rights and prerogatives conferred upon the office by the Persian kings.

Whilst the situation was thus essentially the same as it had been under the preceding regimes, there was a decisive change in the attitude of the people to the Hellenistic civilization. Many Hellenistic cities sprang up in Palestine, bringing Jews and Greeks into close contact, socially as well as commercially. Characteristic Greek ideas and practices began in consequence to infiltrate and make themselves felt powerfully more and more, attracting particularly the members of the aristocracy and of the upper classes.

Unfortunately, the Hellenism that reached Palestine in common with other oriental countries from the West was not the Hellenism of classical Greece, the Hellenism that flowered in the genius of a Pythagoras, Socrates, Aristotle, Plato. It was a debased kind of Hellenism, decadent, wily, voluptuous, such as was purveyed by the soldier, the trader, the slave-dealer, and the brothel-keeper.

The devastating effects of this new civilization upon the religious and moral life in Judea is indicated in the Book of Jubilees, written about this period. The biblical ordinances were disregarded, the Sabbath was desecrated, the rite of circumcision neglected. Jewish youth would strip themselves naked for Greek athletic games, and even idolatry made its appearance again among Jews. In the domain of morals, the degeneration had reached so low a point that even the oath had lost its sanctity. Ben Sira, too, another contemporary writer, speaks in his Ecclesiasticus of Jews who are ashamed of the Torah and of ungodly men who have forsaken the law of the Most High (41).

For some time those who had embraced the Greek ways of life did not interfere with those of their countrymen who preferred to remain loyal. But shortly after the accession of

Antiochus IV (175–164), the son of Antiochus III and the brother of Seleucus IV whom he succeeded, a number of renegade Jews made a determined effort to Hellenize Judea by force. Whatever fascination Greek fashions and customs had for these renegades, their Hellenistic zeal was derived from political considerations. They saw the tiny Judean state as a mere weak and helpless plaything in the hands of two rival powers, and they believed that its future security depended on its complete integration within the great Syro-Greek empire, and identification with its institutions. This attitude precisely suited the book of Antiochus. A megalomaniac of the first order, as his self-conferred title *Theos Epiphanes* – 'the Evident God' – indicates, he pursued a policy of unification, which he sought to achieve by imposing his national culture upon all his subjects. Recognizing the formidable foe he would have to encounter in the Jewish religion, he resolved to extirpate it root and branch throughout the land. All religious precepts, particularly circumcision, and the keeping of Sabbath and the Festivals, were prohibited on pain of death. Copies of the 'Book of the Law of Moses' were destroyed, and the possession of such a book was made a capital offence. The whole of the Jewish sacrificial cult was proscribed. The Temple itself was converted to the worship of the Olympian Zeus. Swine's flesh was offered on its altar, harlots were brought within its sacred precincts, and heathen altars were set up in towns and villages, worship at which was made a test of loyalty.

What was most perilous for Judaism in this crisis was the fact that Antiochus in his paganizing measures was aided by treacherous high priests, first Jason and then his supplanter Menelaus, both men of vaulting ambition, who for the sake of their personal advancement sought to ingratiate themselves with Antiochus by displaying a flattering zeal for his policy. Nor was the solid part of the community, the men of property and position, averse altogether to this Hellenizing process, which they believed was to bring in its wake peace and order in the land, as well as all the privileges of Antiochian citizenship.

The rank and file, however, thanks to the persistent efforts of a succession of teachers, whose names have become lost to posterity, remained loyal and staunch. Refusing to yield, many of them perished as martyrs, whilst others sought safety in refuge and flight.

But this passive resistance soon flared up into open rebellion. Mattathias, an aged priest, who was of the family of the Hasmoneans and dwelt in Modin, a small town north-west of Jerusalem, issued the call: 'Whoso is zealous for the Torah, let him follow me.' This call set the stamp on the character of the revolt. It was to be essentially a war in defence of Torah. Thousands responded to the call. Admittedly not all those whom Mattathias drew to his side were actuated by the same motives. In the main body of the insurgents there were two motives at work, the religious and political. In their judgement the defence of the Torah could best be secured by political freedom, the throwing off of the yoke of the foreign oppressor and the establishment of a self-governing Jewish state. At the same time there were some, known as the *Hasidim* (the Pious), whose motives were purely religious. All that mattered to them was the Torah and no political gains entered into their consideration. While again there were others for whom political liberty was really the end aimed at, and the defence of the Torah was a convenient battle-cry with which to gain the support of those who did not care for the political object. But in the first phase of the struggle, all who threw in their lot with Mattathias sank their differences and took up arms in defence of Torah.

Forming themselves into small groups, the insurgents went up and down the countryside, destroying the heathen altars, harrying the apostates, and engaging in general guerrilla activities against the enemy. In retaliation, Syrian punitive troops were despatched against them, staging one of their attacks on the Sabbath. The defenders, unwilling to desecrate the sacred day, perished without offering any resistance. Thereupon Mattathias enacted a decree, which has since become valid Jewish law, making it obligatory for Jews to defend themselves on the Sabbath Day, if attacked.

On the death of Mattathias the struggle was carried on by his five sons. Head and shoulders above the others was Judas, who was called Maccabeus (generally taken to mean 'the Hammerer', and from whom the Maccabees derived their name). A supreme tactician, he avoided pitched battles, and surprising the enemy in night attacks, he met and defeated several Syrian armies much superior in strength and size to his own. Within a year he cleared Jerusalem of the enemy and obtained possession of the Temple, which he cleansed from all heathen pollution, and restored and reconsecrated to the worship of the God of Israel on *Kislev* (December) 25, in the year 165 B.C. A special Festival, marked with the kindling of lights, was then instituted and joyously celebrated for eight days, under the designation of *Chanukah* (Dedication), a festival which has since been kept by Jews annually to the present day.

Soon after the recovery of the Temple, Antiochus died and, following on some further fighting with fluctuating fortunes on either side, peace was made in 163, and the Jews were given full freedom to live 'according to the customs of their forefathers' (I Maccabees 6. 59).

The victory of Torah over Hellenism was now complete and final. The Hellenist party slowly melted away, its adherents either becoming absorbed by the enemy or merging with their loyalist kinsmen; and although complete independence had yet to be achieved, a supreme Court was immediately established to administer the internal affairs of the community in accordance with the Torah, which was now once more restored to its dominant position in the country.

The religious cause for which the Maccabeans took up arms was now no longer a living issue, but politically Judea was far from free. It was still held down under the heel of its Syrian overlord. For over twenty years the struggle for political freedom went on, claiming in its course one after another of the Maccabean brothers as victims. Finally, in 143, Simon, the last of the surviving brothers, expelled the Syrians from Jerusalem, and thereby in the words of I Maccabees 'was the yoke of the heathen removed from Israel' (13. 41). Judea was now independent, and Simon was elected by popular assembly as the first High Priest and civil ruler, with the title Nasi, of the newly-established Jewish state.

NOTES

1. Some scholars would place Ezra after Nehemiah, giving the date for the former 398 instead of 458, but this is rejected by the majority of historians.
2. An example of such a 'fence' is the prohibition of handling on the Sabbath day a working implement as a precaution against its _use. Other examples concern 'the washing of hands' before meals and the tithing of certain products not specified in Scriptural law.
3. See pp. 46–7.

CHAPTER II

THE SECOND HEBREW COMMONWEALTH

In all this fight carried on by the Maccabean brothers for national independence, the *Hasidim* took no part. Having secured their religious objective, they withdrew from the struggle and made peace with the Syrians. Nor is this attitude of theirs to be condemned as unpatriotic. Yielding to none in their love for their country and people, the *Hasidim* did not believe it possible for tiny Judea to free itself altogether from foreign subjection, with predatory Syria, Egypt, and now the new looming power of Rome, prowling about to devour small nations.

And subsequent events have, to a considerable extent, confirmed their point of view. Judas himself, despite his brilliant victories, realized the weakness of his position and sought accordingly to strengthen it by entering into an alliance with Rome – an alliance which proved the first step to the loss of Israel's newly recovered national independence.

For the time, however, Judea felt secure. During the rule of Simon, the country enjoyed a large measure of prosperity; and his son John Hyrcanus (135–104), who succeeded him both in the high priesthood and as civil ruler, taking advantage of the internecine strife among the Syrians, added to the extent of his rule. But with his victories he grew more and more ambitious. No longer was it with him merely a question of religious freedom or political independence. He dreamt of a kingdom, an empire. He began to wage aggressive wars on all sides. He employed heathen mercenary troops, with whose aid he conquered the Samaritans and the Idumeans (the earlier Edomites) upon whom he enforced circumcision at the point of the sword.

In his aggressive nationalism, Hyrcanus was violently opposed by the Pharisees who, together with the Sadducees, formed the two principal parties that made the first appearance during that period. As spiritual heirs of the *Hasidim*, the Pharisees could not but condemn a war which had national

aggrandisement for its aim. It was this opposition of the Pharisees, whose influence upon the masses was great, which obliged
Hyrcanus to resort to mercenaries for his military adventures,
short of conscription, which he could not well introduce as this
was forbidden by the Torah (see Deut. 20. 8), the basic constitution of the land. The only support he derived was from the
Sadducees consisting mostly of those former Hellenized elements – the upper classes of priests, and the wealthier land-
owners, who had absorbed many foreign ideas and with them
an intense and aggressive nationalism.

Here we come to the point of cleavage between these two
parties, a cleavage which Hyrcanus' policy had only served to
accentuate. The difference between them is not indicated in the
names by which they had become known in history, for the
meaning of the names is certainly not clear. Both parties were
loyal to the Torah. But whereas the Sadducees, with all their
recognition of the Torah, laid primary stress on the nation, the
Pharisees, with all their attachment to the State, laid primary
stress on the Torah.

This difference of attitude determined the extent and nature
of the authority which Torah was to exercise in the State. The
Pharisees desired that all the affairs of the State should be
governed on strict Torah lines, with no concern for any other
consideration. The Sadducees, on the other hand, maintained
that whilst it was well to recognize the Torah as the basic constitution of the State, it was impossible to carry on a Government which, under changed conditions, necessarily demanded
close relations with heathen powers without making political
expediency and economic interest the final arbiter of things.
Not that the Pharisees were blind to the changes in conditions,
but the issue involved was the validity of the oral Law and its
inclusion in the concept of Torah. If Torah meant only the
written text of the Five Books of Moses, then evidently it was
impossible to obey it under new conditions. If, however, Torah
included the oral Law, then the way was open for its interpreters to discover from the written text its true meaning as applied to the needs of their own times.

The difference of attitude between the Pharisees and the

Sadducees as to the relative importance of Torah and nation stemmed from their respective conception of God. To the Sadducees, God was essentially a national God, the God of Israel only; to the Pharisees He was a universal God, the God of all mankind. This in turn led to the doctrinal difference in matters of eschatology (the end of things). As the history of religion shows, the belief in a universal God tends towards the individualization of religion, whereas the belief in a national God tends in the opposite direction. Because the Pharisees recognized God as the God of all mankind, they held fast to the doctrine of the individual's relation and responsibility to God, and consequently believed in the survival of the individual soul and in retribution in the hereafter; whereas the Sadducees, with their nationalistic conception of religion, rejected all these essentially individualistic and eschatological notions as mere fantasies of the Pharisees.

Hyrcanus was at first an adherent of the Pharisees, and in reconstituting the Sanhedrin, or Great Beth Din, by means of which he ruled, he filled it with Pharisaic members. The Pharisees, however, objected to his combination of the high priesthood with temporal power, and, irritated by their attitude, Hyrcanus broke with them and went over to the Sadducees.

From that time onwards the two parties became active rivals and competitors for the control of the State. Whenever the Sadducees were in the ascendancy, the country was full of aggressive warfare, rebellion, and bloodshed. Such were the tragic conditions throughout the days of the sons and successors of Hyrcanus, first Aristobulus, who had himself appointed King, and then his brother Alexander Jannaeus (103–76) who, as a result of a series of campaigns, ruled towards the end of his reign over a kingdom almost Solomonic in its extent. But notwithstanding these military gains and territorial acquisitions, the Pharisees were as irreconcilable as ever. The masses sided with the Pharisees and did not hesitate to attack the king in person on a certain Festival of Tabernacles for having treated with scorn the ritual of water libation which he, as officiating priest, had, according to Pharisaic tradition, to perform on the altar. A massacre ensued and many Pharisaic leaders were driven to exile. On his deathbed, he advised his wife, Salome Alexandra, whom he had nominated for the succession, to make peace with the Pharisees. Following his advice, Alexandra recalled the Pharisees from exile and placed them in control of the affairs of the State. Restored to power, they had vested in them more influence and authority than ever before. They re-organized the Sanhedrin, filling it exclusively with members of their own group. They re-cast the Temple ritual according to their prescriptions and enacted a number of laws which the needs of the time demanded. Foremost among these Pharisaic leaders was Simeon ben Shetach who, in association with Judah ben Tabbai, was placed at the head of the Sanhedrin, the former as *Nasi* and the latter as *Ab Beth Din*.[1] They both urged the judges to exercise the greatest care and impartiality in the administration of justice; whilst Simeon ben Shetach was responsible for the institution of the *Kethubah*, the marriage settlement, designed to give the wife marital security and to protect her against hasty divorce, as well as for the democratization of the education of children. The Pharisees also carried out the separation between the royal and ecclesiastical powers and prevented the ruling house from embarking upon foreign wars and conquests. The external peace of the country was matched by an internal tranquillity and prosperity, and generations later the reign of Salome Alexandra was looked upon as a golden age in the history of the second commonwealth.

But no sooner had Alexandra died (67 B.C.) than the Sadducees raised their heads again. Impressed with the warlike and martial qualities of her younger son, Aristobulus, they supported his claim to the succession against Hyrcanus, his older brother, who, not content with the high priesthood which he already held, had now seized the throne. The Pharisees, although preferring the pacific Hyrcanus, looked askance at the concentration in his hands of both the kingly and high priestly office, and in consequence withheld their support from him. The conflict ended in a victory for Aristobulus, who wrested the kingship and high priesthood from his defeated brother.

But now, as by way of unconscious revenge, a scion of the

Edomites, whom John Hyrcanus had forcibly Judaized, appeared on the scene to set into motion a course of events which was to bring irretrievable disaster upon the second Hebrew commonwealth. His name was Antipater. Calculating, wily, and ambitious, Antipater persuaded the defeated Hyrcanus to enlist the help of Aretas, the King of Nabatea Arabia on the borders of Judea. Once more, civil wars broke out between the two brothers. Both sides appealed to Rome for help. Pompey answered the call, advanced towards the capital, captured it, and conquered the land (63 B.C.).

Judea was now a Roman province, placed under the charge of Hyrcanus whom Pompey had reinstated as High Priest, but without the title of King. In all these wars, the Pharisees took little part. Whilst prepared to die for the Torah as they lived by it, they refused to give up their lives in the hopeless struggle for national independence where no religious issue was at stake. Hyrcanus and his supporting aristocracy also began to realize that the independence of Judea was lost and that the future depended on submission to Rome. But for Antipater, Hyrcanus' appointment by Pompey as nominal ruler, meant an increase in power, which he was not slow in turning to his own advantage. When Caesar became master of Rome after the defeat of Pompey at Pharsalus in 48 B.C., Antipater, who had prudently all the time sided with Caesar, hastened to ingratiate himself with the new dictator, from whom he won his appointment as Procurator of Judea. He immediately turned over to his son Herod the governorship of Galilee. His chance finally came with the invasion of Palestine by the Parthians, and their appointment of Aristobulus's son, Antigonus, on the Judean throne as King and High Priest. Herod immediately made for Rome where he was named by the Senate King of Judea in 39 B.C. He then returned, defeated Antigonus, captured Jerusalem, and put an end to the Hasmonean dynasty and all their claims.

Nominally still independent, Judea under its Idumean ruler was actually in bondage to Rome. As a puppet of Rome, Herod placed Roman interests above those of his subjects. In character cruel, rapacious, and vindictive, and realizing his tenuous hold on the people, he destroyed all the Hasmonean dynasty and by war and proscriptions reduced the upper classes, among whom the Sadducees were numerous, to a low state. On the other hand, in order to win the loyalty of the common people, he embarked upon extensive building operations, providing employment for many, and also had the Temple rebuilt on a most munificent scale. For the same reason, he sought to secure the goodwill of the Pharisees whose moral and spiritual influence upon the masses was steadily growing in proportion as that of the Sadducees was on the decline, and when the Pharisees refused to take the oath of allegiance to him, he did not insist.

The Pharisees, on their side, were finished with politics. As realists they became reconciled to the tragic fact that there was nothing that could humanly be done to rid their country from the Roman grip which, with the help of the semi-heathen king, was closing tighter and tighter upon them. Whilst they refused to despair of the hope of better days to come, they were content for the time being with the freedom they enjoyed to devote themselves to the study of the Torah, and to the dissemination of its knowledge as well as to the promotion of its observances among all the sections of the people.

This withdrawal, generally speaking, of the Pharisees from politics involved of necessity a separation of the political and religious administration of the country. This gave rise to the two Sanhedrins, the political and religious. The political Sanhedrin, composed primarily of the Sadducean aristocracy and presided over by the High Priest, concerned itself with political matters, and with the relations of the State with foreign countries; while the religious Sanhedrin, known as the Great Beth Din, presided over by pairs of teachers, had full control over the religious life of the people, and all civil and domestic issues, in so far as these did not impinge upon the politics of the State.[2] Taking full advantage of the situation, the Pharisees taught and interpreted the Torah, adjudicated in its name in all matters, religious and moral, and proceeded to adjust its ordinances to changed conditions, while all the time labouring with their countrymen for more faithful observance of the divine precepts and fanning in them the messianic hopes for the restoration of Israel to its ancient national glories and greatness, and the enthronement of the one and only God among the sons of men.

Foremost among the Pharisaic leaders at this time were Hillel and Shammai, Hillel being the *Nasi* and Shammai being the *Ab Beth Din*. Hillel came from Babylon to Jerusalem when already a mature man, whilst Shammai was a native of Jerusalem. These two teachers differed in temperament: Hillel was a proverbial saint – patient, gentle, and humble. His ethical influence on his own generation and generations that came after him was immense, and he epitomized Judaism in the golden rule 'Do not unto others that which is hateful unto thee'.[3] Shammai, on the other hand, was of a sterner disposition. Yet, with all their contrast in temperament, Shammai shared with Hillel a common humaneness. Hillel's maxim 'Be of the disciples of Aaron, loving peace, pursuing peace, and loving human creatures'[4] is paralleled with a saying of Shammai 'Receive every man with a cheerful countenance.'[5] These two teachers differed also in their interpretations and applications of the law, Hillel displaying a tendency towards leniency, Shammai towards rigorism.

The difference of attitude between Hillel and Shammai was not merely a question of temperament. In the last analysis it stemmed from divergent exegetical principles, which at times in fact worked in the opposite direction, Hillel holding a more rigorous view than Shammai. On the whole, it seems that Shammai, unless there was a clear tradition to the contrary, followed closer the literal meaning of the text. Hillel, however, operated more freely with certain principles of Biblical interpretations which he had seen applied by scholars before him, and which enabled him to adjust the law to the conditions of the time. A classical example of Hillel's application of his method for the adjustment of the law is the institution of the *Prozbul*,[6] a legal instrument which secured creditors against the operation of the year of release which according to Biblical law (Deut. 15. 1) demanded the cancellation of debts.

The difference in method employed by Hillel and Shammai

in the interpretation of the law perpetuated itself among their disciples, who, after the death of the two masters, formed two rival schools – the House of Hillel and the House of Shammai. The opposing views of these two schools stretched themselves practically along the whole gamut of Jewish life – ritual, domestic, social, and economic. Yet, despite their manifold differences, their basic allegiance to the written and oral Torah prevented them from degenerating into separate sects, and the two schools would often meet in conference in order to discuss their respective opinions and reach a decision by a majority vote.

Contrasted with the national-religious ideology of the Pharisees was that of the Essenes who made their appearance for the first time about this period. Little is known of the Essenes apart from the short references in Philo, Josephus, Pliny the Elder, and Hippolytus. In any event, having regard to the historical background, it would seem reasonable to connect the Essenes with the oppression and misery suffered by the Jews in the time of Herod, and to see in the sect the effort of men who forsook the wicked world in order to live their life of piety, in peace and safety. Living in seclusion for the most part, in isolated communities, in the neighbourhood of the Dead Sea, they practised a life of rigid asceticism, they abstained from marriage, attached importance to daily lustrations, took their meals in common and amid complete silence, and shared their possessions. Like the Sadducees they refused to be bound by the scriptural interpretations of the Pharisees, though unlike the Sadducees who were latitudinarians in life, the Essenes adhered strictly to the letter of the Holy Writ and their observance of the Biblical laws was accordingly marked by an excessive rigorism. This is exemplified in their observance of the Sabbath, on which, contrary to Pharisaic interpretation but in accordance with the literal sense of Exodus (16. 29), they would not move from their place. This deviation of the Essenes from the Pharisaic teaching in matters of practice also extended to matters of belief. They dabbled in mysteries, such as foretelling the future, casting out demons, and resorting to supernatural invocations for curative purposes.

They also held to a rigid predetermination, which denied man all freedom of action and effort. The Essenes in departing from the Pharisaic teaching lost that sense of harmony between life and religion, with the result that they withdrew from the world and sought to make up by the strictness of their asceticism for the failure to take a share in facing the temptation and sufferings of life. As such the Essenes were a kind of forerunners of the hermits and monks of the Christian church, who may indeed have learned part of the lesson of the Essenes. On the whole, the Essenes seem to have been a break-away from Judaism, with the exaggeration of some features which were recognized as belonging to Judaism, and the repudiation of others; because not only the practice of asceticism, properly so-called, but also the policy of withdrawal from the world to escape its burden of suffering, has never been approved by Jewish opinion generally at any time as a line for Jews to follow. No wonder that they faded away and came to count for little or nothing in the subsequent development of Judaism.

Akin in spirit to the Essenes, though not necessarily belonging to their circle, was a class of visionaries whose notions have come down to us in that body of literature known as the Apocalypse (Revelation), dealing with eschatology (the doctrine of the last things), and comprising such works as the book of Jubilees and of Enoch. Despairing, like the Essenes, of human conditions, the Apocalyptic writers directed their hopes to a future in which the present natural and temporal world-order would give way to a supernatural and eternal world brought about catastrophically by divine intervention. With this eschatological future is connected a heavenly Messiah, the Anointed One of God, gifted with divine authority, who would reign in splendour and glory over a restored Israel. To this consummation man can do nothing to contribute. No action of his can serve either to speed it on or retard it. Its rise has been predetermined from the beginning in the counsels of God, and the faithful are but bidden to have patience and trustingly await the miraculous deliverance and the reward which is theirs.[7]

As the product of a despair seeking relief in the hope of a

birth of a new supernatural world, Apocalypticism could not
fail to make appeal to a certain type of Jewish mind in times of
national tribulations and sufferings, from which there seemed
to be no earthly escape. This, in turn, gave rise to the formation
of the Damascene body of new covenanters and its closely
related Qumran community, the knowledge of the existence of
the former having come to light by the discovery in 1898, in the
Cairo *Genizah*[8] of the so-called *Zadokite Document*, and of the
latter by the Dead Sea Scrolls, first tumbled upon in the
spring of 1947. Besides certain striking ethical tendencies
which these two sects shared in common, they each believed
that they were living at the end of time, and looked for a
'Teacher of Righteousness' who was to be followed by a
Messiah who would bring salvation to those who kept away
from the world with its impurities, whilst handing over the
rest to destruction. The date of these two sects is still disputed
and their further history remains unknown. But so much is
certain that they both, in their beliefs and practices, were inspired by the Apocalypse, as is evidenced by the fact that the
Jubilees and Enoch were their favourite book, and, in the case
of the Qumran community, by the discovery in its library of
the Scroll known as *The War of the Sons of Light and the Sons
of Darkness* which, alike in theme and imagery, runs true to
the general pattern of Apocalyptic writings.

In stressing the depravity of human nature, the Apocalyptists stood in opposition to the teachings of Judaism, with its
doctrine of man as a being possessed of moral and spiritual
qualities, enabling him to overcome all evil and sin, and to
make an effective contribution towards the consummation of a
blessed future within the framework of the present; with the
result that the Apocalyptists, too, like the Essenes, remained
outside the main-stream of Judaism and had little influence on
its development.

But if the Essenes and the Apocalypists represented a kind of
negative reaction against the misery and oppression of the
times, the Zealots represented the positive reaction, the attitude of men who were not going to run away and hide themselves for the sake of peace, but were out to fight against the

oppressor and make an end of his tyranny. In this they differed from both the Pharisees and the Sadducees. The Pharisees were always on the side of peace, and though they looked for the coming of the Messiah to restore Israel and set up the Kingdom of God, they held that it could not be brought about by violence, but only through righteousness of conduct and loyalty to Torah. So, too, even more were the Sadducees opposed to the Zealots, because by their violence and open hostility to the Romans they upset all diplomatic relations and endangered the very existence of the State.

The Zealots, however, were not fanatical nationalists pure and simple, as were the latter Maccabeans. They were deeply ardent patriots who combined with an intense love of their country a devotion to Torah and were ready to fight and die for both.

Combining the religious and political motives in their extreme form, they took Torah as their warrant for hurling defiance against all enemies of God and His people. The Torah was the divine revelation of the Will of God and of His ways to Israel, God being the God of Israel, and Israel His chosen people, and their land His land where the presence of the heathen was a defilement and all foreign rule and acceptance an invasion of His rights. They thus thought it a mortal sin for a son of Israel to submit to the Romans and to recognize their lordship.

The first to lead the way in the direction of violent resistance to the Romans was Hezekiah, whom Herod had executed at the beginning of his reign. But it was Judas of Galilee, his son, who organized the Zealots as a band of desperate men who would stop at nothing in a cause which they held sacred. The Zealots' rise to power was accelerated by the complete subjection of Judea to Rome following the death of Herod in 4 B.C. Appealed to by Herod's sons in their rival claims to the throne, Rome interfered further only to annex Judea in 6 C.E., making it but a part of the Roman province of Syria.

On the whole, conditions in Judea even as a vassal of Rome could have been favourable. The Romans, in pursuance of the policy of interfering as little as possible with the internal affairs of conquered provinces, granted the Jews a large measure of autonomy. The religious Sanhedrin continued as hitherto to exercise its jurisdiction in all cases, whether religious, civil, or capital, involving an infraction of Jewish law, and the people were allowed full freedom in their religious pursuits and practices. Acting as intermediaries between the Roman administration and the people, was the political Sanhedrin, constituted at the will of the High Priest, and with a membership drawn largely from the politically-minded Sadducees. This political Sanhedrin had also to deal with cases of sedition and insurrection, its verdict however being subject to review by the procurators.' But unfortunately the procurators who governed Judea abused their power and did everything to render the lot of their Jewish subjects miserable and bitter. Most notorious among these procurators was Pilatus. His administration (26 C.E. – 36 C.E.) was characterized by corruption, violence, robberies, and continuous executions without even the form of a trial.

Caring little for the elementary human rights and feelings of his subject people, he outraged Jewish religious sentiments in every possible way. Contrary to all precedent, he ordered his legionaries to carry standards bearing imperial images through the Holy City and plundered the Temple in order to construct an aqueduct. He also sought to weaken the power and influence of the religious Sanhedrin by depriving them of the penal jurisdiction hitherto vested in them in capital cases which were of no concern to Rome. On the other hand, he saddled the political Sanhedrin with the responsibility of maintaining the Roman rule in the province. Theirs was the duty to order the arrest of any persons suspected of plotting against Rome, and where there was a clear capital charge to hand over the defendant to the Romans for actual judgement. It was before this political Sanhedrin that Jesus was brought for examination on the political charge that he had attempted to make himself King of the Jews. Fearing that, unless they followed the normal procedure in a capital charge which was considered sufficiently proved, the Jews would lose the little national independence they still retained (see John 11. 48–50), the Sanhedrin handed over Jesus to Pilatus, at whose order, Jesus, like many other Jews charged with sedition, was nailed to the cross by Rome.[9]

The Pharisees stood aloof from the whole affair. Their differences with Jesus were essentially religious. Never once did they reprove him for his messianic claims. In every case where they did rebuke him it was because of his disregard of their traditional interpretations of the laws of the Torah and the 'fences' erected round it.[10] As such their differences had no bearing whatsoever on the political charge for which Jesus appeared before the High Priest and his associates, and in which they could not intervene even if they would. Consequently not a single Pharisee is found to have participated in the trial, much less in the decision to hand over Jesus to the Romans.

The crucifixion of Jesus put an end to all political-national hopes which his followers had pinned on him. Instead they turned to apocalypse for an explanation of his death and sought to reassure themselves by exalting him into a heavenly Messiah who was to reappear speedily on earth as a supernatural ruler. Thus arose in that century the Judaeo-Christian sect which in time tore itself away from Judaism to found the Christian Church. The earliest adherents of this sect were Jews in all respects but one – they regarded Jesus as the Messiah. They made no other changes. They continued to go to the Temple, and presumably to the Synagogue, as they had been accustomed to do, and to all appearances conformed in every respect to the usual Jewish observances. Their belief that the Messiah had come was not a ground of division between them and other Jews. But within a few decades the Christian church under the influence of Paul was altering its conception of Jesus in a way that meant that he was no longer thought of as merely human, and implied that he was in fact a second God – a belief which was a denial of the unity of God as Jews understood the term. Once this development had taken place accommodation of Jewish Christians within Judaism was no longer possible and the final rift between the two became inevitable.

The removal of Pilatus in 36 C.E. on account of his tyranny brought little peace to the land. In 38 C.E. the Emperor

Caligula, claiming divine honours, demanded that worship be offered to him and that a bust of him be erected in the Temple for the purpose. The Jews refused, declaring that they would rather die than comply. His assassination in 41 C.E. automatically brought his order to nought.

Under Claudius, his successor, the Jews enjoyed a measure of peace and prosperity. He abolished the rule of procurators and replaced it by that of Agrippa I, a grandson of Herod, whom he made king over all the countries of his grandfather. The Jews once more had their own king, and the country the semblance of an independent kingdom. Agrippa was strict in religious observances and on very friendly terms with the Pharisees. For this reason he won much popularity, and on one occasion when he tearfully avowed in public assembly that as an alien, racially, he had according to Biblical injunction (Deut. 17. 15) no right to be king of Judea, the populace hailed him with acclamation 'Thou art our brother'.

On his death in 44 C.E. Agrippa I was succeeded by his Roman-educated son, Agrippa II. He, however, was king only in name. The real authority lay in the hands of the procurators whose rule was once more restored to Judea. These new procurators were much worse than the earlier ones and did all they could to outrage Jewish national self-respect and religious sentiments.

The prosecutions and humiliations of the Jews under these procurators gave increasing provocation to the Zealots. In the year 66 C.E. the Zealots under the leadership of Menahem, the son of Judas,[11] the founder of the party, rose in revolt and appealed to the people for a life and death struggle against the oppressor. The Pharisees in vain tried to restrain the people from plunging headlong into war and ruin. They were teachers of Torah and had only a lesson of submission to teach, of faithful acceptance of the divine will, even if it meant the endurance of oppression and cruelty. The conditions of the times in the country, however, were all against the Pharisees, with the result that the Pharisees were overborne. The Zealots dragged the people to war and the outcome was as calamitous as it was inevitable. In the summer of the year 70, after a siege of unbelievable horror and slaughter conducted by Titus, Jerusalem fell and the Temple went up in flames. The Jewish state had ceased to be.

But the Jews lived on.

NOTES

1. See p. 89.
2. The first to advance the theory of the two Sanhedrins was Dr Adolf Büchler, a former Principal of Jews' College, London, in his work *Das Synedrion in Jerusalem und das grosse Beth Din in der Quader-Kammer*, Vienna 1902. His theory has since gained an increasing number of adherents.
3. *Babylonian Talmud, Tractate Shabbath*, 31a.
4. The Mishnah, *Ethics of the Fathers*, i, 12.
5. op cit. i, 15.
6. The term *Prozbul* is generally explained from the Greek *pros Boule* – '(declaration) before the Council', and is the name given to a legal instrument drawn up by the creditor before the incidence of the year of release empowering the Court to collect the debt due to him. The principle underlying the *Prozbul* is founded on the Biblical passage 'that which is thine with thy brother, thine hand shall release' (Deut. 15.4). This has been interpreted by Hillel to exclude from the operation of the year of release such debts as had already been secured by order of the Court before the advent of the seventh year, such debts being virtually no longer 'with thy brother', but regarded as already 'exacted' – that is, collected.
7. It is the denial of the transcendental reality of an earthly future which in the last analysis marks off sharply Apocalypse from the Book of Daniel, whose imagery has been borrowed by one Apocalyptic writer after another. In the general solution of the problem of justice, Daniel follows the Prophets (see pp. 59–60) in depicting an earthly future which, save for the supremacy of righteousness, will not be unlike the present, a future in which even sinners will after trials and sufferings share in its bliss (Dan. 12. 10) – which explains the inclusion of the Book of Daniel in the Canon, notwithstanding its Apocalyptic elements.
8. *Genizah* (Hiding Place) is the name of the store-house in the Ezra Synagogue in Cairo which contained a large collection

of discarded ancient works and fragments of works in manuscript, shedding considerable light on Jewish literature and history, the large majority of the contents of which were transported by Dr S. Schechter in 1898 to form part of the collection at Cambridge University. Among these fragments was the *Zadokite Document* which Schechter first published in 1902. The sanctity attached to sacred works forbade their destruction and made the storage of discarded books a prized custom.

9. See Tacitus, *Annals* xv, 44: 'Auctor nominis eius Christus Tiberio imperitante per procuratorem Pontium Pilatum supplicio adfectus erat (Christ, the founder of the name [Christian] had undergone the death penalty in the reign of Tiberius by sentence of the procurator Pontius Pilatus).

10. See p. 87.

11 Some scholars identify this Menahem as 'The Teacher of Righteousness' of the *Dead Sea Scrolls*; see p. 104.

CHAPTER 12

THE JEWISH NATIONAL
SPIRITUAL CENTRE

IT was on a bedecked and beflagged Rome that the sun rose on that summer day in the year 71 C.E. The youth of thirty who had blazed across the fields and mountains of Judea, leaving fire and sword in his trail, was on his way to receive the glories and honours of an Empire. A triumphant procession awaited his victorious return; and the conquering hero, followed by Jewish captives and trophies of war, led the procession. Among the spoil carried in triumph was a Scroll of the Law. But the youthful warrior was not happy. He had misgivings and anxieties. He was haunted by a fear of Resurrection. He had heard Jewish soldiers being urged on to the defence of their beloved homeland by the assurance of immortality. Might not the corpses of the valiant Jewish defenders, lying scattered hither and thither amid the ruins, suddenly become repossessed of the enlivening spirit and, rising to take up arms once more, undo all the great work achieved by him at such unspeakable cost and anguish! It was in order to forestall such a contingency that Titus, we are told, left behind at Jerusalem the tenth legion of the Roman army.[1]

But all was in vain. True, the dead bones did not stir, nor did the captured Scroll return. But neither was the Jewish people robbed of its Torah, nor the gift of immortality denied to Israel. For this invincibility and deathlessness the Jewish people are indebted mainly to the Pharisees. They it was who generated among the people a spirit that proved mightier than the sword, and a loyalty that has stood the test of centuries.

Of all the parties and sects that existed at the time of the Destruction, and according to an ancient source[2] there were twenty-four of them, the only one to survive the national cataclysm was the Pharisees. All the other parties failed their people in the time of dire need. The Judeo-Christians at the very outbreak of the war made for the safe retreat of Pella beyond the Jordan, while the Sadducees, Zealots, and Essenes, and all the other sects, vanished gradually from the scene. The Pharisees alone stood at their post and were left to rebuild the shattered fabric of the spiritual life of Israel.

The Pharisees were indeed the party eminently suitable for coping with the needs of the times. For some time the Pharisees had been moving away from the national unit and the territorial state in the direction of individualism and universalism – the only foundations on which a reconstruction of Jewish life was now possible. The God of the Pharisees was not limited to Palestine. His benign providence extended over all the earth; nor was He the God of the nation alone. He was also the God of every individual. This indeed held a comforting assurance that, in spite of the national disaster, God still ruled. He was still the master of events, and He would, in the end, shape all things for the ultimate good of the nation, the individual, and the race. Moreover, in Judaism, as the Pharisees conceived it, the loss of political autonomy and the destruction of the Temple broke no essential links. They had developed the institution of the Synagogue with its elaborate liturgy, which could now take the place of the Temple for prayer and worship. Furthermore, the conception of the oral Law enabled them to reconcile development and change with loyalty to tradition, and to undertake the far-reaching adjustments in Jewish life which the new conditions demanded.

A leader in the work of reconstruction was Rabbi Jochanan ben Zakkai. Already before the termination of the war, seeing that Jerusalem was doomed to destruction, he left the city and went to the coastal town of Jabneh in order to establish there a cultural centre for the Jewish people. The story is told that he simulated death and had himself carried out in a coffin by his trusted disciples. Once outside the gates of the city, he went to seek the Roman general Vespasian and asked him for the gift of Jabneh and its school, for which the town was famed. The request appeared to the Roman general too trifling to be refused, and it was granted. Thus for the first time was Jerusalem and its Temple given up by men representing those elements in the Jewish people who, with all their patriotism and attachment to the Holy Land, did not want spiritual progress to be subjected to geographical limitations. Against this attitude militated that of the Zealots and Sadducees, who could not believe that a people without a country and State of its own could survive. Is not such a people like a soul without a body? To this Rabbi Jochanan and his followers might have answered: 'Certainly it is; and we believe in the survival of the soul.'

When the appalling news of the fall of Jerusalem and the burning of the Temple reached Rabbi Jochanan, he rent his garments but consoled his disciples and followers with the thought that all was not lost. They still had the Torah which was to become the rallying force of the Jewish people, and the task before them was not to weep over the past but to reconstruct a new future out of the shambles of the present. He immediately set about to create in Jabneh a spiritual centre which was to reinforce the national bonds now that the bonds of the Fatherland had been lost. A sovereign body, an academic Sanhedrin, was set up after the model of the Supreme Council of pre-Maccabean days[3] and entrusted like it with the combined functions of education, legislation, judicature, and government. Entering upon its tasks, this Sanhedrin lost no time in providing for a wide range of religious, civil, and criminal law as far as the Roman rulers would allow. A number of measures were adopted to meet the confusing problems that arose in the numerous observances which centred round the Temple and the priesthood. The divine services and liturgy were recast and readapted by the substitution of prayers for animal sacrifices and the insertion of supplications for the speedy restoration of the Temple and the ancient Hebrew polity.

The Sanhedrin very soon established itself as the central religious authority with jurisdiction recognized by Jews in Palestine and beyond, even to distant Persia and Media. One of the most direct means for the exercise by the Sanhedrin of its authority over world Jewry was the prerogative, hitherto reserved for the Jerusalem Sanhedrin, of regulating month by month the calendar, and communicating to most distant communities the day of the new moon on which the whole of the

Diaspora no less than the Palestinian Jews depended for the celebration of the ensuing feasts and fasts.[4]

The Sanhedrin also became through its *Nasi* (President) the nation's accredited representative before the Roman authorities, and a semblance of royalty was imparted to its authority by appointing a Rabban Gamaliel, who was a descendant of Hillel and hence of Davidic lineage, as its *Nasi*.

Educationally, the tasks that devolved on the Sanhedrin was to teach and transmit the oral Torah. This teaching was carried out by means of the two methods which had been practised in the schools long before the destruction of the Temple.

The one method was to teach the oral Torah in the form of an exposition of the Biblical text. This was the *Midrash* method – a term derived from the Hebrew root meaning 'to teach, to investigate'. When the exposition yielded a legal teaching, the result was a *Midrash Halachah* (lit. 'walking', with reference to Ex. 18 20: 'And thou shalt show them the way wherein they shall walk'); if a non-legal, ethical, or devotional teaching, it was a *Midrash Aggadah* (lit. 'narration'). The other method was to teach the oral Torah independently of the scriptural basis which was claimed for it. This method was appropriately designated *Mishnah*, from a Hebrew root meaning 'to repeat', as it was only by dint of repetition that an oral teaching, transmitted without the aid of a written text, could have been imparted and fixed in the memory.

The Midrash method, which was the older of the two, was first employed by Ezra and his associates, and represented for centuries after Ezra the most important medium for the expression of Jewish thought and teaching. Midrash was, in fact, during the whole of the Soferic period, the 'Queen' of Jewish spiritual life; but whilst Midrash was an admirable vehicle for transmitting oral teachings that stemmed directly or indirectly from Scripture, it could not be used in connexion with that large body of traditional usages that came into being and established themselves independently of Scriptural sanction. This led to the introduction of the Mishnah form.

With the rise of the Sadducees, who not only denied the binding character of the oral law but opposed the scriptural text in its literal sense to the interpretations transmitted by the Pharisees, there was little advantage to be gained by appealing to the written text in support of oral traditions. What was required was the building up of a definite system of directives which were considered binding by virtue of the authority whence these emanated. Thus did the Mishnah, about the end of the first century B.C., begin to be given preference to Midrash, even in connexion with Halachic teachings that were derived directly from scripture; and those who specialized in teaching Mishnah were named *Tannaim*, from the Aramaic root corresponding to the Hebrew one from which the term Mishnah is derived.

The adoption of Mishnah did not, however, altogether oust the Midrash form. Not only was Midrash allowed to retain the Aggadic field all to itself, but even in the realms of *Halachah*, its sway, though disputed, did not entirely cease, with the result that Midrash and Mishnah continued to exist side by side as media for teaching *Halachah*.

This teaching activity by means of Midrash and Mishnah had all along been carried on orally for fear lest such teaching, if committed to writing, might be confused with the written Torah. But by the time the Temple was destroyed the accumulated traditions as a result of the activities of the schools since the days of Ezra had become so great that the best memory could normally be no longer trusted; much less could memory serve as a reliable guide considering the convulsing effects of the political upheavals extending over a long period which the nation had been passing through. Furthermore, the absence of written records was responsible for the growth of conflicting traditions and these had introduced uncertainty into the religious and legal practices. There were also as we have seen differences between the schools of Shammai and Hillel,[5] and these differences, which concerned basic laws and their application in detail, only served to aggravate this uncertainty extending it over the entire religio-legal life.

Such was the situation which faced the Jabneh Sanhedrin, and to which it applied itself with singular devotion and energy. One of the first tasks it set itself was to resolve the outstanding differences of opinion. Every problem and dispute was brought to the test of scripture, or recognized tradition, or logical reasoning, and decided upon by a majority vote. Next came the task of conserving the body of traditional laws and teachings. Valuable traditions began to be collected and re-dacted in Mishnah form by pupils of Jochanan ben Zakkai and his younger contemporaries. The activity of Jabneh provided a stimulus to other schools which had sprung up in various parts of the country and where scholars made their contributions towards the preservation and development of oral traditions and teachings.

Foremost among Mishnah teachers was Rabbi Akiba (c. 50–135), with whom the real systematization of the contents of the traditional law in Mishnah form began. He it was who was the first to arrange Halachic teachings according to subject-matter with divisions and sub-divisions, facilitating the task of the teacher in the handling of new problems as they arose and in making the law more accessible to disciples. Several attempts in the same direction were made by Akiba's disciples, notably Rabbi Meir (c. 110–175).

Parallel with the attention given at Jabneh to Mishnah went its cultivation of Midrash. It was from Jabneh that there emanated these series of Midrashim in which the centuries-long process of Biblical interpretation reached a high point never since surpassed. The first of this series was the *Mekilta*, a Midrash on the Book of Exodus compiled by Rabbi Ishmael (60?–140?).

Akiba also contributed greatly to the development of the Midrash. Evolving a new method of interpretation which at-tached the utmost importance to every single jot and tittle of the Biblical text, Akiba opened up new vistas in Midrash lead-ing to enrichment of law, morality, and religion. Akiba's method was opposed by Ishmael, who maintained that 'the Torah speaks in the ordinary language of man'. Yet, stimulated by the Master, Akiba's disciples, Rabbi Judah ben Ilai (100?–180?) and Rabbi Simeon ben Yochai (100?–160?) adopted his method and applied it respectively in the Midrashim – the Sifra on Leviticus, and the Sifra on Numbers and Deuteronomy –

they themselves had compiled. Simeon also compiled a Midrash on Exodus, also named *Mekilta* which has come to light within recent years.

It was also at Jabneh that the process of canonization, about which there is much uncertainty but which by every indication began centuries before the Babylonian exile, was brought to completion by the acceptance of the Song of Songs, Ecclesiastes, and Esther (or their retention) within the Canon. The Jabneh academy also determined which of the Hebrew texts of the Bible in circulation at that time, as illustrated by the Dead Sea Scrolls, was to be deemed authoritative, and thereby established what in all essentials constitutes the consonantal text of the Hebrew Bible of today.[6] Furthermore, in order to support that text, Akiba and Rabbi Joshua ben Chanania, another famous member of the Jabneh academy, commissioned the proselyte Aquila, from Sinope in Pontus, to render it with exact literalness into Greek for the use of the Greek-speaking Jews who had been relying on the various Greek Septuagint versions which diverged from the text now declared authoritative. Thus was produced the famous Aquila Greek version, of which only fragments and quotations have been preserved in the Origen Hexapla Bible (*c.* 240 C.E.) and palimpsests found in the Cairo *Genizah*.

The work of reconstruction, religious and social, proceeded generally speaking apace until it was completely wrecked in the days of Hadrian (117–138). This emperor began his reign by showing friendship to the Jews, but before long things took a turn for the worse. Conceiving it his task for political reasons to achieve a measure of cultural and religious uniformity among his subject peoples, Hadrian gave orders for the erection, on the site of the ruined Temple of the Lord, of a temple to Capitoline Jupiter. Driven to exasperation, the Jews under Simeon ben Kocheba ('Son of the Star'), whose real name, as shown by the two letters written by him and discovered in 1951[7] at Murabaat, was Bar Kosiba, rose in revolt in 132. Many of the spiritual leaders were for peace. However deeply outraged, they held that the most important element of Judaism was the study and teaching of Torah, and as long as no restrictions were imposed on that score, Judaism could continue to live on and survive. But acclaimed by Akiba as a military Messiah, Bar Kocheba carried most of the population with him. For three and a half years Bar Kocheba and his followers fought on, defeating the best of Roman troops sent against them. But in 135, under the command of Severus who was summoned by Hadrian from Britain, the end quickly came with the fall of Bethar (a few miles south-west of Jerusalem) where Bar Kocheba met his death. Then began an era of unparalleled persecutions. Hadrian rightly realized that the Jewish strength was derived from the Torah, and he was not going to repeat the mistake of his predecessors in allowing the Jews to practise their religion, and to enjoy a measure of self-government, through the agency of an academic Sanhedrin. He was going to destroy alike Israel and the Torah, from which Israel drew its strength. He accordingly suppressed the Sanhedrin, closed its centre at Jabneh, and issued an edict forbidding on pain of death the study of Torah and the practice of its observances. Many, young and old, gave their lives rather than comply. The number of those ready to suffer martyrdom became so great as to imperil the very existence of the Jewish people. This led a Council of sages, who met at Lydda, to decree that a Jew, in order to save his life, might violate any of the commandments of the Torah except those which forbid idolatry, murder, and incest (including adultery). This decree was destined to become the fundamental guiding principle of Jewish life in all the centuries that followed. Akiba, however, held himself bound to defy publicly the prohibition of teaching Torah and in consequence met his death. Jerusalem was renamed Aelia Capitolina, and the Jews were forbidden to enter the Holy City, except on the 9th Ab, the anniversary of the destruction of the Temple, when they were allowed to come to weep by the Wall.

The failure of the Bar Kocheba revolt deprived the Jews of the last vestige of self-government and of all the material attributes of nationhood. But the Torah, functioning for generations in synagogue and school, had struck too many roots in the heart of the Jewish people in Palestine and in many distant lands to be materially affected by the national débâcle. In hundreds of schools and synagogues there were teachers who continued the work of past generations. They taught the Torah, interpreted its laws, developed its traditions, and guided the people in the rules of personal and social conduct and in the understanding of the world and led them to worship in spirit and in truth the God who is tabernacled in the hearts of good men everywhere. Thus were the Jewish people scattered to the four corners of the earth without a state, country, or government, but united through the knowledge of Torah and allegiance to the one and only God, able to fashion for themselves a new nationhood, not bound up with a national territory or fixed homesteads, but with a national literature, religion, and culture which were destined to preserve their national consciousness and ensure their survival as one distinct people among the nations of the world.

The Jewish Christians, however, were unable to follow the idea of a nation divorced from its territory. For them the end of the Jewish state meant the loss of the foundations on which Jewish spiritual and cultural life was built. Thus was the way open for a complete separation from their people which the force of tragic events only served to hasten. In order to escape Hadrian's common proscription of the Torah and to gain some temporary advantages, the Jewish Christians did not hesitate to renounce all the religious practices they had observed for about a century and, cutting themselves adrift from their own people, finally joined the mass of pagans who under the influence of Paul had during the intervening period been attracted to Christianity.

NOTES

1. See. M. Schreiner, *Jahrbuch fur jüdische Geschichte und Literatur* (Berlin, 1899), p. 55.
2. *Jerusalem Talmud*, Sanhedrin, x, 5.
3. See pp. 89–90 ff.
4. The Jewish Calendar is lunar. The ordinary Jewish year consists of twelve lunar months, a little more than $29\frac{1}{2}$ days each, with every new moon a minor festival. The fixation of the

New Moon was in Temple times determined not only by reference to calculation, but also on the basis of observation; that is to say, it was not declared until witnesses had appeared before the Great Sanhedrin at Jerusalem (or any other place in Palestine where it had its seat) and given evidence that they had seen the new moon, provided such evidence was available not later than thirty days after the previous new moon. Where no witnesses appeared on the thirtieth day, the new moon was fixed on the following day without witnesses, since there could be no doubt that the moon had by that time renewed itself. On the declaration of the new moon, messengers were sent out to outlying districts of Palestine informing the communities the day when the new moon was fixed, so that they might know on what day the festival in that particular month might be observed. Jewries in the Diaspora, whom the messengers could not reach in time to inform of the exact day of the new moon, had to observe the festival two days, in order to be sure of observing the right day. Thus arose the two festival days of the Diaspora. This practice for the Jews outside Palestine to keep two festival days has remained in force even after the introduction of the calendar by Hillel II (a Patriarch of the fourth century), in virtue of which all festivals are fixed solely by reference to calculation (see *infra*, p. 128). This is not only in deference to ancestral custom, but also to show, as in days of old, their dependence on Palestine.

5. See p. 102.

6. According to the Mishnah there existed in the Temple long before the common era a copy of the standard text of the Pentateuch on the basis of which Scribes would correct privately owned copies (see T. Kethuboth, 106 a). This copy was known as 'the Scroll of the Temple Court', or according to a variant 'the Scroll of Ezra' (see H. H. Danby, *The Mishnah*, Oxford University Press, 1933, pp. 210, 626). Josephus, *Contra Apionem*, i, 42, speaks of the extreme care taken to safeguard the accuracy of the scriptural text.

7. Fifteen more letters from BarKocheba, bearing the signature of Shimeon bar Kosiba, were discovered on 11 April 1960, in a Dead Sea cave three and a half miles south of Ein Geddi where the remnants of his army perished after the fall of Bethar.

CHAPTER 13

THE TALMUD IN THE MAKING

THE Hadrianic persecutions had decimated Palestinian Jewry. Those who had not been slaughtered or sold as slaves or forcibly deported, fled the country, particularly to Babylon, and organized Jewish life in Palestine was on the verge of complete extinction. But the death of Hadrian in 138 brought an immediate improvement in the situation. His successor, Antoninus Pius, moved by appeals made to him, revoked many of the edicts of his predecessor. Soon Pharisaic activity sprung to life again, centred this time in Galilee, which had been spared much of the ravages of the Hadrianic wars. A new academic Sanhedrin was at once established in Usha under the presidency of Rabbi Simeon ben Gamaliel, whom Antoninus Pius recognized as the Patriarch, and as such, the supreme head of the Jews. The schools were re-opened, religious life reorganized, and, although a shadow of the former Jabneh Sanhedrin, this new Sanhedrin lost no time in taking over the functions of its predecessor and in exercising like it control over the Jewries within and outside the land.

The academic Sanhedrin in Galilee reached its zenith under Simeon ben Gamaliel's son and successor to the Patriarchate, Judah, the Prince I (135–217), called 'Rabbi', the teacher, *par excellence*. He is said to have been on friendly terms with one of Antonine emperors. The identity of this Emperor is still a matter of debate. Many identify him with Marcus Aurelius; but however it may be, there is no doubt that it was due to Rabbi's high standing in court circles that the Jews, notwithstanding the serious difficulties, economic and political, with which they had to contend, enjoyed during Judah's patriarchate, which covered more than fifty years, a measure of peace and tranquillity which gave a fillip to the activities of the academy. Judah, however, well knew that these favourable conditions could not last and that it was only a question of time whether the academy would be able to maintain itself, much less to exercise its unifying authority over the scattered Jewries of the world.

Appraising the gravity of the situation, Judah resolved to create some instrument to take the place of the authority wielded by the central academy. This instrument, completely fashioned, became to be known as the Mishnah.

Attempts at the compilation of traditional teachings in Mishnah form had, as we have seen, been made before. In addition to Akiba and Meir, other Tannaim were busy at the same time in compiling similar works. Frequently the traditions transmitted by one were lacking in another, and opinions expressed by one were contradicted by another. Yet, as long as there was a central academic Sanhedrin in existence, these diversities of tradition and divergencies of opinion did not matter. The task of scrutinizing and testing the differences as they arose, and of choosing among them, devolved upon the academic Sanhedrin. But with the decline of this central authority and its possible disappearance, there came the necessity of an authoritative compilation setting forth the standard law. At the same time, provision had also to be made to safeguard the power of development, which was basic to the Law, but which a compilation of this nature would only tend to impair.

It was the intrinsic merit of Rabbi Judah's Mishnah that, whilst teaching the authoritative norm, it maintained the flexibility of the Law. This Judah achieved by making his Mishnah serve both as a code and as a digest of the oral Law. As a code, the Mishnah indicates the standard law as fixed either by preceding academies or in the academy of 'Rabbi'. As a digest, it includes all that 'Rabbi' considered worthy of preservation, even divergencies of opinion that had originated either among earlier generations or among his own contemporaries. In this way 'Rabbi's' Mishnah contributed towards the standardization of the Law, whilst leaving, at the same time, ample scope for further research and study, investigation and development.

The Mishnah, which is written in pure and fluent Hebrew, is divided into six orders (*Sedarim*). Each order is divided into tractates (*Massechot*) of which there are sixty-three, whilst the contents of each tractate are grouped into chapters (*Perakim*) and paragraphs. The orders are as follows:

Zeraim (Seeds) sets forth and elaborates the Biblical precepts relating to the rights of the poor, the priests and Levites, to the produce of the harvest, as well as the rules and regulations connected with agriculture – the tillage, cultivation, and sowing of fields, gardens, and orchards. These laws are appropriately introduced by a tractate which has as its theme the daily prayers and worship of the Jew, for the faithful observance of these laws depend on the faith in God which Jewish worship and prayer inspire.

Moed (Appointed Seasons) deals with the laws of the Sabbath as well as of the festivals and fasts, whether Biblical or extra-Biblical, and the rules for the fixation of the Jewish calendar.

Nahsim (Women) sets forth the laws of marriage and divorce, and other regulations governing the relations between husband and wife as well as of the sexes in general.

Nezikin (Damages) treats of Jewish civil and criminal law and procedure, and appropriately includes the 'Ethics of the Fathers' (*Pirke Aboth*) which traces the chain of oral tradition from Moses to Shammai and Hillel, and also sets forth ethical standards which should govern the conduct of judge and judged, teacher and disciple, in fact of every man in all his relations, social, domestic, economic, and political.

Kodashim (Holy things) is devoted to the regulations of the sacrificial cult, the Temple, and its appurtenances, as well as of the officiating priests and their duties. It also contains a special tractate which prescribes the rules regarding the slaughtering of animals and birds and their ritual fitness for use, which constitute an integral part of the law of Holiness which, as we have seen,[1] lies at the basis of the sacrificial cult.

Tohoroth (Purifications) deals with the laws of ritual cleanness and uncleanness in things and persons.

The Mishnah soon established itself as highly authoritative, second only to the Scriptures themselves, and already during the lifetime of Rabbi Judah was becoming the standard work of study in schools, both in Palestine and Babylon.

Rabbi Judah died in 217. With his death, in the words of an ancient source, 'Glory departed from Israel' and also in the words of another, 'Troubles multiplied manifold'. By a combination of untoward events – persecutions, heavy taxation, economic hardship, bad harvests, epidemics – life in Palestine was becoming more and more difficult for the Jews. A number of schools were obliged to close, and Palestine was gradually giving way to Babylon as a cultural centre of the Jewish people. There, with the advent in 219 of Abba Arika (175 - 247) who had been a disciple of Judah, arose the famous school of Sura where Abba Arika taught his master's Mishnah. Thousands of disciples flocked to his school and his reputation rose so high that he became known as Rab, the 'teacher', *par excellence*.[2] About the same time a rival school was established in Nehardea by Samuel (180–250), who was likewise a disciple of Rabbi Judah and considered the leading authority on matters of civil law. Samuel is the author of the well-known dictum *dina demalchutha dina* (the law of the State is law), which has proved of tremendous influence on the development of Jewish civil law. Somewhat later as a result of the sacking of Nehardea by Odenathus (Zenobia's husband) in 258, a third school was founded by Judah ben Ezekiel (d. 299), in the neighbouring Pumbeditha. These three schools cooperated with each other as well as with the dwindling schools in Palestine in maintaining and developing the traditions of Jewish learning.

The main basic text of study, investigation, and research, both in the Palestinian and Babylonian schools was now the Mishnah of Rabbi Judah. The teachers called *Amoraim* (lit., 'speakers') worked through the Mishnah word by word, interpreted its contents, discussed its meaning, and sought to harmonize its contradictions and to trace back its teachings to scripture. But that was only part of their activities. The Mishnah contained only a minor fraction of the legal material current in the Palestinian academies. There were many additional and rival collections made by younger contemporaries of Rabbi Judah, such as Bar Kappara and Rabbi Hiyya, which preserved teachings which Rabbi Judah had for one reason or another thought fit to exclude. These 'external' or 'additional' teachings (*baraitha* or *tosefta*), which were of the utmost importance for the study of the origin and development of the law, could not be ignored in the discussions centring round the Mishnah; nor could the oral traditions and teachings in Midrash form, such as emanated from the school of Akiba and Ishmael among others be overlooked by the *Amoraim*. Theirs was also the task of making final decisions of *Halachah* as well as of formulating new legal judgements (*Halakoth*) in answer to problems which arose out of the changed conditions of life.

This intellectual activity of centuries was finally crystallized in the Gemara (lit., 'completion'). Both the Gemara and the Mishnah constitute the Talmud (from a Hebrew root meaning 'to study'), of which there are two versions – the Palestinian and the Babylonian.

The Talmud is therefore primarily the Mishnah of Rabbi Judah with a commentary thereon. As such the Talmud is essentially Halachic in character. The result of this Talmudic development is the compilation of exclusively Aggadic writings which became synonymous with the Midrashim. Some of these Midrashic creations, however, found their way into the Talmud. This happened particularly when Aggadic motives of one kind or another entered into the course of Halachic discussions. Thus it is that the Talmud is rich in Aggadic material covering, in fact, the whole field of religion and ethics. Moral reflections, homilies, apologues, maxims on wordly wisdom, metaphysical speculations, tales of Israel's past, both historical and legendary, visions of its future, and of the universal messianic salvation, as well as *obiter dicta*, often showing remarkable powers of observation on geometry, medicine, astronomy physiology, botany, and other scientific subjects – such are the constituents of the Talmudic *Aggadah*. The aim everywhere is to inspire, edify, and elevate and to supply those finer qualities of heart and mind moving men to that righteousness of action which the *Halachah* prescribes.

As a product of two distinct centres of learning, the Palestine and Babylon Talmuds are dissimilar in subject matter, method, presentation, and language.

In bulk the Palestine Talmud is about a third of its sister-version, and its dialect is that of Western Aramaic. The foundation of the Palestinian Talmud was laid by Rabbi Jochanan ben Nappacha (d. 279). A disciple of Rabbi Judah the Prince, he excelled all his contemporaries by his great intellectual gifts, and founded the Academy at Tiberias which became the principal seat of learning in Palestine and the main 'workshop' of the Palestine Talmud.

In its present shape, the Palestine Talmud is a product of the middle of the fourth century. By that time Christianity had already, as a result of the conversion of Constantine (306–37), been established as the official religion of the Empire, and Jerusalem converted into a capital of Christendom. Judaism was now a political as well as a religious heresy, and a militant Church backed by the power of the State was making life for the Jews in Palestine unbearable. Under such adverse conditions, the compilers of the Palestine Talmud had neither the time nor the peace of mind to apply themselves leisurely to their work. This fact accounts for the shortcomings of the Palestine Talmud, its incompleteness and lack of continuity, as well as the corrupt state of its text. But, notwithstanding its defects, the Palestine Talmud remains invaluable for the study of Jewish law, as it represents the *Halachah* in its unbroken line of development in the home of the Mishnah. It also derives additional importance from the Aggadic material it contains, which provides a veritable mine of information on the internal and external relations of the Jews in Palestine which, in turn, on account of its relative antiquity, is of the greatest historical significance.

The Babylonian Talmud, written in an Eastern Aramaic dialect, recalls the discussions on Rabbi Judah's Mishnah as they were carried on in the schools of Babylon. There the Jews enjoyed full rights and were allowed a large measure of autonomy. At their head was the Exilarch, or Prince of the Captivity, who had conferred upon him by the Persian king great powers and was surrounded with semi-royal statue. The Jewish academies were fully organized and well supported and enjoyed material conditions which were conducive to intellectual pursuits and activities. A particular feature of the Babylonian academies were the public sessions held bi-annually in Adar (February–March) and Elul (August–September), known as the months of *Kallah* (probably meaning 'bride', and suggestive of the idea that the Torah is compared to a bride), which attracted scholars in large numbers from near and far, including many professional and business men. Under such favourable conditions the editors of the Talmud could take their time and were thus able to produce a work which is superior to the Palestine Talmud alike as regards system, arrangement, text, and content, and one upon which all subsequent codifications of the Jewish Law primarily rest.

A constant intercourse and interflow of ideas alike in the realms of *Halachah* and *Aggadah* existed between Babylon and Palestine, and statements of Palestine Amoraim enjoy high authority, and occupy an important place in the Babylonian Talmud.

Like its sister-version, the Babylon Talmud abounds in *Aggadah*, constituting about a third of its contents, and mirroring much of the knowledge, secular and religious, of the rabbis of the time.

The intensive activities of the Babylonian Amoraim reached their climax under Abbaye (283–338) and his halachic opponent, Raba (299–352), whose dialectics, which were of a high order, set the pattern for the studies pursued in Babylonia. Layer upon layer of Halachic and Aggadic material continued to be added during the several generations which followed, each generation interpreting, arguing, and debating the opinions and judgements of generations preceding. The mass of the orally transmitted traditions and teachings accumulated through the centuries assumed such proportions that the time came for the redaction of the vast material, involving the sifting, summarization, and systematic arrangement of the whole, in accordance with the various tractates of the Mishnah.

The work of redaction was undertaken by Rab Ashi (died 427) who was for fifty-two years head of the Sura Academy, the affairs of which he directed with singular brilliancy and success. The result of his labours on which he spent thirty years constitute the bulk of the contents of the Talmud. Ashi's work was carried on by his successors, especially Rabina II (d. 500), who redacted the new material accumulated since the days of Ashi. Rabina was the last of the *Amoraim*, the last to teach the Torah on the basis of oral transmission; and with his work the Talmud may be regarded as having come to a close.

The period that followed the compilation of the Palestine Talmud saw a rapid deterioration in the position of the Jews in Palestine. Hemmed in by the growing power of the Church and the dreadful restrictions imposed, Jewish organized life became practically impossible. More and more the Judean Sanhedrin found it difficult to meet for the purpose of regulating the calendar and communicating their relevant decisions to distant communities. To meet the situation the Patriarch Hillel II (330–65) decided on a revolutionary, and self-effacing step which proved of incalculable benefit for his contemporaries and subsequent generations. He made available to the communities a permanent calendar based on astronomic calculations,[3] though this involved a surrender of the most significant function of the Patriarchate for world Jewry. Reduced in its authority over world Jewry to a mere shadow, the Patriarchate was shorn in Palestine itself of much of its power, and finally about 425, under Theodosius II, abolished altogether. Henceforth, the academic Sanhedrin was forced to close, and Palestine lost its influence as a centre of Jewish learning, though it continued to live in the hearts and minds and daily prayers of Jews everywhere.

The closure of the academies in Palestine did not bring to an end all literary activity. While it affected the Halachic disciplines, it led to an increase of interest in *Aggadah*, to which the people turned more and more for solace and comfort in their plight and misery.

The result was the compilation of a series of Aggadic compendia designed to provide the people with ready Aggadic, or homiletical, material for use in their homes and schools. These compendia, known as *Midrashim*, fall into two classes. Some are cast in the form of comments and reflections on the Biblical text, more or less in its order of sequence. Others consist of homilies based on Biblical readings for special Sabbaths and Festivals.

To the former class belong the *Midrash Rabbah* (Large), which covers the whole of the Pentateuch and the five 'Scrolls' (Canticles, Ruth, Lamentations, Ecclesiastes, and Esther). The oldest among these collective works are the Midrash on Genesis and on Leviticus, the compilation of which can be safely placed about the beginning of the sixth century.[4] Besides the *Midrash Rabbah* are the *Tanchuma Midrashim*, named after Tanchuma bar Abba, a famous Palestinian Aggadist of the fourth century, whose homilies largely figure in these collections. A characteristic of the *Tanchuma Midrashim*, which are contemporaneous with *Genesis Rabbah*, and of which we have several versions, are the words 'Would our Master teach us' (*Yelammedenu Rabbenu*), positing a legal problem with which the homilies are frequently introduced and which, having been first disposed of by the preacher, provide him with an opening lead for his homily.

To the latter class belong the *Pesikta Midrashim*, the oldest of which, commonly known as *Pesikta de-rab Kahana* (a Babylonian-Palestinian scholar of the third century), is probably a product of the sixth century.

A fate similar to that of the Jews in Palestine befell the Jews in Babylon shortly after the compilation of their Talmud. Signs of the gathering storm began to appear shortly after Ashi's death, when Yezedgerd II (438–57), instigated by the fanatical fire-worshipping magian priests, instituted persecutions against all other religions. These persecutions grew in intensity under Firuz (459–86), Yezedgerd's son, when the Academies of Sura and Pumbeditha were closed, and reached their climax in 501 with the appearance on the scene of Mazdak, the founder of Zendicism, who preached community of property and of women. The execution of Mazdak in 528 brought about an improvement in the situation. The Jews began to breathe more freely and the schools to resume their functions. A new succession of teachers arose, named *Saboraim* (from a Hebrew root meaning 'to reflect'), who 'reflected' upon the sayings and teachings of the *Amoraim* contained in the Talmud, interpreting and expounding them, and made certain additions to the Talmudic text, principally of an explanatory character. But the heyday of Babylonian Jewry was now a thing of the past, and it was only 200 years later, under the Caliphate, that the Babylonian academies were able to recapture some of their former glories.

The Jewish centres in Palestine and Babylon which for centuries had helped to weld together the scattered Jewish communities had lost much of their influence. Their place was now taken by the Talmud, which proved in turn the greatest single cohesive force in Jewry. For it was out of the Talmud's scriptural interpretations and discussions that there emerged those dynamic principles of religion, law, and morality, which made it possible for Judaism to adapt itself to every time and place, to every state of society, and every stage of culture and civilization, as well as those regulative standards and rules of conduct which injected into Jewry that uniformity and vitality that have preserved it throughout all its trials and tribulations. Widely though the modern world is separated from the world of Talmudic times, the Talmud still remains, after the Bible, the most fruitful, spiritual, moral, and unifying force in Jewish life. The ritual, the liturgy, the marriage laws of the modern Jew all derive directly from the Talmud, even as it is the Talmud which has given shape to these religious and ethical doctrines which largely constitute the Judaism of today.

NOTES

1. See p. 25.
2. 'Rab' is the Aramaic form for the Hebrew 'Rabbi', and was the designation by which the Babylonian Talmudic teachers were known.
3. See p. 119, n. 4.
4. In course of time similar collections were made in other Books of the Bible, of which the most comprehensive is the *Yalkut Shimeoni*, a kind of Midrashic Thesaurus on the whole of the Hebrew Scriptures, compiled from numerous sources, some of which are no longer extant, probably in the first half

of the thirteenth century and attributed to a certain Simeon of Frankfort. There is also a voluminous Midrash on the Pentateuch ascribed to David ha-Nagid (1212–1300), a grandson of Maimonides, preserved in manuscripts in the libraries of Paris, London, Berlin, Jerusalem, and Moscow, the existence of which in the last named has been first made public by A. Katsch of the New York University, at the World Congress of Jewish Studies in Jerusalem in July, 1957.

Another Midrashic thesaurus (recently discovered) is the Yemenite *Midrash ha-Gadol*, variously ascribed to David ben Amram of Aden (13th century) or to Abraham, son of Maimonides. This Midrash has been brought over to Europe in manuscript form by a dealer of antiquities towards the end of the last century, and has since then engaged the attention of a number of scholars who have edited and published different parts, making the bulk of it now available in print.

CHAPTER 14

TALMUDIC JUDAISM (I): ITS FAITH

THE Talmud, as will have been seen, is the written story in Hebrew and Aramaic dress of Biblical interpretation, of the making of byelaws, and of the adding to the store of practical guidance and wise counsel, which the intellectual and religious leaders of the Jewish people taught during a period covering almost one thousand years, from the time of Ezra to the end of the fifth century of the Common Era. As such, it might be compared to the History of the British Parliament, now in progress of publication, which is intended to give a summary account of what has been done, spoken, and debated in the British legislative assembly since its earliest days to the present time.

But whatever comparison such a work, when completed, may afford, man's relation to God will be in it at the most an inconspicuous detail; and it is just this which is most prominent and fundamental in the Talmud. For amid all the diversity of opinions and variety of subjects which the Talmud presents, we find in its pages the heart and mind of a people seeking God. It is this which makes the Talmud into the greatest Jewish classic, and the richest fount of religious guidance and inspiration, after the Bible.

What, however, imparts to the Talmud its particular authoritative place in Judaism is the fact that it is founded on Scripture and that its teachings and principles are in the direct line of development from those communicated in the Torah, the Prophets, and the Holy Writings.

This applies equally to religious and moral doctrine and to ritual and legal practice. Employing their methods of interpretation, the rabbis of the Talmud were able to penetrate to the deeper sense that lies beneath the letter, and in consequence to find in Scripture the loftiest conceptions of God's character and man's duty, conceptions which in some important respects were in advance of the teachings of the Scripture text itself.

The rabbis of the Talmud were, however, neither philosophers nor theoreticians. Like their spiritual fathers, the Prophets, they were essentially practical men concerned primarily with conduct. As such, they were on the whole little interested in arid speculations that had no bearing on human behaviour. But their mind was greatly exercised by the religious doctrines of the Bible because of their relevance to life and conduct. They thus set themselves the task of interpreting, elucidating, and applying these teachings and of communicating them by means of homily, parable, and wise saying, not as mere theoretical principles but as guides to the practical.

This pragmatic attitude of the Talmud in matters of religious doctrine extends to the very belief in God. Faith is extolled only in so far as it leads to right action. To profess belief in God and act as if He did not exist is indeed of little value. On the contrary, from the Talmudic standpoint, to know God and act in rebellion to His will is worse than to deny His existence altogether.

This attitude of the Talmud has remained consistently the attitude of Judaism, both in the popular apprehension and in the explicit affirmation of its religious leaders in all periods. While insisting on the definite establishment of doctrines, it refuses to be bound by any particular form in which these doctrines are to be understood. Given the faith, the means whereby this faith is to find expression in presentation is considered of no practical moment. God is a reality; how exactly He is to be apprehended is a philosophic, not a religious problem, which, strictly speaking, does not concern Judaism. The unity of God is axiomatic; and that excludes whatever tends to obscure the sublime conception of God as the One and Only Being, but precise intellectual definition is a task left to philosophy. Judaism affirms the divine attributes of Justice and Mercy, without attempting to explain the relation of the attributes to the being of God. Revelation is a fact; yet the *modus operandi* of this divine communication with man does not trouble Judaism. The Messianic redemption is sure, but how, and when, and under what conditions it would be fulfilled is left to individual imaginings. Immortality and the Hereafter are a certainty, though no specific attempt is made to describe what these terms connote. Thus Judaism presents, in some of its details in matters of faith, contradictory opinions, which, however, do not affect the central core of its beliefs.

The principal religious doctrines of Scripture have already received attention.[1] It remains here to deal somewhat more fully with the presentation of these doctrines in the light of the Pharisaic interpretations which, by the time the Talmud came to a close as a written book, had already for centuries been, generally speaking, accepted as the norm of Judaism by Jews in all lands.

Judaism rests on two basic doctrines: (1) the belief in the One and Only God; (2) the election of Israel to be the bearers of this belief. These two doctrines, which are so inextricably bound together as to form one, receive their classic formulation in the great Deuteronomic utterance, known as the *Shema* ('Hear!') – from the first word with which it begins, 'Hear, O Israel! The Lord is our God, the Lord is one' (6. 4) – an utterance which has become Israel's ages-long primal confession of faith.

There is no assertion here of the unity of God in the metaphysical sense. The idea of God as pure, simple being, belongs to the realm of philosophy rather than of religion. Nor is there any claim made that the one God is only Israel's God and of no other people; this would be contrary to the universalism inherent in Judaism. What is here affirmed is (i) that there is but one God, with none other beside Him; and (ii) that the one and only God is the One whom Israel confesses and worships. The negations are as emphatic and insistent as the affirmations. They negate all embodiments and notions of the Deity which, however refined and sublimated, veil the one and only God of Israel more than they reveal Him. Thus are excluded, not only all dualistic no less than polytheistic creeds, but also the 'Trinity in Unity' of Christianity which, however much it may be explained away so as to make it compatible with the *one* God in the metaphysical sense, remains a direct denial of the *only* God who, from the beginning, had chosen Israel in His service.

The one and only God to whom Israel owes absolute homage and is called upon to give witness is no abstraction, but the living God whose creative energy is ever at work in the universe. The beginning of this power was made manifest in creation when God called the world and man into existence. The problem of creation itself – whether the world came into being *ex nihilo* (out of nothing) or out of some pre-existent matter – is principally philosophic and of no direct concern to Judaism. What Judaism insists in its doctrine of creation is that the world and all that it contains is not the product of chance, the outcome of accidental collocation of atoms, but the handiwork of God.

Interlinked with the Jewish doctrine of creation is the doctrine of God's providential activity which preserves the world He called into existence from collapsing into non-being. Were God to withdraw His providence but for a single moment, the whole existence would collapse into nothingness. This is the truth which Scripture never tires of asserting. 'He hangeth the earth upon nothing' (Job 26. 7). 'Thou hidest thy face and they are confounded' (Psalm 104. 29); and it is a truth equally affirmed by the Talmudic sages: 'God created the world and He provides; He made and He sustains.'[2] And what applies to the totality of the universe applies more specifically to the fate of nations and individuals. 'He increaseth the nations, and destroyeth them. He spreadeth the nations abroad and bringeth them in' (Job 12. 23). 'No man wounds his finger below, unless it has been so decreed against him above' (T. Hullin, 7b).

The two primary principles of God's dealings with nations and individuals are, as we have seen in a previous chapter,[3] Justice and Mercy (which includes Love). These two attributes, according to rabbinic interpretation, are represented respectively by the two divine names, *Elohim* ('God') and YHWH (usually rendered, 'the Lord'). They are thus by no means divided into two separate powers, as in the Pauline system where the world of Satan and the world of Christ are in constant conflict with each other. In Judaism, the God of Justice is the God of Mercy (Love), one and inseparable, both

Justice and Mercy being but complimentary aspects of God's character as exhibited in His moral government of the world and His particular providence.

Divine justice carries with it the affirmation of God as Judge, confronting humanity with His demands and judgements. 'Shall you say the world is *hefker* (ownerless)?'[4] In this Talmudic dictum is announced the indomitable conviction that the world is not left with no one to care about what is happening therein. There is no human action that is allowed to go by unrequited. There is no moment in human history over and against which God does not stand in judgement.

Divine mercy is an expression of God's character as Redeemer, with whom 'there is loving-kindness and plenteous of redemption'. (Psalm 130. 7). As Redeemer, His judgements upon individuals and nations for rebelling against Him are not vindictive in character. They have, that is to say, as aim the redemption of humanity from its sins, miseries, and follies, for its ultimate happiness and salvation.

Linked to creation, divine providential activity in the universe provides the foundation for the emphasis laid by Judaism on the meaningfulness of human history and human life. In the face of the divine activity in creation, judgement, and redemption, all that happens in time is of fundamental significance. No longer are the happenings in the history of nations and the lives of individuals products of chaos and interplay of blind forces. All is living drama, unfolding itself through manifestations of divine judgement and redemptive acts towards a purpose for the fulfilment of creation.

The conception of divine purpose fulfilling itself through human history and human life determines all the teachings of Judaism about God.

Next to the doctrine of His unity is that of His omnipotence. God in the Talmudic phrase is 'The Might' (*ha-Geburah*), omnipotent and powerful. His power has no other limit than His will. Even the forces of Nature are subject to His will, and all events, whatever their character – whether so-called natural or super-natural – are equally the immediate work of His hands.

Judaism further emphasizes God's omnipresence, and the Talmud has coined a special term to describe this divine attribute. God is *Shechinah* ('The Indwelling'), immanent and omnipresent, not necessarily in the sense that God is co-extensive with creation, but that His providence extends over all creation. 'The *Shechinah* is everywhere' (T. Baba Bathra, 25a); 'There is no place without *Shechinah*' (Midrash Exodus Rabbah, ii, 9) – are some of the dicta by which Talmudic teachers seek to give expression to this doctrine of divine omnipresence.

The fact, however, that God is omnipresent does not mean that He is identical with the world or limited by it. He is of the world and yet beyond it. 'He is the Place of the World, but the world is not His place' – is the Talmudic phrase which expresses the Jewish doctrine of divine transcendence. God is thus near and afar off. He is 'our Father in Heaven' – a Father ever near at hand to His children on earth, though His transcendent being is, so to speak, far off in Heaven. This rules out all pantheistic doctrines that would identify or compound God with nature.

Closely connected with the idea of the transcendence of God is that of divine incorporeality. God is, in Jewish teaching, pure spirit, free from all limitations of matter and weaknesses of the flesh. The doctrines of divine incorporeality is among the oldest in Hebrew scriptures and lies at the basis of the prohibition of graven images. The anthropomorphic descriptions of God that abound in the Bible have from the earliest times been understood as mere figures of speech employed to impress upon the mind the reality and providence of God and to instruct man in the knowledge of His ways. 'We describe God,' in the words of the Talmud, 'by terms borrowed from His creation in order to make them intelligible to the human ear.' (Mekilta on Exodus 19. 18).

Another attribute stressed by Judaism is God's omniscience. Even the secret deeds of man and his innermost thoughts are laid bare before Him. He is 'the Lord of thoughts' (*Baal Machashavoth*), and no concealment or deception can avail aught with Him.

God is also 'living and existing to eternity' (Midrash Leviticus Rabbah, vi, 6). He is 'the everlasting' (*Chei-ha-Olamim*). There is thus no place in Judaism for any notions of dying and reviving Gods such as are to be found in other religions.

The interest of Judaism in making these affirmations about God is not philosophic but immediately religious and practical. They all relate to His purpose. Even His unity, the cornerstone of Judaism, is stressed not because the association with Him of any other being independent of Him would obscure the philosophic or theological conception of the one and only God, but because such an association would involve a limitation of His power and in so far interfere with the fulfilment of His purpose.

His omnipotence holds out the certainty of His over-ruling power to control all things towards the ultimate triumph of His purpose. His omnipresence and omniscience carry with them the assurance that no machination, whether in thought, word, or deed, can circumvent the ultimate realization of His purpose. His transcendence and incorporeality free Him from all limitations of Nature or matter, which would prove a hindrance to fulfilment; whilst His eternity is a guarantee that His purpose, however thwarted and delayed, will in the end prevail. 'For the Lord of hosts hath purposed, who shall disannul it?' (Is. 14. 27).

But for the fulfilment of divine purpose human cooperation is necessary. Developing the Biblical idea of man as co-worker with God, the Talmud conceives man as having been chosen by God as his *shuttaf* 'partner' for the fulfilment of creation. Not for material interests alone has man been called to his great task. He was also selected as a special agent for the fulfilment of a purpose that transcends the physical boundaries of the universe, though it is through the physical domain that the purpose can work itself out.

Obedience to the moral law, which we have seen in a previous chapter lies at the basis of this divine cooperation, involves, in the rabbinic phrase, 'the imitation of attributes of God': 'As He is merciful, so be thou merciful; as He is gracious, so be thou gracious; as He is righteous, so be thou righteous' (Sifra on Lev. 19. 2). Life accordingly becomes for

Judaism a task for moral culture, and man in his spiritual and moral capacity has the power and the duty to fit himself to become increasingly a co-worker with God in the development of the human race towards righteousness, by growing in likeness to Him, through the imitation of His gracious and merciful ways.

The idea of fulfilment is associated in Jewish teaching with a vision of the Kingdom of God. But this kingdom is not relegated to the celestial stage of another existence, unconnected with the struggles, problems, hopes, and aspirations of the present. It is a kingdom to be built *here* on earth, under divine guidance, by the hands of man. Human endeavour, which determines the whole complexity of human destiny along the high road of fulfilment, is none other than that which is translated in terms of personal and social righteousness; and the universal realization of these ideals of righteousness in all human relations constitutes the quintessence and distinctive element of the Jewish conception of the Kingdom.

The kingdom of God, in its terrestrial and social setting, provides the key to the understanding of Judaism in all its varied manifestations, and, indeed, the solution to the riddle of the existence of the Jewish people. The Jews, it has been said, believed in hope against hope. No people has suffered more cruelly from 'man's inhumanity to man' than have the Jews, but they have refused to despair either of the world or of humanity, and never gave up the belief in man's ultimate regeneration and perfection. This belief is not a product of a later age, born from the sense of a disillusion and despair seeking relief in the vague hope of better days to come. It is a genuine historical tradition, based on the conviction that this is God's world chosen by Him to become the scene of a divine order wherein goodness and truth are to reign supreme.

The Kingdom of God in the scheme of Judaism will be ushered in by the Messiah. The Messiah will be the central dominating figure of an age which will witness the reign of righteousness on earth, a righteousness which will bring universal peace and plenty, plenty of the things necessary for a righteous life, without taking away the need for sacrifice on behalf of ever-widening and growing ideals. But the Messiah in Jewish teaching is not a supernatural being, nor a divine being, having a share in the forgiveness of sin; much less is he to be confused with God. At the highest the Messiah is but a mortal leader who will be instrumental in fully rehabilitating Israel in its ancient homeland, and through a restored Israel bring about the moral and spiritual regeneration of the whole of humanity, making all mankind fit citizens of the Kingdom. Then shall the reign of the Lord be universal. In the words of the prophet 'The Lord shall be King over all the earth, in that day shall the Lord be one and His name one' (Zech. 14. 9); and in this universality a true religion, professed by all men and realized in their lives in all their relations to God and their fellow-men, shall divine purpose on earth find its fulfilment.

The Kingdom of God in its Messianic setting and earthly fulfilment is but preparatory to the consummation of the Kingdom in the supra-historical and supernatural world to come, a world which in rabbinic parlance 'No ear hath heard, nor eye hath seen' (cf. Isa. 64. 3 [4]). With this supra-historical and supernatural order of things are associated the doctrines of the resurrection of the dead and the universal Day of Judgement, when the end of all the ways of God will be made known, and the fullest consummation of His purpose shall be accomplished.

The belief in the fulfilment of divine purpose in the supra-historical and supernatural is shared by other religions; but what is distinctive in Judaism is its insistence that the consummation in the Beyond is conditioned by the fulfilment in the historical and social context of daily life.

This attitude to the common religious doctrines of the final end is fundamental to Judaism. Unlike other creeds, Judaism refuses to admit the dualism that opposes the earthly to the heavenly, the temporal to the eternal, and consequently considers suffering and misery inseparable from the present world and the lot of human life. On the contrary, the earthly and the heavenly are in the view of Judaism in harmonious relationship to one another, the latter being regarded as inevitable result and development of the former.

This essential harmony in Judaism between the heavenly and the earthly determines also its distinctive doctrine of man. Although composed of two different elements, the earthly body and the heavenly soul, man is a unity. Judaism rejects the dualistic idea of a pure spirit imprisoned in a body which is impure and hostile to the immaterial and spiritual. For Judaism body and spirit have been united to one another in order to give rise together to a higher form of earthly life – the righteous man – and thereby contribute to the rearing of righteousness on earth in fulfilment of divine purpose.

The conception of man as co-worker with God, both now and in eternity, gives a new and higher significance to the doctrine of immortality which, as we have seen,[5] is indigenous to Judaism. It is grounded in God and in His purpose in which man is called upon to cooperate. Immortality is thus no longer merely a survival beyond the grave, but the homegoing of the spirit or the soul of man to the further cultivation and development of the divine relationship made manifest on this stage of life. 'Then shall the dust return to earth and the spirit shall return unto God who gave it' (Eccl. 12. 7).

To become a co-worker with God in the development of the human race towards righteousness in fulfilment of His purpose in the temporal and eternal sphere is the task which Judaism sets before individual man. In this there is no difference between man and man, class and class, nation and nation. The difference lies only in the content and character of the contribution. Common to all mankind is the obligation to observe the 'Seven Precepts of the Sons of Noah'.[6] These precepts, which the Talmudic teachers deduced from their interpretation of Biblical texts, are the abstention from (i) idolatry, (ii) blasphemy, (iii) incest, (iv) murder, (v) theft, (vi) the eating of a limb torn from a living animal, and (vii) the command for the administration of justice. Any individual regulating his life by these 'Seven Precepts' fulfils according to Talmudic teaching his immediate task as a co-worker with God. But fuller in content and higher in character must be the contribution of the son of Israel. As God's elect people charged with the duty to promote divine righteousness on earth, the Jew must be thoroughly obedient to the Torah (Written and Oral) in which is revealed the moral will of God.

This summons from God imposes on the individual a tremendous responsibility. Failure to respond to the call from God is a sin, a personal offence against God. Such an offence leads to the alienation of God, with all the frustration and ruin of life this entails. Yet the effects of sin are not irrevocable. If by straying from the right path man lapses into sin, regret and penitence will repair the ravages of his transgression and will restore the harmony between him and His Creator. But for the restoration of harmony, in Jewish teaching, man does not stand in need of a mediator. The various mediating terms in use in the Bible such as the 'Holy Spirit' and the rabbinic *Memra* (Word)[7] denote only aspects or qualities of the Deity, and are not to be regarded as beings of any kind, much less as personal beings. So are the angels considered mere instruments used by God, and not intermediaries to bridge some imaginary gulf between God and the world, or God and man.

Judaism further denies the existence of original sin, needing a superhuman counterweight, and allows only the free choice to sin, an inevitable concomitant of free will. True, the idea that the sin of Adam had brought death on all mankind is not unknown in Jewish teaching, but the reference is invariably to physical death, and is not to be confused with the spiritual death from which in Christian doctrine none can be saved except through faith in the risen Saviour. Man can therefore achieve his own redemption by penitence, being assured that God himself is ever-ready in His abundance of loving-kindness to receive the penitent sinner and purge him of all iniquity.

Persistence in sin, however, provokes divine judgement and retribution. Obedience, on the other hand, or return to God after offending, carries with it divine favour and reward. The exact relation between sin and suffering in this world is not always to be established, but must be left to the righteous and inscrutable Will of God. Classical in this connexion is the Talmudic saying 'It is not in our power to explain either the prosperity of the wicked or the afflictions of the righteous' (*Ethics of the Fathers*, 4. 19). Being chiefly interested in doctrines for the sake of the moral and religious significance in them, Judaism is satisfied with a mere establishment of the belief in retribution, without concerning itself with the manner in which it would be affected. This applies particularly to retribution after death which occupies an important place in Talmudic doctrine. Judaism teaches there is a *gehenna* which is identified with the pit of fire mentioned in the Bible (Isa. 30. 33), and that there is an abode of bliss, the *Gan Eden* (the Garden of Delight), and there it leaves the matter. In the *gehenna* the wicked are said, except in exceptional cases, to spend twelve months, after which they enter the *Gan Eden* to enjoy in company of the righteous, in the rabbinic phrase, 'the effulgence of the *Shechinah*' (Divine Presence) and everlasting life. And not to an existence of sheer inactivity. The cooperation with God in His purpose begun in this life stretches in Jewish belief beyond the earthly life. Even after the individual has thrown off his mortal coil, his immortal spirit continues its mortal progress, adding to the store of moral forces that make for the ultimate consummation of God's eternal purpose. 'The disciples of the wise (the Righteous) have no rest either in this world or in the world to come' (T. Berachoth 64a).

Nor is the *Gan Eden* reserved only for Israel. In Jewish teaching there is reward in the Hereafter in store for 'the pious of the nations of the world'. Judaism makes salvation depend on right conduct and, accordingly, all nations are admitted to the bliss of the life to come. From an early date Rabbinic Judaism differentiated mankind into those who did and who did not obey the Noachian Laws. Those who observed these Laws were accepted as 'proselytes of the Gates' and were included among the pious of the nations of the world who have a share in the world to come as an Israelite.[8]

Belief in the one and only God was not demanded, provided there is no idolatry, which Judaism condemns not so much because it is a false religion as because it is a false morality; the Son of Noah is not charged to confess the one and only God of the son of Israel. He may be a dualist or a trinitarian, as he wishes. This conception of the Noah laws reveals the real significance of the theocratic constitution of Israel: it rested not on the unity of the state and religion but on the unity of the state and morality. This pragmatic attitude to other creeds is also reflected in the Rabbinic law that whoever accepts Judaism must not commit his young children, who must be allowed to choose for themselves when they grow up whether they are to follow Judaism or remain Noachians.

The conception of the Noah laws also determined the attitude of Judaism to conversions. Confronted in the Graeco-Roman world with a paganism which was at once omnipotent and universal, Judaism was a missionary religion, but its missionary activity was of a restricted character. No organized attempt was made by official Judaism to propagate the observance of the practices of the Jewish religion which were never intended for any other people than Israel by virtue of her priestly calling. All that Judaism was concerned with in its missionary work was to substitute the religion of humanity, communicated to Noah, for the false gods and false morality of the pagan world. But when paganism gave place to Christianity and later also to Islam, Judaism withdrew from the missionary field and was satisfied to leave the task of spreading the religion of humanity to her daughter faiths. The reason for this was not indifference to the fate of other peoples, but the recognition that Christianity and Islam, though lacking the true vision of the one and only God, shared in common many truths, religious and moral, with the mother faith. The improvement, so Judaism teaches, will come, nay, it must come, in God's own time, with the coming of His Kingdom. Such is Israel's undying hope; and it is this hope which provides the dynamic content of the Jewish religion, as well as the unifying motive running through the whole of Jewish religious life and action from the earliest times to the present day.

NOTES

1. See Chapters 2 and 3.
2. Midrash Tanchuma ed. Buber, I, p. 50.
3. Chapter 3.
4. *Yalkut Shimeoni*, Exodus, 396; also Midrash Lamentations Rabbah, i, 53: 'Have you seen a *Hefker* world'.

5. See p. 29.
6. Cf. pp. 19–20.
7. See p. 196.
8. *Tosefta Sanhedrin*, xiii, 2, and *Mishnat Rabbi Eliezer* (ed. Enelow, New York, 1934), p. 121: 'The pious of the nations of the world who observe the seven Noachic precepts will inherit the world to come as Israel'. The *Mishnat Rabbi Eliezer* is ascribed by its editor to the fourth century.

CHAPTER 15

TALMUDIC JUDAISM (II):
ETHICS AND VIRTUE

THE Talmudic genius for penetrating the text of the Holy Writ and discovering in it new ideas of far-reaching importance is nowhere more conspicuous than in the sphere of ethics. Here is evidence of a fineness of perception that enabled the Talmudic teachers to draw out the full consequences of the moral injunctions and admonitions of the Bible for the enrichment of Jewish ethical teaching and the general moral culture of mankind.

In a former chapter consideration was given to the general contents of the Scriptural moral law with its basic principles of justice and righteousness and the human rights and duties they respectively entail.

It is the purpose of the present chapter to deal with the subject in some detail, and at the same time to show how in Talmudic teaching these rights and duties have been developed so as to bring within their scope rules of conduct which no ordinary interpretation of the Biblical text could disclose.

To begin with human rights – the right of life, as interpreted in Talmudic teaching, is designed not simply to offer security in life and limb but also to provide a safeguard against a mere *threat* to life and limb. Even to lift a hand against a fellow creature without actually striking him is branded as an infamy. 'He who lifts a hand against his fellow although he did not strike him is called a wicked man' (T. Sanhedrin, 58b).

Allied to the right of man to live is his right to possess things by which to live. This right to possession forbids in Talmudic teaching any encroachment upon a fellow man's livelihood, such as depriving him directly of a customer or entering competitively by unfair means in his profession or calling, no less than actual robbery and theft. It also condemns cornering, forestalling, graft, and other similar practices which in modern life are associated with big business.

Included among the Biblical safeguards to the right of possession is the prohibition of 'wronging one another' in business dealings (Lev. 25. 14, 17). This prohibition, as interpreted by the Talmud, precludes all kinds of deceit, tricks of trade, or misrepresentation in commercial transactions. The most scrupulous honesty is demanded alike of the buyer and the seller. The seller must not overcharge, underweigh, or give his wares a delusive appearance, so as to deceive the customer. The buyer must not trade on the disadvantage of the seller, or his defenceless position, or ignorance.

What applies to business transactions applies equally to the obligations of employees in regard to their work. The worker who, either by slackness or by deliberate lowering of output or by unpunctuality, does not do his part is violating his employer's right of possession and sins against his fellow man and God.

The right of possession also includes the right of the labourer to his earnings. This denies the right of the employer to hire workmen on his own terms. In Talmudic law the wages have to be fixed with a view to safeguarding the workman's standards of living, and any attempt at curtailing the standard of life of the workman is regarded as a defiance of Jewish law.

The right of the person safeguards man's honour and reputation. The Biblical prohibition of slander is interpreted by the Sages to include both Jew and non-Jew. Included in slander is what the Talmud designates as the 'dust of slander', which few can avoid, and which covers any uncharitable remark or suggestion regarding our fellow-men. Even commendation is condemned where it may call forth in reaction some disparaging remark from someone present.

The right of person also forbids inroads upon a person's self-respect. To put a fellow-man to shame in public is considered in Talmudic ethics as bloodshed, 'the red in the face disappearing, and the pallor taking its place' (T. Baba Metzia, 58b). Particular care must be taken not to hurt feelings of aliens who are prone to be sensitive to the least affront to their person. It is therefore forbidden, even under provocation, to remind an alien of his foreign antecedents and origins. It is similarly impermissible to recall to a reformed character his former delinquencies and conduct.

In its concern for the right of person, the Talmud has taken the greatest pains to explain what kind of acts offend against this fundamental human right. It is, for example, sinful to give someone an address without being sure that it is the correct one. It is likewise sinful to go into a shop and ask the price of an article when there is no intention of buying it. Offences of this type are designated in the Talmud as 'wronging through words' (*onaath debarim*) and considered graver than wrong caused to fellow-men in respect of material values, called in Hebrew *onaath mamon*, since they are an affront to human personality.

Closely allied to wronging with words is *genebath daath* 'stealing (a fellow-man's) mind'. The chief idea of *genebath daath* is that of misrepresentation of the truth, such as is practised by the confidence trickster who seeks to influence his victim to think or to act against his own interest or what would have been his better judgement. Among the examples given in the Talmud of 'stealing of the mind' is to invite a fellow-man to a meal knowing that he would not accept, or to borrow money on the pretext of buying food whilst in fact it is intended for less needy purposes. All such deceptions, whether practised on a Jew or on a non-Jew, come under the category of 'stealing of the mind' and are forbidden.

Respect for the human person forbids also deception by lying speech, no matter to whom it is addressed. 'You shall not lie to one another' (Lev. 19. 11). Lying is not restricted to the formal meaning of the words. The words may be verbally accurate but used with the intention to deceive they become lying words. This brings immediately under condemnation all mental reservation. 'Let your *Yea* be righteous and your *No* be righteous' (T. Baba Metzia, 49a). Thus, to say one thing with the mouth, and another in the heart is lying.

Respect for the human person forbids also hatred. This Biblical command (Lev. 19. 17) as understood by Talmudic teachers is of universal significance 'Whoever hateth any man hateth Him who spoke and the world came into existence'

(Sifre Zuta Numbers 18) – *any* man, that is, whether Jew or non-Jew.

Bracketed in the Bible with the command not to hate is the one forbidding revenge or harbouring a grudge (Lev. 19. 18). This is another Biblical injunction relating to the right of the person which in Talmudic teaching is of universal significance. 'If a man cuts off one of his hands with a knife, would he avenge himself by cutting off his other hand which did the damage?' (J. T. Nedarim, 6). Here is a dictum which makes the law not to avenge or bear a grudge a universal law. Nor may even an enemy be denied this aspect of the right of the person. 'I should have denied the One above if I rejoiced at the destruction of him that hated me or exulted that evil overtook him' (Job, 31. 28–9).

The right of person also upholds human liberty and human freedom. Freedom is an inalienable human right which must not in any circumstances be tampered with. This general principle found its expression in a number of rules in Talmudic legislation, such as the right of the workman to retract before completing his work, provided he can be replaced and his retractation does not involve the employer in any financial loss. His obligations to his employer are regarded as material only, and not personal.

Allied to the right of human liberty is that of human equality. In Job the full right to equality, even of the slave, is upheld when it declares, 'If I despise the cause of my manservant (slave) or of my maidservant, when they contend with me; what then shall I do when God riseth up? And when He visiteth, what shall I answer Him? Did not He that made me in the womb make him? And did not one fashion us in the womb' (Job, 31. 13–15).

This principle of human equality has entered into the Talmudic rules governing the relations of slave and master. It was forbidden to let the slave perform any degrading work, or work which was not absolutely necessary; and a disabled slave had to be cared for with the same solicitude as the one who was sound and healthy.

These, and similar rules and regulations – Biblical and

Talmudic – designed to safeguard human rights – belong to the demands of justice. But supplementing the demands of justice are those of righteousness which, laying stress on the acceptance of duties seek to confirm positively in many ways the fundamental human rights of individual and classes.

Confirming the right of the individual to live, righteousness bids man not to stand idly by the blood of his fellow (Lev. 19. 16). Whatever the peril he may find his fellow to be in, whether, in the words of the Talmud, he is seen drowning or attacked by robbers or wild beasts, he is in duty bound not only to come to his rescue, but if personally unable to do so, to organize rescue work at his own cost (T. Sanhedrin, 73a).

Righteousness also demands that man shall furnish his fellow with means whereby he can live. In ancient Israel those who could not earn enough were provided for by the Biblical laws which assigned part of the harvest – the corners of the field and certain gleanings – to the poor. By reason of national economy, these Biblical laws ceased with the destruction of the Jewish State. But there still remained ample scope for righteousness to confirm man in his right to live. One of the earliest forms in which his righteousness found expression was charity – almsgiving. Almsgiving in the form of money, food, or clothing is indeed in Talmudic teaching one of the regular duties of daily life. This is a universal duty which must be performed to all in need, irrespective of creed or origin, not excluding even a personal enemy. 'Even if your enemy has risen up early to kill you and he comes hungry and thirsty to your house, give him food and drink' (Midras on Proverbs 25. 21). Nor may anyone claim exemption from this duty. Even a poor man who himself subsists on charity, should give charity to those in greater distress than himself (T. Gittin, 7b).

The highest form of charity, however, is that which might be called 'constructive charity' – offering the poor man a loan so as to open for him a new avenue for his socially useful energies. This, too, is universal law embracing Jew and non-Jew alike. '"If thy brother be waxen poor and his hand fail with thee, then thou shalt uphold him, yea, though he be a stranger or a sojourner that he may live with thee" (Lev. 25.

35) – 'provide him with means whereby he can live,' is the Talmudic comment (T. Baba Kamma, 112a). No interest may be accepted for the loan, the aim of which was to prevent a fellow member of society from breaking down (Lev. 25. 36); nor is it permissible according to Talmudic law, to levy or execute upon the debtor's tools, which he may require for earning a livelihood (T. Baba Metzia, 115a). Furthermore, in order to keep his mind clear from the threat of execution whilst he is engaged in building up for himself an economic future, the creditor is forbidden to press him for the repayment of the loan (Ex. 22. 24). What is even more, if he is known to be in no position to pay, his creditor must avoid meeting him so as to cause him no embarrassment (Midrash Exodus Rabbah, 31. 6).

The poor man's right to live carries with it also the right to clothing and shelter. And it is in confirmation of this right that the creditor has enjoined upon him what Scripture describes as 'an act of righteousness' – the duty to return to the debtor any raiment taken in pledge which he may require either for day wear or covering at night (Deut. 24. 13).

It is not without significance that *Zedakah*, the Hebrew term for righteousness, came to designate any work directed towards relief of the poor. The poor in Jewish teaching have a claim on the support of the more fortunate as a matter of *right*. Consequently, Jewish ethical teaching made it a point not to taunt those who received alms with the reproach of indolence.

As a right or just act towards the poor, it is the duty of the donor to enter with sympathy and understanding into the experiences of those who turn to him for succour. Stress is particularly laid in Talmudic ethics on tender words which are to accompany the gift to the poor and which, in fact, may mean more to the poor than the gift itself (T. Sukkah, 49b). At the same time, there is a responsibility fixed upon the giver to see that his gifts are not put to unworthy use. Simply to give away money for the sake of giving is not considered a satisfactory contribution to charitable activity and endeavour. In Jewish ethics charity was never looked upon as a source whence there flow gifts of heavenly grace to the donor irrespective of the need or character of the recipient. All relief is essentially looked upon as having for its object the *benefit* of the recipient, the alleviation of his distress, without encouraging idleness and loafing. Applicants for relief, unless it is for immediate relief – food to the hungry, drink to the thirsty, and clothes to the naked – must therefore have, so Talmudic law ordains, their cases investigated and due discrimination is to be exercised between the genuine and deserving poor and the professional beggar and impostor.

As an act of righteousness charity must not contain in it an element of injustice or unrighteousness. Talmudic ethics accordingly consider it reprehensible to give charity whilst not paying debts or proper wages to the employees (Yalkut Shimeoni, Proverbs, 947); or to use alms as a cloak for unjust practices, or to associate the making of gifts to the poor with personal advantages (Midrash Exodus Rabbah, 31. 18).

The claims of the poor upon the consideration of the more fortunate are derived from the idea of divine ownership, involving the recognition that whatever man has he holds from God, and that his right of possession is justified only by the opportunities this provides for service. This was the principle underlying the Biblical laws already referred to regarding the reaping of the harvest. The landowner, whilst enjoying the reward of his toil and diligence, had to recognize that whatever rights he had in the land and its produce were derived from God and were subject to the overruling consideration that He alone had the ultimate ownership. From this followed the corollary that all God's children were entitled to a share in the land as a common heritage. It was this common human right, flowing from the idea of Divine ownership, that the Bible sought to safeguard in assigning to the poor part of the harvest.

The Biblical attitude in respect of the gifts of Nature inspired the Talmudic teachers in their attitude to other gifts which fall to man by good fortune. Though they recognized private property rights, they sought to circumscribe these by social considerations, and only in so far as they provided a basis for service were the claims of private possessions justified. For a man, therefore, to refuse to others of what he possesses simply on the ground that what he held is his own is a conduct for which, in the eyes of these teachers in Israel, there is no warrant. Provided it involves no loss or damage to the owner, others too are entitled to avail themselves of the benefits and advantages which private property could offer. A typical example to which the Talmud applies this principle is a field which has been cleared of crops at the end of the harvest, when it is considered unethical for the owner to refuse to allow the public to enter the field simply because it was his private possession (T. Baba Kamma, 81b).

Righteousness as a mainspring of human action is not limited to human beings, but includes all brute creation. Consideration for the beast was from ever regarded as the mark of the righteous man. 'A righteous man regardeth the life of his beast' (Prov. 12. 10). Some of the laws enjoined by the Bible for the treatment of animals have already been set forth in a former chapter. On the basis of these and similar laws the Talmudic teachers have, under the term *tzaar baale hayyim* (distress of living creatures), declared the least disregard of the needs and feelings of animals to be a crime. Thus they ruled that it was forbidden for a man to partake of his meal before he had given food to his animals, or to purchase any animal or bird whether tame or wild before having first made adequate provision for its food. It was the same concern for the claims of dumb creatures on human pity that lies behind the many elaborate precautions whereby Jewish law had hedged about the slaughter of beasts or birds for food so as to minimize, if not to suppress, pain altogether.

And not only to animal creation. Righteousness is a principle which in Rabbinic ethics is to govern the attitude of the Jew to the whole creation, inanimate as well as animate. The Biblical prohibition against the destruction of fruit-bearing trees (Deut. 20. 19–20) has been extended by the Talmud to apply to all kinds of things useful under the general prohibition of *bal tashchith* (thou shalt not destroy) (Deut. 20. 19). Food, particularly bread, may neither be damaged nor wasted. It is also forbidden to destroy unnecessarily any object no longer required by the owner but which can be of some use to others.

Transcending the demands of justice and righteousness and

embracing them all are those of love as formulated in the Biblical command 'Thou shalt love thy fellow as thyself' (Lev. 19. 18). The implications of this golden rule are left undefined in the Bible, but in Talmudic ethics they are made to cover any kind of personal service to one's fellow-men. Such acts are designated in the Talmud as *gemiluth chasadim* (the practice of goodly deeds). The inner meaning of the Hebrew term is making good – a making good to fellow-men for the goodness of God – and is connected with tenderness and mercy to all men and all classes.

Among the more specific 'goodly deeds' on which the Talmudic teachers lay stress are visiting the sick, providing the poor bride with a dowry, paying the last respects to the dead, and comforting the mourners.

Gemiluth Chasadim expresses itself not only in conferring temporary benefits upon our fellow-man but also in attempting to lead him or bring him back to the right path of conduct (T. Tamid, 28a). It also finds expression in courtesy and considerate behaviour towards all men, in greeting all peoples, irrespective of faith or origin (*Ethics of the Fathers*, 4.15): and receiving every man with a cheerful countenance (*ibid.*, 4. 15).

The rule of love as expounded in the Talmud also demands that man shall act *lifenim me-shurat hadin* (within the line of his legal rights). A man who acts in this manner does not insist on the legal rights accorded to him in a lawsuit – compensation, damages, or what not – but renounces them in favour of his economically weak litigant.

The command to love one's fellow-man with all its implications is all-embracing, extending to all men, of whatever race or creed. Unmistakable in this connexion is the Biblical injunction 'to love the stranger as thyself' (Lev. 19. 34). In the words 'as thyself' is enunciated the great principle of human equality: the non-Jewish stranger is *as* thyself. Any distinction which Judaism makes between the Jew and non-Jew is only of religious significance. Politically and socially no distinction is recognized between the two. 'One law and one ordinance shall be for you and for the stranger that sojourneth with you'

(Num. 15. 16). The law is one and the same for all. 'Judge righteously between a man and his brother, and the stranger that is with him' (Deut. 1. 16). The stranger requires no patron as in Greece and Rome to take legal action. 'For the judgement is God's' (*ibid.*, 17). It is God who gives the stranger his share and full rights in the law of the land.

This equality is stretched even in regard to the land: 'And it shall come to pass that ye shall divide it (the land) by lot for an inheritance unto you and to the strangers that sojourn among you, which shall beget children among you; and they shall be unto you as homeborn among the children of Israel; they shall have inheritance with you among the tribes of Israel' (Ezek. 47. 22).

The Biblical attitude to the non-Israelite is also manifested in the teachings of the Talmud. Characteristic of such teachings is the saying of Hillel, 'Be thou of the disciples of Aaron, one that loves peace and pursues peace, that loves human beings and brings them near to the Torah' (*Ethics of the Fathers*, 1. 12).

At the root of all Jewish ethics lies the concept of personal holiness. The great texts 'Love thy fellow as thyself', 'Hate not thou thy brother', 'Avenge not', 'Bear no grudge', 'Love the stranger' – are all part of the Law of Holiness enunciated in the command 'Ye shall be holy' (Lev. 19. 1).

Holiness, as has already been pointed out in more than one connexion, has a two-fold connotation, negative and positive. On the negative side, holiness demands self-control. Self-control must be exercised in regard not only to evil acts but also to evil desires which, because of their tendency if unchecked to develop into habitual vice, are at times considered in rabbinic ethics in their effects worse than the evil act itself (T. Yoma, 29a).

Among the vices which are regarded in Talmudic teaching as most dangerous are envy, greed, and pride. These are the vices which are declared to drive out man from the world (*Ethics of the Fathers*, 4. 2), in that they embitter social relations and lead to the destruction of man's usefulness to society. Another vice which counts in Talmudic ethics as most dangerous is anger. 'It is certain that the iniquities of the angry man outweigh his merits' (T. Nedarim 22b). In this Talmudic saying attention is fixed on the danger of anger which, often resulting in the complete loss of self-control, is liable to destroy much of the good done by the person thus affected.

Self-control in Jewish ethics is not to be confused with asceticism. The ascetic ideal as an end in itself is alien to the spirit of Judaism. Essentially optimistic, Judaism does not consider this world to be inherently evil, nor existence to be under a curse. Though it glorifies future life, it does not do so at the expense of this life. This life too is very good, and it is the will of God that man should enjoy all the good things of which the earth is full. '"And the Lord saw everything that He had made and behold it was good" (Gen. 1. 37) – that is, both this world and the world to come' (Midrash Genesis Rabbah, 9. 3). Nor did Judaism ever regard the body as contaminated, and the appetites as rooted in evil. The human body is a sacred vessel comprehending a Divine spark – the soul, and as such must be kept healthy, sound, and clean. To neglect the body and its physical requirements is to offend against God, and to wash daily is a religious duty which the Jew is bidden by the Talmud to perform, in the glory of His Creator (T. Shabbath, 50b). Abstention from anything not proscribed by the Law is accounted as sin. 'A man,' so runs the Talmudic saying, 'is to give account in the Hereafter for any permissible pleasures from which he abstained' (T. J. Kiddushin, 4. 12). Individual fasting is likewise looked upon with disfavour, and the habitual faster is a sinner (T. Taanith, 11a). In the same spirit, Judaism repudiates the view which condemns wealth and regards marriage with no particular favour. On the contrary, 'wealth and riches' are among the blessings promised by Jewish teaching to the man who fears God (Psalm 112. 13), and the High Priest was not to perform the solemn service on Israel's most sacred day in the year, the Day of Atonement, unless he had a wife to make his home holy.

Materialism in Jewish teaching is not wrong because it deals with material things, but because it deals with nothing else. But when it gives up its exclusiveness and the senses which it satisfies are put under control, the enjoyment of the goodly things of the earth is a fulfilment of the Will of God.

But self-control, with all the eradication of vice it involves, is not enough. It represents only the negative side of holiness which is concerned with the avoidance of transgression and the eschewing of evil. But there is a positive side to holiness which must be expressed in terms of righteousness and love. This necessitates the cultivation of positive virtues which, though personal, derive their special quality from the relation to the social context in which they come to fuller realization, making man conscious of what he ought to do rather than merely what he ought not to do.

The first of these virtues is contentment, contentment with our own mind. 'Who is wealthy?' is a Talmudic question; and the answer is 'He who is contented with his lot' (*Ethics of the Fathers*, 2. 1). A contented man is not merely only saved from many offences such as envy, lust, etc. but what is more he is a source of joy to society. 'A merry heart is a continual banquet' (Prov. 15. 16).

Contentment springs from a conscious faith in God's providential and beneficent ordering of human life. The result of this attitude is a calmness and serenity of mind that assumes the deeper and richer hue of joy – 'Joy in God'. Joy in God is a quality of the soul that enriches the whole content of life and that has always proved a saving strength in time of national turmoil or social upheavals. 'The joy of the Lord is your strength' (Neh. 8. 10).

Faith in God involves also man in the willingness and readiness to recognize his dependence on God and the insufficiency and weakness of his position apart from Him. The vivid apprehension of this truth leads to humility, the virtue which protects man from the danger of pride in his material worth and achievements and thus makes him a 'beloved on high and desired below'.[1]

'The reward of humility is the fear of God' (Prov. 22. 4). The sincere recognition by the individual of his moral unworthiness in the sight of God cannot but act upon him as a deterrent against any act or thought which would only serve to lower him still further in the Divine estimate. Thus does humility become the foundation of all human behaviour, religious and social – the fear of the Lord.

Whilst the fear of the Lord is the motive which applies to the whole range of ethical conduct, it is specially stressed by Talmudic teachers in matters which they designate as 'committed to the heart' (*masur laleb*), that is, matters which are not susceptible of exact definition and quantitative determination, but must be left to individual conscience and the moral discernment of the person concerned. Generalizing from a number of Scriptural texts (Lev. 19. 14, 32; 25. 36, 43) the Talmud points out that 'all commandments that are committed to the heart are accompanied by the exhortation 'Thou shalt fear thy God' (T. Kiddushin, 32b).

The fear of the Lord is, however but 'the beginning of Knowledge' (Prov. 1, 7) – the first step to right action.

Higher than the fear of the Lord is the love of Him – a love evoked by the contemplation of His glorious perfections and His loving-kindness that fills the earth. Both motives of the fear and love of God are stressed in Judaism. Whilst the fear of God is urged as a restraint on evil-doing, the love of Him is upheld as the most impelling incentive to virtue.

The love of God leads to the 'sanctification of His name' *Kiddush Hashem*, which has been recognized as the most characteristic feature of Jewish ethics both as principle and as motive. The idea underlying *Kiddush Hashem* is that every act which exhibits the elevating power of the Jewish religion and sheds lustre on the name of Israel is a sanctification of the name of God. So is every act of self-denial, self-restraint, and self-sacrifice in the service of God or our fellow-man, a *Kiddush Hashem*. Conversely, to act in any manner which tarnishes the honour of the Jewish name and brings into discredit the religion of Israel is a *Chillul Hashem*. The highest form of *Kiddush Hashem* is, however, that exhibited in the cause of God – an heroism, that often leads to martyrdom. The hero in such a case may be called upon to defend with his very life his manhood as leagued companion of God. Even a whole people may hear such a call. The Jews had often to make the choice in the cry

'Sacrifice to idols or die'. Their life down all the ages can well be called a continual *Kiddush Hashem*. Private defects there are – defects which in many cases have been characterized by generations of persecutions; that does not change the historical fact of Israel's martyrdom in the cause of the truth and of the ethical and religious ideals of mankind. And the strength and inspiration that moved the Jew to take upon himself this martyrdom in the service of humanity came from no other source than the Torah and the practical observances of his religion.

NOTES

1. *Tanna debe Eliyyahu* (Ed. M. Friedmann), p. 197. On this Midrash see p. 185.

CHAPTER 16

TALMUDIC JUDAISM (III):
RELIGIOUS OBSERVANCES

THE Talmudic contribution in the domain of ethical conduct has its counterpart in the domain of religious practice. Applying their methods of interpretation, adaptation, and development to the religious prescriptions of the Bible, the Talmudic teachers were able to erect a system of Jewish observance which, notwithstanding the cessation of the sacrificial cult, was sufficiently rich and colourful to satisfy completely the religious needs of Judaism. Subsequent generations, it is true, have made their own contribution by the introduction of a variety of rites and customs, but all these additions were designed to enhance the effectiveness of the system as the norm of Jewish observance, and to maintain its supremacy as the guide of all Jewish religious life and action.

In proceeding, therefore, to an account, however brief, of the religious observances of Talmudic Judaism, it will not be incongruous if, for our purpose, reference is also made to supplementary rites and practices introduced since the close of the Talmud and still in force to the present day.

The practical duties prescribed by the Talmud begin with the very first moments of the Jew's waking hours. As soon as he opens his eyes in the morning he has to utter thanks to the Almighty for having restored unto him his soul, refreshed and reinvigorated, ready for the tasks of the day.

'Cleanliness is next to godliness' – to the idea expressed in this proverb of unknown origin the Jew is bidden by the Talmud to give practical demonstration in a number of ritual ablutions he has to observe on a variety of occasions. Washing hands immediately on rising in the morning is enjoined at once as an act of elementary hygiene, and as a rite of consecration. The same twofold motive enters into the ritual washing of hands prescribed before meals.

Indeed, many are the consecrating rites attending the meals

of the conforming Jew. Before and after the partaking of food or beverage of any kind, he utters a grace. His diet is regulated by law. No meat whether of animals or birds is eaten by him unless it belongs to the class of what is Biblically termed 'clean' or, in popular usage, 'kasher' (fit), properly slaughtered by expert *shochet*, under strictly prescribed regulations ensuring the minimum of pain, and the elimination of blood which by the Bible is rigorously forbidden. The meat, in addition, has to be free from any lesions or organic diseases, and has to be salted and well rinsed to drain off the remaining blood. The distinction between 'clean' and 'unclean' species also exists in fish. These regulations are all designed to impart to the animal process of eating an element of spirituality.

In this connexion mention should also be made of the observance derived from the Biblical law not to 'seethe a kid in its mother's milk' (Ex. 23. 19; 34. 26; Deut. 14. 21), and demanding the complete segregation of meat and milk alike in diet and kitchen.

Consecration is also the keynote of the multiplicity of rites that encompass the life of the Jew. Chief among them are the outward symbols: the fringed garment (*tzitzith*), the 'phylacteries' (*tefillin*), and the sign on the doorpost (*mezuzah*). The fringed garment worn at all times, formerly outwardly, but, since the thirteenth century as an undergarment under the name of *arba kanfoth* (four corners), is to serve as a constant reminder to the Jew to consecrate his whole being to the service of God. The 'phylacteries', worn during morning prayer on the head and on the arm near the heart, contain Scriptural texts (written on parchment) exhorting the Jew to love God with all his heart, soul, and might and to subject all the powers of common life – thoughts, feelings, and actions – to the service of God; while the part of the same Scriptural texts, affixed in a case to the doorpost of the main entrance as well as of every living-room of the house, and constituting the *mezuzah*, summon the Jew to consecrate his home, making it an abode worthy to be blessed by the presence of God.

The set times of prayers are three in number daily: morning, afternoon, and evening. The morning prayer can be recited from dawn till the day has reached about one-third of its length, the afternoon prayer from after mid-day till somewhat before sunset, and the evening prayer from some time before nightfall till the rise of the dawn. These hours correspond with the hours of the daily sacrifices that were offered in the Temple and for which the prayers are nowadays a substitute.

Most solemn of the three regular daily prayers is the morning prayer, before which it is not permissible to have a meal or perform any work. In keeping with its solemnity the morning prayer is recited with a praying shawl, fringed at the four corners, the *tallith*, and on weekdays also, as already mentioned, with the *tefillin*. The *tefillin* are, however, not worn on Sabbath and Festivals, as the days themselves bear testimony to the consecrating ideas that the *tefillin* enshrine.

The principal feature of each of the three daily prayers is the *tefillah* (lit., 'prayer' – the Prayer *par excellence*) so called in the Talmud, because of its supplicatory contents and antiquity, but now more popularly known as the *Amidah* (lit., 'standing') on account of the standing posture in which it is recited. The *Amidah* consists of nineteen (originally eighteen)[1] benedictions, the first three of which are in praise of God's sovereignty, omnipotence, and holiness, and the last three in thanksgiving to Him for His continuous bounties, closing with a prayer for peace; whilst the intervening thirteen are offered in supplication for a wide range of human needs – material, spiritual, and physical – and include prayers for Israel's national restoration.

On Sabbaths and festivals, when the sadness awakened by supplications is not in keeping with the joyful spirit of the day, the intervening thirteen benedictions are replaced by a single one, which has for its subject the celebrations of the particular day and its proper observance.

In the morning and evening the *Amidah* is preceded by the *Shema* which, as mentioned on a previous occasion,[2] constitutes Israel's primal confession of faith. The *Shema* is in its turn introduced by two benedictions: (i) in praise of God for creating light (in the morning prayer) and for ordering day and night (in the evening prayer), and (ii) a eulogy of His love for Israel as shown in Revelation. Following the *Shema* is a eulogy of God as Redeemer to which there is added in the evening an additional prayer for peaceful repose. Each of the daily services ends with the *Alenu* (Upon us [is the duty]) prayer, which gives eloquent expression to the Messianic hope for the universal sovereignty of God, when the world will be made perfect in the Kingdom of the Almighty, and all the wicked of the earth shall turn to Him in recognition of His Kingdom.

For the purpose of daily prayers it is proper for the worshipper to meet in congregation with a quorum (*minyan*) of at least ten males of over thirteen years of age, and this insistence on a quorum for prayer guarantees the corporate and social character of Jewish religious loyalty. Prayers, however, may be said in private, except for certain features which are reserved for congregational worship. Among the features which are restricted to congregational worship are the 'sanctifications', the *Kedushah* and the *Kaddish*, as it is only amid a communion with his fellow-men that the Jew can sanctify the name of God and give witness to His Holiness. The *Kedushah*, which is attached in the morning and afternoon prayers to the third benediction of the *Amidah* proclaims, in the thrice-repeated 'Holy' of the Seraphs (Isa. 6. 3), the Holiness of God; whilst the *Kaddish*, which marks off the close of parts of the service, is a prayer for the hallowing of the name of God and the coming of His Kingdom. It is not without significance that the *Kaddish* is written in Aramaic, the recognized *lingua franca* of the times when it was composed, thereby emphasizing the universal character of this prayer.

Another feature of worship for which Talmudic law prescribes a quorum is the public reading of the Torah (the Pentateuch and the Prophets). This prescription is designed to emphasize the need of social contacts for a proper study and observance of the Torah. The Pentateuch is read from a scroll, *Sefer Torah*, written on parchment by hand, under certain minute regulations as to the materials to be used and the mode of writing. From the earliest days the teachers of Judaism saw to it that at least no three days should pass without the Jew coming under the influence of the Word of God. They accordingly instituted public readings of portions of the Pentateuch to take place on Monday and Thursday mornings, and on the Sabbath morning and afternoon. For this purpose the Pentateuch was divided into 54 *Sedarim* (sing. '*Sidra*' – order) and arranged to be completed in the course of one year. In Palestine in early days, the Bible was completed in three years. This Palestinian cycle, called the Triennial, ultimately gave way to the Babylonian annual cycle which became the usual practice. On Sabbath mornings one *Sidra* is read and is followed by a reading from the Prophets which has some bearing on the contents of the particular *Sidra*. On Mondays and Thursdays the first section of the *Sidra* of the coming Sabbath is read. This is also the reading on the Sabbath afternoon service. On festivals and other festive days and fasts, special selections from the Pentateuch are read, as well as from the Prophets. To the Scriptural readings a number of persons are 'called up', each of whom recites a benediction before and after the reading of his portion by the officiating Minister. The lesson from the Prophets is generally read by the person 'called up'.

In Talmudic times in Aramaic-speaking lands (Palestine and Babylon) the Scriptural readings were accompanied by a translation (*Targum*) in the vernacular. This custom is traced back to Ezra in whose time Aramaic was supplanting the various native tongues and became the general language of government, commerce, and culture throughout Western Asia. The translation which was in charge of a special interpreter (*Meturgeman*) was given orally, so as not to confuse it with the sacred text, and although the accepted interpretation in Judaism remained determinative, the translator was allowed a measure of freedom as to the form in which the interpretation was to be cast, thus giving rise to different Aramaic versions varying from place to place.

The oldest of the officially adopted *Targums* on the Pentateuch is that of Onkelos,[3] which dates, perhaps, from the second century, and which for the most part follows the text closely, and in many ways shows affinity to the exegesis of the school of Akiba, although the *Targum* did not receive the present definite form before the fifth century. The *Targum* Onkelos is highly revered, and although Aramaic is no longer spoken, it is still the practice for the pious Jew, who reads privately the weekly *Sidra*, to accompany it with the Onkelos version. For the Prophets the official *Targum* was the one ascribed to Jonathan ben Uzziel, a disciple of Hillel, which, however, in its present form is of the same date as that of Onkelos.

On Sabbath, Festivals, and new moon days after the scriptural reading, an additional *Amidah* (*Musaf*) is recited in analogy to the extra sacrifices that were offered on these occasions in the Temple. The structure of the *Musaf Amidah* is the same as all Sabbath and Festivals, morning, afternoon, and evening *Amidahs*, except for the petition section, which consists of a prayer for the restoration of Israel and the building of its Temple, and of biblical passages detailing the additional sacrifices of the day.[4]

In addition to the daily prayers, the Talmud prescribes benedictions for various occasions in recognition of man's dependence on God and his gratitude to Him, for the good and wonderful things with which He has filled the world.

Apart from the grace which has to be said before and after meals, there are special benedictions to be recited for gratifying the senses through odorous plants or fragrant spices; on witnessing some natural phenomena, such as thunder, lightning, or a rainbow; on seeing a great sage (Jew or non-Jew) or a king; on hearing tidings, good or bad; on buying a new house and acquiring new clothes.

All statutory prayers, as distinct from private devotions, have to be recited in Hebrew, as being the only language deemed by Talmudic teachers adequate to give expression to the deepest Jewish feelings, hopes, and aspirations. Nor is it permissible, according to Talmudic teaching, to recite prayers with the head uncovered, an act which it regards as savouring of irreverence.

Just as the Jew's waking thoughts of the day are directed to God, so are his last thoughts at night filled with the awareness of the Divine Presence. He retires with a prayer of peaceful and undisturbed repose, the recital of the *Shema*, and an expression of confidence and trust in God.

The home is the foremost institution in Judaism, where the ideals of the consecration of life are to be inculcated, developed, and fostered. The foundation of the home is the sanctity of the marriage tie. The sacred character of Jewish marriage is already indicated in the term *kiddushin* (sanctification) given to a Jewish marriage ceremony, as well as by the fast of the bride and bridegroom on the day of the wedding up to the solemnization, in preparation for the consecration of their wedlock.

The marriage ceremony is performed under a *Chuppah* (canopy) which, in Talmudic teaching, denotes the voluntary entrance of the bride upon the estate of matrimony. Under the canopy the bride meets her bridegroom in the company of her parents, or others *in loco parentis*, for the solemnization of the marriage. In Talmudic times the marriage ceremony, which celebrated the entrance of the bride into her husband's home, followed some time after the betrothal ceremony, at which the ring was given. It was only gradually that betrothal and marriage became merged in a single service which, retaining however a vestige of the ancient distinction, falls into two parts.

The first part of the marriage solemnization consists of the 'Benediction of Betrothal', which is recited over a cup of wine in praise of God for the institution of marriage. This is followed by the act of *Kiddushin*, in which the bridegroom, in the presence of two persons specially appointed to act as witnesses, places the ring upon the forefinger of the right hand of the bride, with the declaration, 'Behold, thou art sanctified unto me by this ring according to the Law of Moses and Israel.'

In order to enable the bride to enter upon matrimony with a free and easy mind, Jewish law demands that no marriage may be performed unless the bridegroom has first drawn up a document providing his bride with some safeguard to her marital security. This document, known as *Kethubah*, 'marriage settlement',[4a] is read out immediately after the giving of the ring, and includes among its clauses a promise made by the bridegroom to the bride in the words, 'I will work for thee, I will honour thee, I will support and maintain thee, as it beseemeth a Jewish husband to do.'

The second part of the solemnization consists of the recital over a cup of wine of the seven 'Benedictions of Nuptials', which include praises to God for the creation of man and woman to be companions and helpmeets to each other, and for His gifts to mankind of the joys of matrimonial bliss; a prayer for the happiness of the bride and bridegroom; and a blessing linking the hopes cherished on behalf of the bridal couple with the Messianic hopes of the Jewish people.

The cups of wine over which the 'Benedictions' have been recited are drunk by the couple as an indication of their resolve to share whatever destiny Providence may allot to them in the years to come. At the end of the solemnization a glass is broken by the bridegroom, as a reminder of the destruction of the Temple, in observance of the national pledge expressed by the Psalmist (Psalm 137. 6) not to forget Jerusalem, even amidst the chief joys of life.

The object of marriage in Talmudic teaching is not only procreation in fulfilment of the divine command 'to be fruitful and multiply' (Gen. 1. 28), but also the promotion of chastity and purity of life, which is hardly attainable in an unmarried state. The basis of the marriage relationship must be accordingly not only fidelity, but unity in aim and purpose between the two partners. Where, however, discordant natures and unequal tempers have rendered such indispensable relations impossible, the Talmud (in accordance with Deut. 24. 1–4) provides for a bill of divorcement, *Get*, which secures for the wife freedom to re-marry. Polygamy, though not forbidden either by Biblical or Talmudic law, has since the eleventh century become outlawed, except among a small number of Jewish communities in Moslem countries, by a ban of excommunication (*Cherem*),[5] enacted in response to an inner Jewish moral sense, which already, in Talmudic times, felt a pronounced aversion to polygamous marriages.

The centre of importance in Jewish marriage relations is the children. Their importance is derived not only from the fact that they ensure the continuity of the family, but also because they are the guarantors in the fulfilment of the role divinely assigned to Israel. For this reason a religious and moral task devolves upon the parents to instruct their children in the practice and knowledge of Judaism from their earliest years. The first formal introduction of a Jewish boy into Jewish life takes place normally on the eighth day of his birth, when he is initiated by circumcision into the covenant of Abraham (*Milah*). This rite, described in the Bible as 'a token of covenant' between God and Israel, carries with it the idea of national consecration. It is, however, by no means to be conceived as a sacrament, giving the Jew his religious and legal character as a Jew. Indispensable for the admission of a non-Jew to the membership of the House of Israel, a Jew born of a Jewish mother is a full Jew, whether or not he has submitted to that rite. Moreover, the status of a Jew, once acquired, whether in virtue of birth or by adoption, is inalienable and cannot be surrendered by apostasy or conversion to another religion.

The obligation of positive commands begins, strictly speaking, on the completion of the thirteenth year when the Jewish boy reaches his legal majority, *Bar Mitzvah* (Son of the Commandment). On attaining that age he is confirmed in his duties and privileges by putting on the *tefillin* and being 'called up' to the public reading of the Torah. The training of the Jewish child to his tasks as a son of Israel begins, however, from an earlier age. 'As soon as the child can speak,' declares the Talmud, 'his father teaches him the Torah' (T. Sukkah, 42a). Among the first texts which the child is made to learn by heart is the verse 'Moses commanded us the Torah as an inheritance to the congregation of Jacob' (Deut. 33. 4); and the *Shema*, exhorting him to fill his soul with the love of God and His commandments, and instilling in him the faith in the consecration of daily life. As the boy grows older he is made to wear the fringed garments (*arba kanfoth*). Thus is the Jewish boy trained gradually in the practice of the observances of his faith.

Women are exempt from many of the positive commands which must be performed within certain prescribed times. This exemption is not a mark of the women's inferiority, but is in accordance with the Talmudic principle that 'one who is engaged in one religious act is exempt from the claims of another upon him' (T. Sukkah, 26a). The vocation of womanhood is in itself considered of a sufficient sacred character as to engage a woman's attention to the exclusion of any other religious duty which must be performed at any given time and which consequently might interfere with her special tasks. Women are, however, obliged to fulfil all such duties as are not restricted to time, and subject to all prohibitions equally with men. The religious majority of girls begins at the age of twelve years and one day, with no particular celebration to mark the occasion as, in the absence of positive commands in their case, confirmation in the Judaic sense of the word is of little relevance. Some modern communities have, however, adopted a kind of general confirmation or consecration service for girls who have attained their majority, held in many cases on the Feast of the Giving of the Law (Pentecost).

Next to the home, the most important institution in the scheme provided by Judaism for the training in the consecration of life is the Synagogue. What the home is to the individual, the synagogue is to the community. It is alike a place of worship, study, and social service, and is designed to make the Jew conscious of his vocation both as a member of the House of Israel, and of the human race. Like the home, the synagogue has its special symbols. The most prominent of them is the Ark, in which the Scrolls of the Law are deposited, and towards which worshippers in prayer turn their faces. There is also the perpetual Lamp, comparable to the seven-branched candelabrum which was kept ever alight in the Temple. In addition there is the *Almamar*, the Reading Desk, reminiscent of the Altar in the Temple, and like it placed, in most congregations, in the middle of the building. Attached to the synagogue are classes, known in the Talmud as *Beth ha-Sefer* (House of the Book), where children receive instruction in the teachings of Judaism, and also, in many places, a house of Learning (*Beth ha-Midrash*), where adolescents and adults meet for instruction and study. Some communities maintain higher schools of Learning (*Yeshivoth*) for young men who devote themselves to the cultivation of Israel's lore – ancient and modern, as well as special institutions for the training of spiritual and religious leaders of Jewry.

Centred round the synagogue is much of the benevolent

endeavour and social service of the community. From the synagogue are launched the numerous appeals in support of local institutions and charities and for the relief of the poor, the sick, the downtrodden, the oppressed, within and without Jewry. An opportunity for responding to the claims of charity is afforded at the reading of the Law, when it is customary for the person 'called up' to make a donation.

The social aspect of the synagogue is reflected even in the services. The worshippers in the synagogue meet in prayer as one large family, sharing each other's joys as well as sorrows. Special ritual features are introduced in the services to congratulate an affianced couple, or the parents on the occasion of the birth of a child, as well as for the consolation of mourners.

A rich contributory factor in the consecration of life are the 'appointed Seasons', the Feasts and Fasts that constitute a highly distinctive feature of Jewish life. Foremost amongst these is the Sabbath, the weekly day of rest. On this day the conforming Jew will abstain from all kind of work, labour, or business occupation, from travelling or handling any tool or working implement, except in cases of danger to life, when all Sabbath laws are set aside. The motives that enter into the observance of the Sabbath are twofold. It is a memorial of the Creation, serving to impress upon the mind man's dependence on God for all he has, including the work of his own hands; and it is also celebrated as a reminder of the great deliverance from Egyptian bondage, and as such is a symbol of human equality and freedom. But the mere cessation of labour on the Sabbath is not enough. The Sabbath is described as a 'Holy day'. As such, it is a day of religious inwardness and moral regeneration, a day when man is free from all working activities to attend to the claims of his relation to God and his fellowman. In conformity with this spirit the Jew sets the Sabbath aside for religious worship and religious instruction as well as social visits, particularly to the infirm, the mourners, and the sick. Nor does the holiness of Sabbath impose on the Jew a flight from the pleasures of life. On the contrary, Sabbath is rendered holy by making it a day of festive delight, joy, cheerfulness, and gladness. Its entry is greeted by the kindling of at least two candlelights, and by the *Kiddush* (sanctification), a benediction recited, preferably over a cup of wine, in praise to God for the gift of the Sabbath. The meals of the Sabbath day, at least three in number, are accompanied by Hebrew table songs. At each meal two loaves of bread are used, recalling the double portion of the manna that fell on the Sabbath eve in the wilderness. The loaves are plaited, symbolic of a bridal wreath, the Sabbath being, from olden times, personified as a bride. The end of the Sabbath, like its entry, is marked by a special benediction, in praise of God for the distinction between the Sabbath and the six working days of the week, recited over a cup of wine or any other popular beverage, and over a light, usually of a plaited wax taper. Spices are also smelt, a ceremony which is explained as affording comfort to the Jewish soul which grieves at the departure of the Sabbath.

In addition to the weekly Sabbath, the Jew celebrates annually three great holidays which are also days of rest, though, unlike the Sabbath, the kind of work which is performed in connexion with the preparation of food is permitted on them. Associated with the harvest of the Holy Land, these festivals are also commemorative of historical events in the life of Israel.

At the head of these festivals is the Passover, which falling on the 19th of *Nisan* (March–April), lasts seven (outside Palestine eight)[6] days, and is observed by the eating of unleavened bread and the total abstention from all leavened food which, in fact, must be removed from the house even before the incidence of the festival. As the spring festival,[7] the season of Nature's rebirth, Passover celebrates the birthday of Israel as a nation on the Exodus from Egypt. The festival is introduced by a touching and beautiful home service, *Seder* (order) which enshrines the Jewish people's most precious memories and most exalted hopes. The principal features of the *Seder* are the unleavened bread, bitter herbs, and wine, recalling the anguish and joys of the Israelites, rescued from the Egyptian bondage in the historic divine redemption. An invitation to all who are hungry to come and eat, forms the exordium of the *Seder*. The youngest child asks four questions introduced by one general question, 'Why is this night different from all other nights?'; and the answer tells of the eloquent story of deliverance with its implicit promise of an even grander because universal redemption. The service is interrupted with a festival meal, and concludes with Psalms, hymns, and popular folk-songs in hopeful anticipation of the coming of the Kingdom of God.

In Temple times the festival was inaugurated by the slaughtering and eating of the paschal lamb; and the agricultural aspect of the Festival was celebrated by the offering of a sheaf of barley on the altar in gratitude to God as Giver of the Harvest.

Seven weeks after Passover the Jews celebrate *Shavuoth* the Feast of Weeks, the wheat-harvest festival. This festival, which is of only one day's duration (outside Palestine two), is now chiefly associated with Israel's spiritual harvest, the Revelation at Sinai, the giving of the Ten Commandments, which is looked upon as the goal and objective of the Exodus. Reminiscent of the preparations which the Israelites had to make for the receiving of the Ten Commandments, it has become customary since the sixteenth century to keep awake and spend the whole night in the study of the Torah.

In modern Israel, the connexion of the festival with Nature has been renewed by a symbolic revival of the ancient ceremony of the offering of the first fruits (*Bikkurim*), which was discontinued with the destruction of the Temple. On the days following the feast, offerings of first fruits are brought for the benefit of the Jewish National Fund which has for its purpose the rehabilitation of the ancestral soil. Outside Israel a memory of the cultural aspect of the festival is preserved in the custom, comparatively recent in origin, of decorating the synagogues with plants and flowers.

The third harvest festival is that of *Sukkoth* (booths). The festival, which falls on the fifteenth of *Tishri* (September–October) lasts seven days and is celebrated at the close of the vintage season in gratitude to God for His bountiful gifts. The observance of the festival is marked by the Four Plants: the *ethrog* (citron), the palm-branch, myrtle, and willow, waved in concert in all directions of the compass, upward and downward, to the accompaniment of the recital of psalms and hymns and carried in procession in the synagogue in thanksgiving to God – the Dispenser of all things. These four plants represent in Jewish tradition different types of men all united in cooperation. The specially erected branch- or straw-covered booths (*Sukkah*), in which meals are taken during the festival, constitute an additional feature of the celebrations. These booths help to recall the divine loving care that enfolded the Israelites during their migrations in the wilderness, and are appropriate to the season when the plentiful harvest is apt to fill men with a sense of self-sufficiency.

At the same time, the festive booth has always been looked upon as an emblem of the divine Booth which will one day enfold all children of men as one brotherhood under One Heavenly Father. It is this association of the festival with the ideals of Messianism that inspired the prophet Zechariah's vision of all nations gathered in Jerusalem in celebration of the Festival of *Sukkoth*. Then 'shall the Lord be King over all the earth. In that day shall the Lord be One and His name One' (Zech. 14. 9).

As the season of vintage, the dominant note of the festival is joy, a joy in which the stranger and the poor must be invited to participate. But the joy is infused with deep religious sentiments and is bound up with the study of the Torah. This spirit is carried over to the closing festival on the eighth day, *Shemini Atzereth*, which since the ninth century has become connected with the 'Rejoicing of the Law' (*Simchat Torah*) on the ninth day. On this day the public reading of the Pentateuch is completed and immediately resumed anew from the beginning. The celebration is marked by processions with Scrolls of the Law around the reading desk and the 'calling up' of all boys under thirteen to the reading of the Law under an improvised canopy formed by a praying shawl. In Palestine, where there is no ninth-day celebration, the 'Rejoicing of the Law' takes place on the eighth day.

While these three festivals are essentially historical and national in character, celebrating God's special dealings with Israel, the Jewish New Year, *Rosh Hashanah*, which falls on the 1st of Tishri (September–October), and is celebrated also in

Palestine for two days, transcends all these narrow confines and associations and its significance is universal. It is the anniversary of the Creation. But it is not with mere commemoration that the festival is concerned. As the anniversary of the Creation, *Rosh Hashanah* inaugurates a period of divine judgement, when individuals and peoples are called to give account to God for His creation which He has committed to their care. On this day, in Rabbinic pictorial language, books are opened in Heaven in which the deeds of all are inscribed and judgement is passed according to merit on individuals and nations. Jews everywhere accordingly greet each other with the blessing: 'May you be inscribed and sealed for a good year', and many suggestive symbols, such as the eating of apples with honey, are introduced at the table on the night of the festival as omens for a good year.

But in the administration of divine judgement the chief aim is not punishment but the turning of the sinners to righteous life and conduct. This makes *Rosh Hashanah* the beginning of the 'ten days of penitence'. These are indeed solemn days in the Jewish calendar, days marked by repentance, contrition, prayers for divine forgiveness, and resolves for the restoration of broken harmonies with God and fellow-men. But that is not all. Whilst as the festival of creation it recalls a divine act in the *past*, and the summons to divine judgement and penitence is a call to the tasks of the *present*, the New Year foreshadows the universal divine event in the *future* towards which the whole of creation is moving, and which can be brought about only through human repentance. On this day, the *Shofar* (ram's horn) is blown in all places where Jews meet for worship and all the host of thoughts and emotions, which the fulfilment of this solemn rite cannot fail to arouse, is pressed into the service of the festival. The *Shofar* notes symbolically proclaim God as King of the Universe, call men to repentance and recall them to God, as a prelude to the Messianic redemption of Israel and mankind.

Messianism, with its associated universal ideas of world-salvation and world-redemption, forms the highest point in the liturgy of the day, in which prayers are offered for God's universal sovereignty over man and Nature for the coming of a golden age when mankind shall recognize the Kingdom of God 'and form a single band to do the divine will with a perfect heart'.

The Day of Atonement (*Yom Kippur*), on the tenth of Tishri, which is the culmination of the penitential period is a day of 'self-affliction' (total abstention from food and drink) and contrition, repentance and confession. Before the commencement of the Day, on which the Jew prays to God to forgive him the sins he had committed against Him, he must first seek to obtain the pardon of his fellow-men whom he happened to have wronged. The fast begins with sunset on the previous evening and terminates with the time of the appearance of the first three stars at the end of the day. The evening service is introduced by the *Kol Nidre* declaration, which is sung to a soul-stirring and plaintive melody, and which carries with it the remission of all vows affecting man's relations with His Creator. Going back to the Jewish persecutions in Visigothic Spain in the seventh century, when Jews in their thousands were forced to abjure their faith, this declaration, with its historical associations, is designed to serve as an inspiration and challenge to all those who, through one cause or another, have strayed during the year from the fold of Israel to return on this most sacred of days in the Hebrew calendar to their ancestral faith.

The whole day is spent in the Synagogue in prayer and confession. A distinctive feature of the services is the collective confession, particularly of social and moral sins -- a confession which is recited several times during the day and accompanied by the expression of resolve not to repeat the sins. The highlight of the services of the Day is that part of the liturgy which brings before the congregation the course of the Temple service (*Abodah*) performed by the high-priest on the Day of Atonement (see Lev. 16. 1–34; Num. 24. 7–11), and which is marked by the worshippers kneeling at the mention by the Reader of the Divine name, kneeling not in confession or in prayer for forgiveness, but in homage to the Divine presence whose nearness the devout Jew in prayer feels nearer on that day than at any other time during the year.[8]

The *Neilah* (closing) service held at sunset forms the climax of the devotions of the Day. The prayer 'O May we enter Thy gates', which expresses the ardent desire of the worshipper to be received by God, provides the key-note of the *Neilah* service. The service concludes with the sevenfold proclamation of God's unity in the rallying cry, 'The Lord, he is God', uttered by Israel of old on Mount Carmel (see I Kings 18. 39); and the sounding of the Shofar which follows announces the termination of the Fast. With this watchword, the Jew, morally and spiritually refreshed and regenerated, enters upon the tasks awaiting him in the coming year.

In addition to the 'appointed seasons' prescribed in the Bible, there are a number of festivals and fasts of a minor character in commemoration of events, joyous and sad, in the history of the Jewish people. The most joyous is *Purim*, commemorating the deliverance of the Jews from the evil edict of destruction by Haman. The festival is observed by the reading in the synagogue of the Book of Esther from special parchment-written scrolls, and by feasting and light-hearted merriment and jollity, and the distribution of gifts to the poor as well as choice portions to friends. In modern Israel the reading of the scroll of Esther is broadcast. The streets are decorated with flags and bunting, and the highlight of the celebration is the Great Carnival followed by masquerades and other joyous festivities lasting through the late hours of the night. The feast is celebrated on the fourteenth day of *Adar* (February–March). Jews inhabiting walled cities celebrate the festival on the fifteenth under the name of Shushan-Purim.[9]

Of post-Biblical origin is the feast of *Chanukah* (Dedication), which lasts for eight days in commemoration of the victories gained by the Jews in 165 B.C. under Judas Maccabeus, against the Syrians, and the consequent re-dedication of the Temple.[10] The festival is celebrated by the kindling of the lights of the eight-branched candlestick, beginning on the evening of the first day with one, and adding one on each successive evening.

In consequence of the rise of the State of Israel, a new festival is now in the making, named *Yom Haatzmaut* (Day of

Independence). It is a semi-festival which is held in Israel on the fifth of *Iyar* (April–May), the Hebrew anniversary of the birth of the Jewish State, and is gradually being adopted by the Jewries in the Diaspora. No definite form has yet been given to the festival, but at present the central features of the celebration as governed by Talmudic traditions consists of a special thanksgiving service which includes the reading of the Messianic prophecies in the book of Isaiah (10. 32 to 12. 6) the chanting of Psalms 113 to 118, known as the 'Egyptian Hallel' (Praise), Israel's joyous song of God the Redeemer, which is sung on all festivals; the intoning of special memorial prayers for the members of the Israeli forces fallen in battle, as well as for the martyrs of the Nazi holocausts; and an invocation to national repentance. The service concludes with the sounding of the *Shofar*, followed by the proclamation: 'May it be the will of the Lord our God that as we have been granted to see the dawn of the redemption, so may we be granted to hear the trumpet of the Messiah.'

Of the minor fasts, four in number, the most solemn is that of the ninth of *Ab* (July–August), commemorating the destruction of the first Temple in the year 586 B.C. and of the second in the year 70 C.E. The fast is subject to the same severe restrictions as the Day of Atonement. The nine days preceding the fast are regarded as days of semi-mourning on which many abstain from meat and wine, as are the three weeks preceding the fast on which no marriages are celebrated.

Another period of semi-mourning during which no marriages are celebrated are the forty-nine days between Passover and the Feast of Weeks. The reason for this is wrapt in obscurity, but in Jewish tradition it is associated with the wars of liberation, waged by the Jews against the Romans under Bar Kocheba (132–5), which failed so disastrously for the Jewish people. A break in the mourning takes place on the 33rd day (*Lag Ba'omer*) which is designated the Scholars' Holiday. The central hero of the day's celebration since the sixteenth century is Rabbi Simeon ben Yochai. A noted patriot of the second century, who refused to be cowed by Roman might and tyranny, and the reputed author of the great Jewish classical mystic work the *Zohar*,[11] his name is revered and venerated by all. As the reputed anniversary of his death, on which in the language of the Jewish mystics his soul was wedded in blissful union with the *Shechinah* (Divine Presence), the day is celebrated under the name of the *Hillulah* (the marriage of) Rabbi Simeon ben Yochai. People from all Israel flock to his tomb near Meron, a village in Galilee, where amid much rejoicing and dancing a great *medurah* (bonfire) is kindled in celebration of his memory and in his honour.

Unlike the *Hillulah* of Rabbi Simeon ben Yochai, the death anniversary of a parent, which is commonly observed by all Jews, is pervaded by a note of sadness. The principal feature of the observance is the recital at a congregational service of the *Kaddish*,[12] which, as already mentioned, includes a prayer for the coming of the Kingdom of God. Indeed, the ideal of the Kingdom dominates the whole of the last ministrations to a Jew on earth. To accept for himself with his last breath the Kingdom of God and to close his eyes with a proclamation of His Unity in the words 'Hear, O Israel, the Lord is our God, the Lord is One', is the dying wish of every Jew. Those present at the time of death as well as the nearest relatives bend in submission to Divine judgement by pronouncing 'Blessed be the Judge of Truth', and as a token of mourning rend the top part of the upper garment. For the last ministrations no clergyman is necessary. A Jewish funeral is marked by its simplicity. The shrouded body is placed in the coffin and wrapped in the fringed garment that wrapt it when alive, and the head is laid to rest on earth specially brought from the Holy Land. Conforming Jews do not practise cremation, which is considered in Jewish teaching an undignified method of disposing of the body.

For seven days after the funeral, the nearest of kin remain in the house in mourning. For eleven months the sons, or in the absence of sons (in some communities), the eldest daughter, attend daily public worship to recite the *Kaddish*, and to offer occasionally a prayer in the pious hope that the soul of the dear departed one 'may be bound up in the bond of life with the Eternal', and find peace in the eternal life with God.

NOTES

1. The additional prayer inserted is for the frustration of the designs and machinations of the maligners of the Jewish people, and was composed according to Talmudic sources (T. Berachoth, 28a), by Samuel the younger, about 100 C.E. at the request of the *Nasi* Rabban Gamaliel of Jabneh. See p. 114.

2. See p. 134.

3 Onkelos is an Aramaic pronunciation of Aquilas (Aquila) (see p. 117). Whether the two translators are considered identical is still a moot point.

4. The only exception is the Musaf of the New Year which has three intermediate benedictions, giving expression to three aspects of the festival (see pp. 174 f.). 4a. see pp. 98.

5. See p. 256.

6. See p. 120, n. 4.

7. The Biblical injunction to observe the Passover in the period of springing corn (Deut 16. 1) made it necessary to harmonize the lunar and solar years, the annual difference between them being roughly eleven days. This harmonization is achieved by the addition at frequent intervals of an extra month, making the year consist of thirteen instead of twelve months. This extra month is placed between *Adar* and *Nisan* and is given the name of *Adar Sheni* (Second Adar).

8. This is the only occasion, apart from New Year, on the recital of the *Alenu*, (see p. 163), at the *Musaf* when a Jew kneels, as all acts of kneeling are otherwise reserved exclusively for Temple worship.

9. See Esther 9. 18.

10. See p. 93.

11. See pp. 234 f.

12. See p. 163.

CHAPTER 17

THE CONSOLIDATION OF TALMUDIC
JUDAISM

THE immense influence which the Talmud, particularly the Babylonian, came to exert as a book over the dispersed Jewries dates from about the end of the seventh century. This was the time when the armies of Islam were advancing triumphantly to the conquest of the world. Like a tidal wave they had swept almost irresistibly over Syria, Palestine, Egypt, Babylon, and Persia. They were now spreading farther eastward and reaching out as far as India and even China. Soon they were to turn west, and engulfing North Africa, overrun the whole of Spain. As they extended their conquests, more and more Jews came under Moslem (or Mohammedan) rule.

The first encounter of the Jews with Islam was not an unhappy one. Mohammed himself (571–632) its founder, had originally set out to win the support of the Jews of Arabia for his religion. For this reason he adopted many of their religious beliefs, practices, and customs. Hence his uncompromising monotheistic doctrine, his insistence on formal prayers, fasting, and almsgiving, his adoption of the Day of Atonement, his introduction of dietary laws (such as the prohibition of swine's flesh), and his requirement that his followers turn towards Jerusalem in prayer. But as soon as he found that the Jews refused to accept him he turned his unrestrained fury against them and proceeded to persecute and expel them from Arabia. This policy was followed for a time by his successors, known as 'Caliphs', but before long their inherited fanaticism gave way to almost boundless toleration. They saw in the Jews a people much akin to them in race and religion; and they also found that they could be of great use to them in the consolidation of their world conquests. The Jews had after all contacts all over the world. Commerce, more especially foreign trade, was in their hands. They had in addition a common tongue – Hebrew – with all their brethren in the Diaspora, and the

Arabs could accordingly use them as interpreters, alike in peace and war.

Thus did the lot of the Jews begin to improve wherever the Crescent bore rule. This improvement was very marked in Palestine and Egypt where the Christian Byzantine rulers had interfered not only with the economic and social life of the Jews but also with the internal affairs of the Synagogue and its services. But nowhere did this phenomenon display itself more brilliantly than in Spain, where Jews had been settled for centuries. The Christian Visigothic kings were pitiless, harsh, and cruel. But their Moslem successors not only brought the Spanish Jews relief from their oppressors, but also encouraged among them a culture which in richness and depth is comparable to the best produced by any people at any time.

Babylonia was still for the time the heart of the Diaspora. There, in the Islamic capital, at Baghdad, the Jews rose to positions of distinction and influence. The secular authority of the Prince of the Captivity, the Exilarch, was revived and clothed with renewed magnificence. Spiritual authority, however, resided in the *Geonim* (sing. *Gaon* 'Eminence'), the name by which the heads of the two major Babylonian academies of Sura and Pumbeditha were now known. Although the Gaon of Sura was considered by virtue of his office superior to his colleague at Pumbeditha, they were both looked upon as the spiritual and religious guides of the Jews, and exercised an authority which the conquests of the Crescent only served to extend.

The Geonim derived their authority by virtue of their pre-eminence as teachers and expounders of the Talmud. This was by no means an easily acquired qualification. The Talmud is one of the most difficult books in the world's literature. Its dialectics, presented in a style of pregnant brevity and succinctness, tend to make the Talmud a sealed book, requiring a traditional guide or commentary to unfold its meaning. Besides, the Talmud in its desire to demonstrate the principle of development as basic to living Judaism, refrains as a rule from formulating decisions, but leaves it to the diligent student to find out the solution for himself, by working his way through the labyrinth of contending views and opinions it records.

Then again, in an ever-changing world there must always arise new problems, new questions, for which no ready answers are available in the Talmud, and which call for authoritative decision and action.

Such were the tasks for which the Geonim were eminently fitted, and to which they directed their main activities. They not only taught the Talmud, explaining its difficulties and expounding its contents and developing its principles, but also determined and fixed the law in all matters, religious, civil, domestic, and social on which communities – large and small – as well as individuals from all parts of the Diaspora turned to them for guidance – whether or not provided for in the Talmud. Their teachings, views, interpretations, and judgements have come down to us, mostly in the form of correspondence, *Sheeloth u-Teshuboth* (Queries and Replies), in English 'Responsa', that passed between them and Jewries from near and far; and, accepted as authoritative, these became generally speaking the norm of law for subsequent generations.

Supplementing the Responsa, the Geonim sought to spread the knowledge and practice of Talmud law by the compilation of legal codes. The first of these codes was composed by the blind Gaon Yehudai of Sura (fl. 756–77) in his *Halachoth Pesukoth* which formed the basis of several subsequent codes. The Geonim also sent messengers to distant communities with copies of the Talmud and Talmudic explanations. The first of such copies to reach Spain was provided by Paltoi Gaon (eighth century).

Furthermore, the Geonim, thanks to their eminence and fame, attracted students to their academies from far and near – from the Christian no less than from the Moslem world. From Spain, Provence, Italy, and the Byzantine Empire students flocked to the Babylonian academies of Sura and Pumbeditha, and brought home with them the Babylonian Talmud, the contents of which they in turn eagerly communicated to others.

The Geonim also occupied themselves with the task of fixing the order of divine service, about which, apart from the most important prayers, there existed much uncertainty and confusion. This was particularly the case in congregations lacking historical continuity and tradition. Amram Gaon (d. *c.* 874) composed about 860 a complete Prayer Book accompanied with notes and explanations, at the request of the Spanish Jewish congregations. This work, known as the *Seder* or *Siddur* (Order) of Rav Amram was the first complete Jewish Prayer Book to have been produced, and has had a great influence on Synagogue usages. About sixty years later another Prayer Book, somewhat different in arrangement, was compiled by Saadya Gaon (892–942) for the use of the Egyptian congregations.

At the same time, the Babylonian schools applied themselves to the standardization of the Biblical text. Owing to the absence of vowels and punctuation marks in ancient Bibles, the art of reading the text was a matter of oral tradition. But the same reasons that led a former age to commit to writing the oral Torah made it now necessary to reduce to written form the oral traditions relating to the Biblical text. This work was carried on by a group of scholars in the academies of Sura, Pumbeditha, and Nehardea, known as the Masoretes (from a Hebrew root meaning 'to hand down'). Their task was to supply the Biblical text with vowel points, accents, and other signs by which the pronunciation and interconnexion of words, as well as sentence-markings and paragraph-divisions, were indicated. They also sought to produce a uniform and correct text free from copyists' errors that had crept into it in the past, and to safeguard it at the same time against the intrusion of errors in the future. With this end in view, they noted all the existing variants and peculiarities of the Hebrew text, they counted the verses and even the letters in the different books or parts of the books, and made most minute computations of words, expressions, and spellings. All these labours the Masoretes embodied in notes they wrote on the margins of copies of the Bible, and also in separate treatises and compilations.

In all their work the Babylon Masoretes based themselves on the traditions relating to the sacred books as handed down orally from the period of the Scribes. But it was in Palestine that the Masoretic studies were pursued with particular energy and drive. The Masoretes of Palestine and Babylon differed in their systems of vocalization, as well as in the consonantal text they preserved.

In Palestine itself divergent textual readings were transmitted by the rival schools of Ben Asher and Ben Naphtali, which flourished in Tiberias from the second half of the eighth century until the middle of the tenth. Ben Asher and Ben Naphtali each wrote a Codex of the Bible, embodying the traditions of their respective schools. In the end, Ben Asher's Palestine Masorah prevailed, not only over the Babylonian, but also over that of his rival, and his Codex became recognized as the standard or Masoretic text of the Hebrew Bible.[1]

The seventh century saw also the emergence in Palestine of a new type of synagogue poetry known as the *piyyut* (from the Greek word for 'poet'), the writers of which were called *payyetanim*, whose activities extended well into the sixteenth century. Specially composed for recital at fasts and feasts and other commemorative occasions as poetic additions to the established forms of prayer, the *piyyut* was designed to deepen the religious emotions of the worshippers and stir within them feelings of the intensest piety and devotion. But the *piyyut* had also a didactic aim in view. It sought to bring before the mind of the worshipper the significance and lessons of the respective commemorations and their observances. For this reason, the *piyyut* drew heavily on the *Aggadah* (Talmudic and Midrashic) with its inexhaustible store of teachings and ideas, stories and legends. In this way the *piyyut* became a vehicle of religious and moral edification and instruction.

The earliest of the Palestinian *payyetanim* was Jose ben Jose (d. *c.* 670) who used blank verse but no rhyme. He was followed by Jannai, the first to employ rhyme and name acrostics. But greater and more prolific than either was Eleazar Kalir, who flourished about the end of the seventh century and whose poems, which he composed for practically every important occasion of the Jewish calendar, are still revered and chanted by millions of Jews to the present day.

In the ninth century a Gaonate was established in Palestine, which gained wide recognition not only in the adjacent countries, Syria and Egypt, but also in distant Italy – a country which had never ceased to maintain its affiliations with the Holy Land. The Palestine Gaonate, like its Babylonian counterpart, had its own schools where preference was given to the Palestine Talmud, although the study of its rival Babylonian was not neglected.

Turning to other parts of the world, the study of the Talmud and its ancillary literature was being highly developed in schools that arose in the eighth century in North Africa and Egypt, as well as in several countries in Christian Europe. The earliest of these schools in Christian European countries were in Italy, from which many scholars went forth to spread the knowledge of the Talmud in other countries. There is a tradition that Charlemagne, anxious to attract scholars to his Empire, induced in 787 members of the prominent scholarly Kalonymus family of Italy, to settle in Germany where they established an academy in Mainz. Ten years later, according to another tradition, Charlemagne sent a diplomatic mission to the Caliph, Harun al Rashid (786–809) at Baghdad, with a request that he should send him a Jewish scholar from Babylon to propagate knowledge among his Jewish subjects. The Caliph sent him a scholar named Rabbi Machir who opened an academy in Narbonne in the south of France, which attracted pupils from many parts.

The principal subject of study in the schools of the West was the Babylonian Talmud, except in Italy where, influenced by their close contacts with Palestine, the schools also cultivated the art of the Midrash and *Piyyut*.

It is to Italy that we probably owe (at least in its present form) that ethical Midrash *Tanna debe Eliyyahu* which has been termed 'the jewel of Aggadic Literature', and the universal humanism of which is reflected in the utterance, 'I call upon heaven and earth to witness that whether a person be a Jew or non Jew, bondman or bondwoman – according to the deed which he performs, the Holy Spirit rests on him' (9).

From Italy there also emanated many of the earliest liturgical compositions of European origin which have been received in the Synagogue liturgy. The first of the Italian *payyetanim* was Amittai (end of the eighth century and the

beginning of the ninth) who was followed by his son Shephatiah (d. 887). But surpassing both the father and grandfather
was Shephatiah's son Amittai (end of the ninth century and
beginning of tenth), several of whose poems express a deep
longing for the Holy Land. Other prominent early Italian
payyetanim were Solomon ben Judah, called 'the Babylonian',
who followed the method of Kalir, and Meshullam ben Kalonymus of Lucca (b. *c.* 976) whose composition for the *Abodah*[2]
service has been incorporated in the ritual of most congregations.

The connexions of the Jews of other Christian European
countries with Palestine were rather limited. Nevertheless, in
the absence of any other direct centre of influence, they were
guided in many matters relating not only to ritual but also to
marriage and divorce and civil law by usages that obtained
in the Holy Land. On the other hand, the Jews who lived in
Mohammedan countries had their centre of influence in the
Babylonian academies with which they were in constant communication by correspondence and by which they were guided
in all their religious usages and practices.

Thus began to take shape those two great Jewish traditions
which, by the eleventh century, came to be represented, on the
one hand, by the Jews who lived in the Moslem world and in
Spain, and called Sephardim, reflecting Babylonian influence,
and, on the other hand, by those designated Ashkenazim,
reflecting Palestine influence, who lived in Italy, France, and
Germany.

The effect of the combined efforts of all these various schools
was a consolidation of Talmudic Judaism throughout Jewry.
Increasingly the study of the Talmud came to absorb the
intellectual interests of more and more Jews everywhere in the
Diaspora, and its teachings to be accepted by Jews in all lands
as standards of all life and action.

But this consolidation was not achieved without a struggle.
About the middle of the eighth century there arose a movement which, for a time, rocked the entire Jewish world and
threatened it with complete disintegration. The founder of this
movement was Anan ben David, who was next in the line of

succession to the Exilarchate. He was, however, suspected of subversive views and tendencies, and consequently passed over in favour of his younger brother. Angry over the failure of his candidature, he renounced the Talmud and founded a new movement, which, like the Sadducees of old, denied the validity of the oral tradition and took its stand exclusively on the Bible in its literal simplicity. This movement was called Karaism (from the Hebrew root meaning 'to read', specifically, 'the Scriptures'), and its followers, Karaites ('Readers of Scripture') to distinguish them from the adherents of the Talmud, who now became known as Rabbanites.

In matters of dogmatic belief there was, generally speaking, no essential difference between Karaite and Rabbanite theology. Where Karaism and Rabbanism parted company was in matters of religious practice. Keeping to the strict letter of the law, Karaism burdened life with rigorous restraints and restrictions which are totally alien to Rabbinic Judaism. This was particularly the case with the application of the Sabbath Law. Karaite literalism forbade anyone on the Sabbath to leave the house, to carry anything from one room into another, to wash the face, to wear a coat, shoes, girdle, or anything except a shirt, to make a bed, to carry food from the kitchen into another apartment, and similar other necessary activities of daily life. Likewise, the Biblical injunction 'Ye shall kindle no fires throughout your habitation on the Sabbath day' (Ex. 35. 3) was pressed to its literalness, and accordingly understood to prohibit the use of light and fire on the Sabbath. The Karaites consequently were obliged to put out all the lights and fires on the incidence of the day of rest and had to spend Friday night in total darkness, and the Sabbath, even in the most wintry season, in the cold.

Forbidden degrees of relationships were so extended as to make it increasingly difficult for Karaites to intermarry with each other without incurring the guilt of incest. The laws of ritual cleanliness, of food and clothing, and fasts were rendered more severe than in the Talmud. In civil and criminal law the Karaites refused to accept the Talmudic interpretation of the Biblical 'an eye for an eye' as denoting a money fine, but insisted on its literal application. So was the Biblical verse 'For I am the Lord that healeth thee' (Ex. 15. 26) understood in its extreme literalness, and medical aid accordingly considered a violation of the Will of God.

The strength of Karaism was derived from its appeal to the sense of individualism. Anan's principle, 'Search well in the Bible', confided to the individual conscience the task of interpreting the law, and as such could not fail to strike a responsive chord in many hearts.

The movement soon attracted to itself a number of intelligent minds of high calibre, and under their vigorous leadership, enforced by an intense literary-propagandist and polemical activity, Karaism began to spread beyond the borders of Babylonia.

Anan himself meeting with difficulties in Babylonia, withdrew to Jerusalem, where he set up a Karaite community governed by the most rigorous application of the text of the Bible, and from which all traces of Rabbinic Law were banished. In his hatred of Rabbinism, Anan forbade intermarriage and intercourse with the Rabbanites, and abolished all prayers which had been used for centuries, substituting for them prayers which consisted solely of Biblical quotations.

By the ninth century Karaism had established itself in Persia, where Benjamin Nahavendi, a disciple of Anan, was active. Although not as uncompromising in his opposition to the Talmud as Anan, Nahavendi did much for the consolidation of Karaism. Nor was he a stickler to the letter of the text as was Anan. Of a philosophic bent of mind, Nahavendi indulged in metaphysical speculations which he did not hesitate to apply to the interpretation of the Bible. He held to the theory, already propounded by others before him, that God was too transcendental to mingle with the material world and that it was an angel who created the world and not God himself. This led him to allegorize all the passages concerning God in the Bible. He also denied the survival of the soul apart from the body.

Another contemporary of Nahavendi, also in Persia, was Daniel Alkumisi, who differed both from Anan and Nahavendi in important matters of law and belief. Daniel denied the validity of speculation and strongly opposed the allegorizations of the Bible. He had likewise little regard for science, going so far as to condemn as astrology the astronomical calculations made by the Rabbanites for the purpose of fixing the New Moons; only direct observations of the moon being in his view valid.

Despite his anti-rationalism, Alkumisi denied the existence of angels, maintaining that when they are mentioned in the Bible they denoted various forces of nature by which God operates in the universe.

The movement, however, despite its promising start, was destined to failure. Its insistence on the freedom of each individual to interpret the Bible in the light of his own understanding and judgement made unity among Karaites impossible. Instead of presenting a uniform trend, Karaism was broken up into numerous dissident groups, leading to its disruption and final disappearance as a factor of any account from the stage of Jewish history.

But the time for the dissolution of Karaism had not yet come. It continued to progress and flourish, encroaching deeper and wider into Jewish life. By the tenth century, it had established itself also in Egypt and spread to Spain and Asia, and bade fair to become dominant throughout the Jewish world.

Added to this insurrection from within, there were the distressing perplexities that pressed upon Judaism from without. The discovery by the Arabs, through the medium of translations in Arabic, of the ancient monuments of Greek culture – its philosophy and science – produced an intellectual upheaval which had a disturbing effect upon the religious life of Islam. The same upheaval with similar effects took place among the Jews who were by no means behind in the cultural progress of their neighbours. As the new learning came flooding in, doubts arose in many Jewish minds as to the truth of the teachings and traditions of the Jewish religion, and reason entered into conflict with faith. It is true that the challenge to the Jewish faith by reason as represented in Greek philosophy was not new. It had already existed, as will be seen, in the days of Philo, but then it had affected only the intelligentsia, particularly in Alexandria, and not the masses, and in any event never invaded the strongholds of Torah in Palestine where all the speculations of the Greek philosophers had aroused little curiosity. Things were quite different now, when the rationalism affected the mind of the crowd. Works attacking the very foundations of Judaism became the vogue of the day. Most vehement in his attacks was Hiwi al-Balkhi (middle of the ninth century) who wrote a book in which he propounded two hundred questions against the teachings of the Pentateuch. He even denied the unity of God, His omnipotence and omniscience. He denied free will and the possibility of miracles, and objected to circumcision. His book created quite a stir, and his ideas found many adherents and were even taught to schoolchildren.

Such was the twofold danger which threatened Judaism at that time and which the Rabbanites resolved to meet. Realizing before long that the most effective method of fighting the enemy from within and without was by employing his own weapons, the Rabbanites began to apply their minds to a wider range of studies than that covered by Talmudics. Whilst the onslaught of the Karaites led the Rabbanites to pay greater attention to Biblical exegesis, Hebrew grammar and philology, the challenge of rationalism gave a strong impetus among them to the cultivation of philosophy, logic, and the physical sciences. These studies reached their highest point in Saadya ben Joseph of Fayyum in Upper Egypt (892–942) who, at the early age of thirty-six was called from his native land to become Gaon of the famous Babylonian Academy of Sura. Of penetrating intellect and encyclopedic knowledge, Saadya exemplified the combination at its best of Hellenic-Arabic and Hebrew cultures. His independent Biblical researches and philosophical attainments, combined with his vast Talmudic scholarship, enabled him to fight and win many battles on behalf of his faith.

In his early twenties, realizing the danger inherent in Karaism, he began writing against the movement. His first work was a criticism of Anan, the founder of Karaism, a work of which only a few fragments have survived. This was followed by many polemical writings in which Saadya championed brilliantly the cause of Talmudic Judaism against the attacks of Karaism. In his desire to strengthen Jewish tradition Saadya produced an array of books, all of them of abiding value and merit. Apart from his extensive writings, on Hebrew lexicography, grammar, and liturgy, he wrote many Halachic responsa, codified rules of Talmudic logic, clarified problems of the Jewish calendar, and composed, as already mentioned, an 'Order of Service', for public and private prayer. Included among the Saadya's works designed to counter Karaite influence was his Arabic translation of the Bible accompanied by an extensive commentary. This version – the first in Arabic ever to have been undertaken – won such popularity that it became incorporated before long in the public scriptural readings of the Synagogue in Arab countries, contributing thereby in a large measure towards the establishment of the supremacy of the Talmudic interpretation of the Scriptures.

The effect of all these literary activities of Saadya proved devastating for Karaism. From his time Karaism began steadily to lose ground until it found itself reduced to small isolated communities in what is now Turkey and the Crimea, as well as in Egypt, whence the mass departure of Karaites early in 1957 in consequences of the measures instituted by Nasser against the Jews, marked the end of the Egyptian-Karaite community.

Taking up the challenge of rationalism, Saadya, apart from his treatise in refutation of Hiwi al-Balkhi, composed his great philosophic work *Emunoth Wedeoth* (Faith and Knowledge). This work, finished in the year 933, was the first comprehensive and systematic attempt ever made to give a rational basis to Jewish religious doctrine and practice. As such, the work was not only the finest gift which Saadya could have made to the perplexed of this generation, but also proved a landmark in the history of Jewish religious thinking; and a consideration of the work is accordingly reserved for the chapter on Jewish Philosophy, which is the next to follow.

After the death of Saadya the cultural hegemony enjoyed by the Babylonian Jews for almost seven hundred years began to pass gradually to the Spanish Jews. The break-up of the unity of the Moslem Empire into East and West, leading to the establishment at the beginning of the tenth century of independent caliphates in Spain and Egypt, was followed by political upheavals and social and economic disorders from which the Jews, as usual, were the most to suffer. Thereupon, Babylonian Jews, taking their scholars and their books with them, made their way in successive waves to Spain where the ruling caliphs – the Omayads – seeking to make their state intellectually superior to all other Moslem territories, welcomed the Jews as a valuable element in human cultural and scientific progress, and extended to them equal rights and a full measure of freedom. Grasping with avidity the new opportunities offered to them, Jews contributed their part brilliantly to Spanish cultural life in all its branches – philosophy, medicine, mathematics, astronomy; and many of them rose to positions of prominence in the State.

Foremost among the Jewish statesmen was Hasdai ibn Shaprut (*c.* 915–*c.* 990), who was the principal minister and court physician to the first Spanish Caliph, Abd al-Rahman III (913–61) and to his successor Hakim (961–76). A munificent patron of learning, Ibn Shaprut gathered about him and supported Jewish scholars, thereby making Cordova, his home, a centre of Jewish scholarship. He also helped Moses ben Chanoch a learned Talmudist, who is said to have hailed from Italy, to establish in Cordova an academy which not only gave a strong impetus to the study of the Talmud in Spain, but also attracted to itself scholars from all parts of the world.

Mention must also be made of Samuel ibn Nagdela (*ha-Nagid* – the Prince), the Grand Vizier of Granada (993–1055), who was not only a generous patron of learning but also himself a scholar and author of great versatility. He contributed richly to Jewish literature in many of its branches – Hebrew poetry (religious and secular), grammar, responsa – and also wrote an introduction to the Methodology of the Talmud which is still being studied as a standard work.

The result was an efflorescence of Jewish culture embracing all fields of Jewish intellectual and scientific endeavour, Talmudism, religious literature, philosophy, grammar, and biblical exegesis. Hebrew poetry especially attained its high-water mark during this period which became known as the Golden Age of Spanish Jewish culture. To this period belong 'the three fathers of song, whose sun rose in the west', Solomon Ibn Gabirol (c. 1021–69), Judah Halevi (c. 1086–1145), fuller reference to both of whom will be made in the next chapter; and Moses Ibn Ezra of Granada (b.c. 1070), a number of whose penitential prayers and hymns of deepest religious feeling and melancholy beauty have found a permanent place in the liturgy of the Synagogue.

The Spanish-Jewish Golden Age had its parallel in the golden age enjoyed by the Jews of Egypt and North Africa. In both these countries, particularly under the Fatimid Caliphs, the Jews rose to the highest positions in the State and in commerce, and were in the vanguard of a flourishing science and culture. Most famous among them was Isaac Israeli (c. 845–945), who was Court physician and also the author of a number of medical and philosophical works which were rated highly amongst scientists and scholastics in the Middle Ages.

Jewish learning was also at that time in ascendancy in these two countries. About the year 970 an important academy was established by Shemaria ben Elchanan of Italy at Fostat (Old Cairo) and another by Hushiel ben Elchanan, also of Italy, at Kairouan in North Africa. Owing to the geographical propinquity of these two schools to Palestine, special attention was given in them to the study of the Palestine Talmud, which was almost unknown in other parts of the Diaspora. This was particularly the case in Kairouan where the study of the Palestinian Talmud was extensively developed by Hushiel's two disciples – his son, Chananel, and Nissim ibn Shachnin, who were both famous as Talmudic commentators. From the Kairouan school the study of the Palestine Talmud spread to all other parts of the Diaspora.

But the glory of the Kairouan school was not of long duration. After the death of Chananel and Nissim (c. 1055) political events in North Africa led to the disorganization of the community and its intellectual life and to the closing of the schools. Nor were conditions much better in Egypt; whilst in

Babylon where, despite the general Jewish exodus, the torch of Jewish learning had still continued to shine brightly under Sherira Gaon (*c.* 900–1000) and his son Hai (*c.* 939–1038), the schools were by now beginning to shrink into insignificance.

It was in Spain that the centre of Jewish learning had by that time become more fixed than ever. Basking there in the sunshine of the Golden Age, the Jewish genius flowered and produced some of its choicest fruit, among which Jewish philosophy was also the newest; and it is to a sketch of Jewish philosophy that we must now turn.

NOTES

1. A manuscript of the Hebrew Bible copied in 1008 in Cairo by Samuel ben Jacob directly from manuscripts 'prepared by Aaron ben Moshe ben Asher', the youngest member of the Ben Asher family, is now in the possession of the Leningrad Public Library (MS B 19A). The text of this manuscript has been printed in the famous R. Kittel's *Biblia Hebraica* from the third edition onwards. There is also the Aleppo Codex which, though not actually written by Aaron ben Moshe ben Asher was provided by him with pointing and Masora. This Codex, written originally in Jerusalem, has for centuries been deposited in an old synagogue in Aleppo, and was reported to have been destroyed by fire during the Arab attacks on the Jews in Palestine, shortly after the decision of the United Nations on the partition of Palestine in November 1947. An article, however, contributed by Yizhak Ben Zvi, the Israel President, in the Hebrew periodical *Sinai*, Vol. 21 (No. 7–8), April–May 1958, pp. 5 ff. assures us that this Codex has been found and 'is now in a safe place'

2. See p. 175.

CHAPTER 18

JEWISH PHILOSOPHY

THE beginnings of Jewish philosophy go back to the Bible. It is true that there is no Jewish philosophy in the accepted sense of the term. Philosophy refuses obviously to be bound by any conclusions arrived at other than by means of reason and experience, whereas Judaism as a religion is essentially based on revelation and tradition. Yet arguments derived from reason and experience are not uncommon in the Bible. The majestic order of the starry heavens is called upon to give witness to the one and only omnipotent creator (Psalm 19. 2 [1]; Isa. 40. 26; Amos 5. 8). Man's gifts of speech and hearing are used as proof for the existence of an all-seeing and all-hearing providence (Psalm 94. 9); and God's special dealings with Israel are made to testify His overruling power in history. Wrestling with the paradoxes of the moral government of God, the Book of Job makes reason and observation of human life and Nature as the final bar of appeal justifying the ways of God to man, whilst the questioning and doubting spirit which is so characteristic of philosophy is not absent in the Bible, particularly in the Book of Ecclesiastes.

It was this tendency to rationalism, discernible already in the Bible, that enabled the teachers of Israel from the earliest times to arrive at a spiritual conception of God notwithstanding the anthropomorphisms in which Scripture abounds. They could not fail to notice in the Bible an inner contradiction between its insistence on the 'unlikeness' of God, on the one hand, and its descriptions of Him after the human pattern, on the other. They thus inevitably came to the conclusion, without the aid of any external influence, that the Biblical anthropomorphic expressions were mere figures of speech designed to impress upon man God's personal character.

This spiritualization of the conception of God is reflected already in certain changes known as *Tikkune Soferim* (Corrections of the Scribes), which, ascribed to Ezra, were introduced into the Biblical text in order to tone down certain anthropomorphic expressions; and it becomes very pronounced in the Aramaic translations of the Bible, the *Targumim*, in which all anthropomorphisms are avoided. Hence the common use in the *Targumim* of the term *Memra*, 'Word', as a reverent circumlocution for God where the literal rendering would make God act in the same manner as man. This anti-anthropomorphical bias is also characteristic of the Greek translators of the Hebrew scriptures. They likewise sought to spiritualize the conception of God by removing or moderating many of the human qualities or motives attributed to God in the Bible. There is no evidence that these translators were influenced by Greek philosophy. They were mere translators, not philosophers. But they could not help being guided by religious ideas which were already well established in Jewry in their times.

The same rationalism led the Talmudic sages to construct out of the Bible the philosophy of Judaism characterized by a definite and comprehensive outlook on the world and on life. That there was an interpenetration of Greek ideas in early Talmud Judaism there is no denying, but these ideas were admitted because they happened to be expressive of a tendency inherent in Judaism itself, not because they were the product of an attractive process of philosophic thought.

The philosophical movement among the Jews began in Alexandria about the second century B.C. as a result of their close intercourse with their Greek neighbours. The first important literary product of this movement is the Book of Wisdom which is a denunciation of heathen idolatries and customs, and an exaltation of wisdom. The book breathes throughout a lofty monotheism and a staunch belief in a personal God, and as such is in keeping with the spirit of Judaism. But influences of Greek philosophy upon the writer are only too evident. 'Wisdom' in this book is quite different from the 'Wisdom' of Proverbs (8): it is made objective and represented as an intermediary being between God and the world and as that which 'pervades and penetrates all things' (7. 24). Here we have an unmistakable affinity with the Stoic World Spirit, or All-Working Reason (*Logos*). Still more distinctly Greek is the teaching that the world was not created *ex nihilo* (out of nothing), but out of some formless matter (11. 17). Quite contrary to the ordinary Talmudic teaching, but in harmony with the Platonic, is the doctrine that the soul comes into the body from a previous existence and feels itself oppressed in the body as in a prison (9. 15).

The greatest and most famous representative of Alexandrian Jewish philosophy was Philo (*c.* 25 B.C. – *c.* 40 C.E.). He was the first to set himself the task of reconciling Jewish scriptural theology and Greek philosophy. The greatest part of his voluminous writings is in the form of commentaries – a kind of Midrash – on the Hebrew scriptures, in which he naïvely believed he could find all the ideas he had borrowed from the Greeks, particularly from Plato. For this purpose he resorted to the method of allegorical interpretation. Everything in the Scriptures from names and dates to historical narratives and conduct – ritual and moral – is subject to allegory. This does not mean that Philo denied the historicity of the events recorded in the Bible, or the binding character of its laws. What he did maintain was that all these were set forth in scripture not so much to guide man's daily conduct, as to convey to him elevated philosophic thoughts which for Philo meant those he had found attractive in contemporary philosophy. The Exodus, for example, was not narrated in order that Israel might recall the wonderful redemptive acts of God on their behalf, but as an exhortation to escape the disturbances of the spirit. The Sabbath was not to remind man of the Creation and of the Exodus, but of the importance of honouring the mystic number seven.

Philo's most important contribution for the history of philosophic-religious thought was his conception of the *Logos* (Word). Carrying further the idea of the Book of Wisdom, Philo developed the Greek notion of the *Logos*, conceiving it as a personality whom he calls 'the second God' and also sometimes 'the son of God', and who is the instrument of God's creation and revelation, and of His immanent activity in the Universe. The *Logos* is for Philo definitely inferior to God, and therefore not identical with the dogma of the *Logos*, 'the Word made Flesh' of Christian theology. God himself, according to Philo, is not only incorporeal, but also divested of all attributes and qualities. He is pure being, of whom nothing can be predicated. He is abstract, static unity, eternally unchangeable, the same, pure immaterial intellect. In this way Philo sought to solve the problem of how to reconcile the Platonic tendency to remove God to a very great distance from the visible world with the Biblical teaching which affirms God to be intimately concerned with the world He created by an act of His Will.

Philo's conception of the *Logos* was totally alien to Judaism. The God of the Bible is a living God, not the impersonal being of Greek metaphysics. He does employ intermediaries to execute His Will, but is certainly not inactive Himself. Furthermore, the conception of the *Logos* as a second God seemed to impair the absolute monotheism of the Jewish religion. Nor was his allegorical method which reduced the scriptures to a mere textbook of Greek metaphysics acceptable to Judaism. Whilst Talmudic teachers did occasionally employ allegory in their interpretation of the Bible, they never lost sight of the fact that the Bible is primarily a revelation of God's Will, and not a guide for ecstatic contemplation of the Divine. Besides, by allegorizing all the narrative parts of the Bible Philo divested it of all the historical-national significance it has for the Jewish people and for Jewish destiny. All this accounts for the little influence Philo exerted on Jewish thought. His works were, however, studied eagerly by the Church Fathers who found in them much material for that synthesis of Jewish and Greek thought that came to be known as Christian theology.

The Alexandrian Jewish philosophy was short-lived, and after the death of Philo, as far as the Jews were concerned, had spent its force. It was only in the tenth century, with the introduction of Greek culture within the Moslem world, that there arose a continuously developing Jewish philosophy that was to shape the subsequent trend of Jewish religious thought. Many Jewish thinkers participated in the movement, but the names chosen for the sketch which follows are only of those who have exerted the greatest influence on Judaism. No attempt, however, will be made, even in their case, beyond a general presentation of those aspects of their teachings which have entered the main stream of Jewish religious thinking, omitting all critical and analytical arguments which would be far too complicated and abstruse to reproduce in this work.

As already mentioned, the first in the line of the Jewish medieval philosophers was Saadya, who has been called the 'father of Jewish philosophy'. Saadya was greatly influenced by the Kalamists (from Arabic *Kalam* – the 'word'), a school of Mohammedan theologians, who insisted on using reason as a means of arriving at true theological knowledge. At the same time, Saadya discusses philosophic problems in an independent manner. In his work *Emunoth Wedeoth* he sought to establish the mutual relationship between revelation (faith) and reason (knowledge). To Saadya any conflict between revelation and reason was inconceivable, since both had their source in the Divine. The only difference between the two is one of method, revelation offering a quicker and more direct approach to religious truth than reason. Moreover, revelation and reason were each for Saadya the necessary complement of the other for making known the truth. Revelation saves reason from the doubts and uncertainties in which it may easily become involved; reason helps to clarify and expand the doctrines communicated by revelation.

Having established the essential unity of revelation and reason, Saadya proceeds to examine in the light of reason the revealed truths of the Jewish religion, and while expounding his own views he combats vigorously opposing theories and concepts. A case in point is Saadya's rejection of the Kalamist doctrine denying natural law and the necessity of cause and effect, maintaining that there is no other casual activity in the world except the Will of God. If the ground, for example, is wet when it rains, it is not, say the Kalamists, because of the rain but because of the Will of God that it should get wet. As against this Kalamist attitude, Saadya strongly upholds the validity of natural law.

On the other hand, following the Kalamists, Saadya finds in creation the most conclusive proof for the existence of the Creator. He accordingly begins the exposition of his philosophic system by proving that the world was created *ex nihilo* and in time; and this provides him with a basis for his proofs for the existence of a Creator who is eternal, all-wise, and all-powerful. He defends the unity of God against the Trinity of Christians and the dualism of the Parsees. God is not only One numerically, but also absolutely simple and pure spirit, free from any physical properties and attributes. The several descriptions of God in Scripture which do violence to this philosophical conception of the Divine are accordingly to be understood in a merely figurative way. Man is the crown of creation and consequently a special object of God's care and love. This means that God seeks man's happiness. For this reason He has given man the Torah, with its commandments, and it is through the very *fact* of obedience to the Torah that man can win for himself the highest good. The commandments of the Torah are divided into two classes – commandments of reason (moral), and commandments of revelation (ritual). This does not mean to imply that the commandments of revelation are void of reason; what it does mean is that they could not have been ascertained by human minds without the help of revelation. The Torah, by virtue of its intrinsic worth, is both eternal and immutable. Furthermore, the eternity of the Torah is bound up with the eternity of the Jewish people. 'Israel is a nation only by virtue of its Torah', and since God has through His Prophets guaranteed the eternity of Israel, the Torah too must of necessity endure to eternity.[1]

The Torah is not unrelated to life, and in fact has little use for those who proclaim that 'the best thing for man to do is to devote himself to the worship of God, fast during the day, and spend the night in praise of God, and relinquish all worldly occupation'. On the contrary, the Torah has little meaning if divorced from human and social activities. If life is renounced for the sake of worship of God, we have, he insists, no chance to obey or disobey many of the religious observances: 'How shall the hermit observe the laws of correct weights and measures? . . . Which part of the civil law will he fulfil with truth and justice? . . . And so with regard to the laws of sowing, of tithes, of charity and similar precepts. . . .'[2]

In order to enable man to obey the law, God has endowed

man with a soul; hence with <u>freedom of will</u> as well as the capacity to distinguish between good and evil, in accordance with the standards set up by the Torah. The soul is a fine spiritual substance, and hence indestructible and immortal. Yet it is distinctly related to the body with which it forms a natural unity, and to the elements of which it will one day be reunited – on the resurrection of the dead. This doctrine of resurrection, whilst it cannot be proven philosophically, cannot be refuted by philosophical arguments. In fact, the doctrine finds some support in reason and is moreover in conformity with natural law. This, however, does not apply to the notion of metempsychosis, or the transmigration of souls, since the union of a human soul with an animal body would be contrary to natural law. With the doctrine of resurrection is also connected the doctrine of Israel's ultimate Messianic redemption, which equally no arguments can be adduced to invalidate.

After Saadya Jewish philosophy developed principally in the highly favourable milieu of Spain. The first great philosopher of Spanish Jewry was Solomon ibn Gabirol. Little is known of his life except that he was born in Moorish Spain about 1021 and died while still in his early thirties. He is the author of one of the most penetrating works of the Middle Ages, *Mekor Hayyim*, ('Fountain of Life').

Unlike Saadya, Gabirol did not set out to prove the existence of God. The problem which primarily concerned him was the relation of God to the world. Philo of Alexandria sought, as we have seen, to solve the problem by the idea of the *Logos*, which he conceived as an instrument used by God for the creation of the world. He thus paved the way for what has become known as the Neoplatonic theories of Emanation, associated principally with the name of Plotinus (*d.* 290 c.e.), which ascribe creative powers to inferior causes proceeding from the Godhead – the Absolute – in stages of decreasing splendour and reality until there arose the concrete world of Matter.

In general, Gabirol adopts the Neoplatonic idea of Emanations except that he departs from its traditional representations in two important respects.

First, Gabirol introduces the conception of the Divine Will

as intermediary between God and the Emanations. The Emanations are accordingly no longer a necessary and mechanical overflow from the superabundant Godhead, as taught by the Neoplatonists, but the result of the voluntary activity of the Will of God.

Second, Gabirol makes Matter one of the first in the Emanations series instead of placing it, as do the Neoplatonists, last. Matter, according to him, is not corporeal but spiritual, and any corporeality that attaches itself to matter is not the property of matter itself as such, but the result of its distance from the source. Indissolubly united with matter, always and everywhere, and standing to it in relation of attribute to essence, is Form. The primary incorruptible source of all reality is the Supreme Being, one and unknowable. By an act of His Will there is produced a World Soul composed of universal matter and universal form. From this World Soul there proceed in turn, through an orderly series of intermediaries, all pure spirits and corporeal things – all sharing in common something of the universal matter and universal form, besides possessing their own peculiar matters and forms which distinguish them from one another.

By introducing the Will of God as mediating between God and the World, Gabirol was concerned first to safeguard the Biblical doctrine of creation which, in its last analysis, seeks to confirm that the world process is not the product of necessity but of the purposive action of God; and second, to mitigate the pantheism as well as the impersonalism which forms an integral element in Neoplatonism. At the same time, the idea of the Will of God acting upon universal matter from which proceed all beings, spiritual and corporeal, meant the spiritualization of the material, all things in nature being the product of the operation of one single dynamic force, the force of the Divine Will.

Although Gabirol, in interposing the Will of God, was keeping in line with Hebrew thought, he never makes any overt attempt to harmonize the Jewish faith with Greek philosophy. Nor does he ever quote a single passage from the Bible or Talmud. His concern was evidently to establish his philosophic views in independence of any dogmatic ties or prejudices. This singular detachment in his work from Jewish sources led to his general neglect by Jews. Unlike other Jewish works of importance, which found their ready translators from the Arabic into Hebrew, Gabirol's masterpiece had to wait for about two centuries before it found a Hebrew translator in the person of Shemtov Falaquera (1225–90), and then only of selected parts. Nor did these selections seem to have had any readers, and but for the discovery of a manuscript of Falaquera's work in 1845,[3] nothing would have been known of its existence.

It was otherwise in the Christian world. There the complete work had been made accessible shortly after the death of Gabirol, through a translation in Latin under the title, *Fons Vitae*, with the name of its author corrupted into Avicebron. Churchmen, supposing the author to have been a Christian, studied the work, which introduced them to Neoplatonic thought, with much diligence, and turned to it as a prime source of inspiration in their scholastic pursuits.

Yet Gabirol came into his own in the thirteenth century with the rise of the *Kabbalah* on which he exercised considerable influence. The doctrine of the Will of God operating through intermediaries to bring the world into being, as well as that of the spiritualization of the material which are basic in Jewish *Kabbalah*, are all traceable to the thought expressed by Gabirol in his *Mekor Hayyim*.

But even before Gabirol had composed his masterpiece, strains of his philosophic thought in all its variations had already reached his people through his religious poems, many of which have been received into the synagogue liturgy. Most famous among these poems is his *Kether Malchuth* (Royal Crown), a glorious meditation on the greatness of God and the wonders of His Universe, in which there is distilled in a style of majestic grandeur and all-embracing simplicity the essence of Gabirol's philosophy, and which is appropriately read in many congregations on the Day of Atonement.

A younger contemporary of Ibn Gabirol was Bachya ben Josef ibn Pakuda of Saragossa, who was the author of one of the most widely read and deeply loved of medieval Jewish

Read to end of chapter

books. Written in Arabic and translated into Hebrew under the title *Hoboth Halebaboth* (Duties of the Heart), the book gives the first systematic presentation of Jewish ethics. The aim of this work, as its title indicates, is to stress the importance of spirituality and inward piety, which it designates 'duties of the heart', as basic motives for all conduct whether religious or moral. These duties, to be more specific, include, *inter alia*, humility, trust in God, gratitude to Him, and finally love of Him as the goal of all human activities. And, significantly enough, these 'duties of the heart' include for Bachya also the study of philosophy and natural sciences and all other allied subjects, for all these serve to deepen man's admiration and reverence for the Creator and His Creation, rendering him thereby ever more and more fit for discharging his duties to God and to fellow men. Bachya is thus the first Jewish philosopher for whom conceptual thinking and philosophical contemplation was more than a mere useful weapon of apologetics, but essentially a religious duty and divine command. For this reason Bachya introduced his work by a philosophical discussion proving the existence of God and explaining the concept of Divine unity, and also by a contemplative study of Divine providence, wisdom, and goodness, as exhibited in Nature and in man as well as in the history of the Jewish people.

Notwithstanding the universality of its ethics, Bachya's work is essentially a Jewish work, being suffused throughout with quotations from the Bible and Talmudic sources. His ethics are, it is true, tinged with a certain asceticism in which there is traceable the influence of Arabic mysticism (Sufism). Yet, even here, the Hebrew spirit prevails, and the ascetic ideal which Bachya recommends is not intended for the generality of mankind, but only for the few elect who may serve as an example leading others to a life of temperance and moderation.

A new departure in Jewish religious philosophical thinking was made by the poet-philosopher Judah Halevi of Toledo (c. 1085–1140). Whilst his predecessors were concerned to defend Judaism, or religion in general, against the attacks of a rationalist philosophy, Judah Halevi sought to demonstrate the excellency of Judaism over that of its two rival religions,

Christianity and Mohammedanism. This task he undertook in his *Kuzari*, written originally in Arabic, which carries as its sub-title 'A Book of Arguments and Demonstration in Aid of the Despised Faith'. The work is written in the form of a dialogue between a Jewish scholar and the King of the Khazars (a Tartar tribe on the Volga)[4] who, together with his people, embraced Judaism in the eighth century. Halevi, in seeking to prove his thesis, was the first to distinguish between the respective claims of philosophy and those of revelation, or, as he puts it, 'between the God of Aristotle and the God of Abraham'.[5] The best philosophy could do was to produce convincing proofs for the existence of a god, a ruler, and organizer of the world. But all this did not touch the fringe of religion which stressed the existence of a close relationship between man and God. Such relationship, however, being essentially personal, could be the result only of an experience, an inner illumination, a revelation. At the same time, in every claim made by any individual to revelation, there was always a suspicion of subjectivism, self-delusion, and self-hallucination. This, could not apply to a revelation in which a whole nation was involved. Such revelation was vouchsafed to Israel at Sinai. Not to a single individual did the Voice speak at Sinai, but to the whole people. The Sinaitic revelation thus becomes for Halevi the only unassailable foundation and fount of all religious knowledge, and the guarantee of the supremacy of the truth of the faith of Israel.

Israel is thus pre-eminently the people of revelation, the people of prophecy. It is this which constitutes the divine selection of Israel. The selection of Israel has nothing of the anomalous about it; in it we have but one of the manifestations of the divine selective process which, at work in Nature, gives rise to the principal kingdoms into which existence is divided – mineral, plant, animal, and man. In the same way there is a selective process in the Kingdom of man whereby certain individuals become endowed with a special divine faculty, the prophetic spirit, which enables them to enter into communication with God.

This divine faculty, which Halevi designates as the *Iynan*

ha-Elohi (Divine Thing), had been first implanted by God in Adam, the direct creation of His hand, who transmitted it by way of heredity through an unbroken chain of chosen individuals among his descendants, until it reached Jacob's sons, from whom it passed on to the entire community of Israel.

By virtue of this hereditary faculty, Israel was selected by God to be the people of Prophecy, and every Jew possesses, at least potentially, this gift, and hence is capable of the highest religious attainments. But this faculty, like all other inherited faculties, is influenced by nurture and by physical environment. It is here that the influence of the Torah and the Holy Land comes into play. The commandments of the Torah, particularly the ritual, are conceived by Halevi as sacramental. They serve, that is to say, as channels for the flow of spiritual energies, capable of provoking the activity of the 'Divine Thing' upon the devotee. As such they provide the methodical nurture for the development of the divine faculty and for the fostering of the prophetic spirit. Similarly, the Holy Land 'the air of which makes one wise' has a sacramental quality and thus provides the physical environment. Associated with the Torah and the Holy Land is the Hebrew language, which by its peculiar structure and beauty of expression is the best suited medium for the communication of the prophetic spirit.

These ideas will appear nationalistic. Yet Judah Halevi was essentially universalistic in his outlook. For him the selection of Israel is but God's universal choosing of mankind. 'Israel', he declares, 'is the heart of the nations', filling the same role in the world at large as does the heart in the body of man[6]. It is the people which is the most sensitive to the woes and sufferings of the world, supplying at the same time civilized mankind with its moral and spiritual lifeblood. Like Israel, all other nations are possessed of the prophetic faculty, except that in their case it is of a lower degree. But in the Messianic kingdom all nations will reach the same degree of spiritual life which is now given to Israel, all of them ripening into the fruit of which Israel is the root.

All these sublime thoughts Halevi, who has been hailed as

the greatest poet since the Bible, expresses in his poems, many of which have been received in the Synagogue liturgy. But it was in his glorious songs of Zion that Halevi pours out his poetic genius. Some of the most magnificent of these songs of matchless splendour and haunting beauty are chanted to the present day in Jewish congregations throughout the world on the 9th of Ab, and never fail to stir the hopes of the mourners. Love of Zion was Halevi's one controlling passion, and it was under its irresistible sweep that Halevi set out, regardless of hardships and hazards of the journey, on a pilgrimage to Jerusalem, at the wall of which he is said to have met his death. As he was kneeling to kiss the holy ground an Arab horseman galloped through the Gate and rode him down.

Whilst Halevi's Kuzari may have proved effective in defending and vindicating the supremacy of Israel's faith against the faith of others, it had left unanswered the onslaughts of a critical philosophy which questioned the validity of all religious beliefs. Nor did the attempts made hitherto by Saadya and others satisfy any longer. The progress of physical studies among the Arabs during the eleventh century led to the gradual abandonment of Neoplatonic spiritualism for Aristotelian naturalism. The whole cosmic process, it was now taken for granted, was governed by the inexorable laws of cause and effect, which could not be tampered with. Matter was neither created by God nor derived from Him; it was eternal and uncreated. This left no room for divine intervention, for providence, in Nature or history, much less for miracles. The effects of these views on the theistic position could not but be most disturbing. A re-statement of Jewish religious teaching was now more imperative than ever. This task was undertaken by Abraham Ibn Daud of Toledo (*c.* 1180) in his *Emunah Ramah* (Exalted Faith), in which we have the first attempt made by a Jewish philosopher to adapt Aristotelianism for the purpose of fusing it with Judaism. Convinced that Aristotle's is the last word in philosophy, even as the Torah is the last word in religion, Ibn Daud affirms at the outset that not only is there no conflict between religion and philosophy but that in fact they both teach identical truths. In contrast to his predecessors,

Saadya and Bachya among others, who based their proofs for the existence of God through the mediation of the doctrine of creation, Ibn Daud adopts the more direct argument of Aristotle which was based on the theory of the nature of motion. Thus, on the supposition that motion (change) lies at the basis of all natural phenomena in the heavens and on earth, Aristotle argued that there must be a 'First Mover' who was 'unmoved' and the cause of all motion. However, whereas this proof, in Aristotelianism, enables God to be recognized only as the originator of motion, Ibn Daud employs it to trace back the existence of the world to God. It is true that the world originated in primary matter, as Aristotle taught, but the prime matter itself was the outright creation of God. He also employed the argument based on the idea of necessary existence and already advanced by the Arab philosophers, Avicenna and Alfarabi. The fact that the existence of all cosmic beings is only 'possible' demands the existence of an absolute 'necessary' being who is at once the cause and condition of all beings.

On the whole, Ibn Daud's attempt to interpret Judaism in terms of Aristotelianism prepared the way for the more thorough-going and comprehensive presentation of the case which was to be undertaken not long after by the great Maimonides in his epoch-making 'The Guide for the Perplexed'.

Moses Maimonides, who was the profoundest religious thinker and intellect of his time, was the climax of the Golden Age of Spanish Jewry. He was born in Cordova in 1134, but when he was still a lad, Moslem Spain had passed under the rule of the Almohades (Unitarians), an Arab tribe which had burst into the country from Africa. The new masters of Spain were fierce fanatics and their persecutions forced many non-Moslems to flee the country. Among the fugitives was Moses ben Maimon, who after an interval of troubled wanderings and serious privations, settled in Fostat (Old Cairo). There he wrote, among other important works, his famous 'Guide for the Perplexed' which laid the foundations for the entire development of Jewish philosophy and remained the exemplar of reasoning faith even for those who could not follow Maimonides all along the line.

Like Ibn Daud, Maimonides had the utmost veneration for Aristotle as the highest representative, after the Prophets of Israel, of human intellectual power, and it was in Aristotle's philosophy that he sought to find a rational interpretation for Jewish religious faith and tradition. For this purpose he employed the allegorical method by means of which he accommodated the Biblical text to Aristotle's teaching. This does not mean that Maimonides discarded Biblical doctrine where no such accommodation was possible. Rationalist as he was, he over and over again insisted that there was something inherently deficient in human reasoning so that it could not be made the final test of truth and that, in consequence, the last word had to rest after all with revelation. What it does mean is that Maimonides was prepared to be guided by reason in all non-essentials provided that what he considered most vital and absolute in Biblical teaching was left unaffected. This distinction between the essentials and non-essentials is the greatest contribution of Maimonides in the domain of Jewish religious thinking, and is nowhere better illustrated than in his treatment of the problem of creation.

Whilst all the predecessors of Maimonides made the doctrine of creation in point of time a religious issue which they sought to defend with all the arguments they could marshal in support, Maimonides was the first to detach this question from the domain of religion. All that mattered for religion, in his view, was to safeguard the element of the Divine Will at creation, without which the whole of the Biblical doctrine of divine intervention in the natural and historical processes could not stand. This being the case, the real problem of creation from the religious standpoint is whether the world is the product of cause and effect or the free activity of the Divine Will. The former view, which is linked with the Aristotelian conception of God as a first cause from whom the world proceeded by a kind of necessity as, say, the rays of the sun proceed from the heat of the sun, was totally incompatible with the religious attitude, and as such had to be rejected; but there was the Platonic view, which, although it also upheld the theory of the eternity of the universe, conceived God as a craftsman working on some pre-existent formless matter and, as such, did not necessarily exclude the element of Divine Will bringing the world into existence. The world existed from eternity because the Divine craftsman always willed it to exist. This latter view had accordingly nothing objectionable in itself from the religious standpoint. The only exception that might be taken to it is that it does not accord with the literal account in Genesis which represents God as having called the world into existence at a certain point of time. This, however, Maimonides did not consider a serious objection, as once this latter theory was demonstrated by reason to be true, the scriptural account could easily be interpreted accordingly. As a matter of fact, however, all the philosophic arguments in support of this latter view are inconclusive and so there is no reason to depart from the clear scriptural teaching on this matter.

Maimonides' readiness to accept the theory of the eternity of the universe (in the Platonic sense), once proven, invalidates the fact of creation as a proof for the existence of God. Maimonides, therefore, proceeds to prove the existence of God even on the assumption that the world existed from eternity. For this purpose he enunciates twenty-six propositions derived from Aristotle's Physics, and based in the main on the impossibility of the existence of an infinite series of causes. By this means Maimonides proves in various ways the existence of God, arguing from creatures to God as necessary being, as first Mover, and as first Cause, in whom the finite series of causes terminate. Omitting his proofs as too technical to be reproduced here, it might be mentioned that they include the two already employed by Ibn Daud,[7] except that with Maimonides they are more elaborate in that they enable him to prove God as an infinite, incorporeal and uncompounded, eternal and unique Primal Being.

But though Maimonides was prepared to compromise on the doctrine of creation in time, he would not depart from that of *Creatio ex nihilo* in favour of the Platonic notion of an eternal, uncreated, matter, for to assume that something else existed from all eternity besides God, and independent of Him, would be a serious infringement of the unity of God. Maimonides' supreme concern to safeguard inviolate the doctrine of absolute Divine unity led him to devote a great part of the first of the three books which his *Guide* comprises to a systematic and exhaustive survey of all the anthropomorphic expressions and phrases occurring in the Bible, to each of which he alone of all Jewish philosophers assigns some definite metaphysical significance. It is also this very same concern which determined his insistence on the negative interpretation of the divine attributes. The doctrine of negative attributes has played an important part in the history of metaphysical speculation, both Jewish and non-Jewish, long before Maimonides' day, but his treatment is more elaborate and thorough than that of his predecessors and his requirements are more stringent. His purpose was to teach the highest spiritual and most absolute conception of the unity of God, anything short of this being in his eyes worse than idolatry. No positive assertions concerning God are thus permissible. To ascribe to God any positive quality is to add something to His essence, and thus endanger his absolute unity. This does not mean to deny God the perfections connoted by the various predicates but, being identical with His essence, these perfections are *unknowable* and, as such, cannot be indicated except indirectly, that is, by negating of Him our own *knowable* perfections. All affirmations regarding God must accordingly be understood in the negative sense. The statement, for example, that God lives, means that He is not inanimate. It by no means connotes the same idea as when we say of a man that he lives. The attribute of life ascribed to man and predicated of God has nothing in common but the name. The same applies to all other attributes which seek to describe God's essence, such as wise, powerful, possessed of will. They are all to be regarded as inverted negations, leading to confirm His unity because in negations no plurality is involved.

The Divine essence, notwithstanding the attributes predicated of God, is beyond human comprehension. The attributes as predicated, are neither identical with God's nature nor able to define Him. All our knowledge of God is confined to the fact that He exists and to the comprehension of the effects of

His activity in the world, in creation and in providence. The actions of God in the world are described by what Maimonides designates as 'attributes of action' which include the thirteen moral attributes revealed by God to Moses at Sinai.[8] Divine Providence embraces the whole of creation. But there is a special providence for those individual human beings who place themselves in right relation with Him, such providence being graded in accordance with the intensity and closeness of this relationship.

The key to the right relationship with God is the knowledge of God. This knowledge is, in the first instance, intellectual and, as such, includes the mastery of all those physical and metaphysical sciences – logic, philosophy, medicine, mathematics, astronomy – which lead to a true perception of the being and essence of God, as far as it is given to the human mind to attain. Such a knowledge serves as a bond of communion with God in this life and prepares the soul for the blessedness of an eternal life with God in the Hereafter which, on the Maimonidean view, is a life of blissful knowledge.

Here Maimonides was following the Aristotelian line of thought which considers intellectual perfection the highest goal of human existence. Yet, despite Maimonides' exaltation, under Aristotelian influence, of the intellectual knowledge of God, he insisted on another aspect of the knowledge of the Divine in which the intellectual finds its completion. This is the knowledge of God's moral character and goodness which constant reflection on His providence, as it stretches itself over all creation, carries with it. This knowledge, once acquired, leads to the love of God. This love, however, does not signify the mystic desire for union with God, but the resolve to imitate His ways in the pursuit of loving-kindness and justice.

By this correlation of knowledge with moral action, Maimonides cuts himself loose from his attachment to Aristotle and his system, and takes his stand on the classical ground of Jewish thinking that conceives the imitation of God[9] as the highest excellence man can attain.

In conformity with his high evaluation of Knowledge, Maimonides agrees with the Platonic, or general Greek, view that prophecy is a natural faculty that may be acquired by all who submit to the necessary training, and can raise themselves to the required moral and intellectual perfection. This is in stark contrast to the view held by Judah Halevi who, as we have seen, regards prophecy as a special gift from God to the people of Israel, and as conditioned by the fulfilment of the ritual precepts and residence in the Holy Land. It is also contrary to the Talmudic teaching which held prophecy to be a peculiar endowment of special individuals chosen by God. Yet also here Maimonides could not escape the influence of the Jewish view, and qualified his acceptance of the Greek notion by declaring that men satisfying all conditions may still be withheld from prophecy by the Will of God.

Maimonides' view of knowledge is also the basis for his interpretation of the commandments of the Torah. The purpose of the commandments is the moral and intellectual perfecting of man. They are intended not only to regulate human conduct, but also to enlighten man in his thinking and make accessible to him the highest intellectual and metaphysical truths concerning God and man's relation to Him. This being the case, the mere practice of the commandments without an intellectual apprehension of their significance cannot be conducive to the highest thinking, and the life with God which it entails. Hence the endeavour of Maimonides in the third part of his *Guide* to offer rational explanations for the commandments of the Torah.

In his interpretation of the commandments Maimonides displays much originality. Many of them were, in his opinion, intended to counteract pagan rites and customs which were in vogue at the time of the Divine legislation. A case in point is the sacrificial system which, in certain of its parts, was designed to wean the people away from the generally prevalent mode of pagan worship. Maimonides, indeed, in his investigation of the origin of a number of precepts, anticipates many a modern standpoint and, as has been rightly remarked, 'his importance in the scientific study of religion has not yet been fully realized.'[10]

Maimonides' reverence for the human intellect determined

also his attitude to miracles. Whilst not denying the possibility of miracles, he endeavours as much as possible to reduce the miraculous elements in the Scriptures to natural processes. In fact, he attaches little importance to miracles as evidence for the truth of any religion. Faith, he maintains, must rest on its intrinsic truth and not on miracles, which may be of a deceitful nature.

It was the same reverence for human intellect which led him to give allegorical explanations to the Biblical story of the Paradise, and also to identify the angels mentioned in Scriptures with the forces or elements in nature or with divinely inspired men. Whilst accepting the existence of angels as the 'separate intelligences' of the spheres that figure in Greek cosmology, he denied, against the traditional belief, that they ever came down on earth in human form. He likewise denied the existence of demons, and maintained that all references to them in the Talmud and Midrash were to be understood only as figurative expressions of physical plagues.

For the same reason, he treats the descriptions of the idyllic conditions of the Messianic age portrayed by the Prophets as metaphorical. The Messianic age, in his view, will not differ materially from the present but will represent a higher type of society patterned on the knowledge of the unity of God and of His righteousness. Towards this consummation Maimonides recognized that Christianity and Islam had an important role to play in paving the way for all mankind to embrace the full truth of knowledge of God with the advent of Messianic times. Likewise, the descriptions of the bliss of Paradise and torture in Hell in terms physical which occur in the Midrashim are all metaphorical and mere attempts to express spiritual imponderables in popular forms. The real bliss of Paradise consists in spiritual communion with God; and the real suffering in Hell in alienation from Him.

This reverence for human intellect Maimonides would also apply to his conception of the power of God. Logical absurdities are, he holds, outside the range of Divine Omnipotence. God cannot square a circle or make a thing to exist and not exist at one and the same time.

Maimonides' conviction that eternal life and bliss depend on the intellectual knowledge of God led him to his formulation of the fundamental principles of Judaism. The earliest attempt to formulate a kind of creed in Judaism occurs in an early Mishnaic passage which denies a share in the world to come to those who reject revelation, or resurrection (with which is associated immortality), and to the 'Epicurean' who does not believe in the moral government of the world (Sanhedrin 10. 1). The lead given by this Mishnah was followed by subsequent generations of Jewish teachers; and it is in connexion with this passage that Maimonides in his *Commentary on the Mishnah* sets forth his creed, which is distinguished from the formulations drawn up by his predecessors in that it makes the acceptance of beliefs, which are essentially derived from philosophic speculation, as a condition of eternal bliss.

According to Maimonides' enumeration, the articles of Jewish creed are the following: (1) Belief in the existence of a Creator and Providence; (2) Belief in His unity; (3) Belief in His incorporeality; (4) Belief in His eternity; (5) Belief that to Him alone is worship due; (6) Belief in the words of the prophets; (7) Belief that Moses was the greatest of all prophets. (8) Belief in the revelation of the Law to Moses at Sinai. (9) Belief in the immutability of the Revealed Law; (10) Belief that God is omniscient; (11) Belief in retribution in this world and the hereafter; (12) Belief in the coming of the Messiah; (13) Belief in the resurrection of the dead.

The motives which determined Maimonides' choice of beliefs for inclusion in his Creed will on examination become evident. His aim was on the one hand to emphasize certain philosophic conceptions concerning God, and on the other to combat the specific claims of Christianity and Mohammedanism in matters of religious doctrine.

Maimonides' *Guide* created a profound impression. It was translated into Hebrew twice during his lifetime and through this medium exercised a tremendous influence on Jewish thought even outside the Arabic-speaking Jewish world. The *Guide* also impressed itself through a Latin translation on the Latin Christian thought of the Middle Ages, and not least on

Thomas Aquinas. In Jewry itself Maimonides' *Guide* became the adopted philosophical textbook of the educated classes, particularly in Provence, where, under the influence of a strong Jewish-Spanish immigration, the Jews had come to participate in Jewish-Islamic culture. Even greater and more widespread was the influence of his Creed, which, before a century had hardly elapsed, had become the theme for the poets of the synagogue, leading eventually to its incorporation in two separate forms – prose and poetry – in the Jewish daily Prayer Book.

At the same time, fierce and prolonged controversy raged about Maimonides' work throughout the thirteenth and fourteenth centuries. The leaders of this controversy were rabbis for whom Maimonides' departure from the notions of God as portrayed in the Bible and the *Aggadah*, as well as from other of their cherished naïve beliefs, was rank heresy. But Maimonides' work came also under the criticism of Jewish thinkers on purely philosophic grounds. The first in the line of important critics of Maimonides was Levi ben Gerson (1288–1334), commonly known as Gersonides of Bagnols, Provence, who was the only one among Jewish Aristotelians who can be compared with Maimonides in speculative power.

Gersonides, in his chief work, *Milchamoth Hashem* (The Wars of the Lord) controverted Maimonides on a number of points. Adopting the Aristotelian doctrine, as portrayed by the Arabic philosopher Averrhoes (Ibn Roshd), that God was not the Unknowable Absolute of the Neo-Platonists, but the Highest Thought, Gersonides argued from this that the ascription of positive attributes to God was by no means incompatible, as Maimonides maintained, with Divine unity.

On the doctrine of creation, Gersonides' views are quite the reverse of those of Maimonides. Whilst insisting on the doctrine of creation in time, he argues in favour of the theory of uncreated and pre-existing matter. The objection that the notion of pre-existing uncreated matter is an infringement of Divine unity, Gersonides meets with the argument that it is God who gave the formless matter its shape, so that this matter cannot after all be said to be independent of God.

A more vigorous speculative critic of Maimonides arose two centuries after his death (1204) in the person of Hisdai Crescas of Barcelona (1340–1410). During these two intervening centuries the centre of Jewish philosophical activity had shifted in the main to Christian Spain, where the knowledge of Aristotle became widespread through Hebrew translations of his work, and Aristotelianism came to dominate the whole scene of Jewish religious-philosophical thinking. It was in this setting that Crescas resolved to free Judaism from the bondage to Aristotle that threatened to blur much of the distinctiveness of Jewish religious doctrine. With this aim in view, he composed his 'Light of the Lord', in which he made a determined attack on Aristotle and also dealt a serious blow at Maimonides. By a chain of analytical arguments, he proved the possible existence of infinite series of causes, and thereby demolished the whole structure of the twenty-six propositions upon which Maimonides had built his proofs for the existence of God.

In this way, Grescas sought to discredit the supposed infallibility of Aristotle and his value as a guide for arriving at the truth of religious knowledge.

For his proof of the existence of God, Crescas falls back on the idea of necessary existence which, as we have seen, has already been employed by Ibn Daud and Maimonides, and the validity of which remains unaffected whether the series of causes are finite or infinite, for even an infinite universe is only of 'possible existence', and as such requires as its ground a necessary existent being.

As a being of merely possible existence, the world is no longer a natural necessity of cause and effect but a product of the Will of God. The highest attribute of the Will of God is Love, and creation is a contingent means whereby God diffuses his Love to give existence to all beings.

With love as the determining impulse of creation, Crescas arrives at a view of creation which, paradoxically enough, appears more radical than that of Maimonides. *Creatio ex nihilo* means for him nothing more than that the world owes its existence to the Will of God. The Divine Will to create, however, though free as far as it proceeds from God Himself and not subject to any influence from without, is grounded in the very nature of God who must will to realize the good and create. Crescas thus finds it possible to accommodate within Judaism even the Aristotelian theory of the universe, provided the universe is conceived not as a product of a natural necessity devoid of will, as it is in Aristotelianism, but of a necessity determined by the eternal Will of God.

Crescas, however, shrinks back from this conclusion, which he regards only as a 'supposition', and in the end declares that 'the perfect truth is after all, as it has come down to us, by tradition, that God created the world and originated it at a given time as we are told in the first chapter of Genesis.'[11] At the same time, Crescas seeks to reconcile the philosophic 'supposition' with the teaching of Genesis by means of the Stoic notion, already mentioned in the Talmud, of a succession of worlds each coming into being after the destruction of the one preceding it. In the light of this notion, Creation could be conceived as an eternal, necessary issue from God, though the present world with which the Genesis account is concerned came into being at a certain point of time.

Crescas's conception of creation as a necessary act of Divine Love leads him to oppose Maimonides' enthronement of the intellectual knowledge of God as the highest goal of human life. In all his teachings about God, man's relation to Him, and the blissfulness of immortal life, Crescas stresses will and emotion rather than intellect and cold reason as all-important. For Crescas communion with God, in this life and the Hereafter, is effected and achieved not through knowledge but through the active love of God expressed in religious observance and moral conduct.

The emphasis on love rather than intellectual knowledge is also reflected in Crescas's formulation of the dogmas of Judaism in which he differs considerably from those enumerated by Maimonides. Crescas criticizes Maimonides for failing to distinguish between doctrines which are fundamental to Judaism and beliefs which though binding are of secondary importance.

Crescas himself classifies the dogmas of Judaism into three categories:

(1) 'Fundamental principles' by which Judaism stands and falls.

(2) 'True beliefs' the denial of which, though involving a strong heresy, does not make Judaism impossible.

(3) 'Opinions', which, though forming part of the general body of Jewish traditional belief, are nevertheless left to the decision of the individual.

Among the 'fundamental principles', Crescas includes the love of God which is altogether absent in the Maimonidean creed. On the other hand, resurrection (including immortality), and retribution, which for Maimonides are fundamental, are treated by Crescas as mere 'beliefs', since the highest ideal of Judaism is to serve God without any hope of reward. So are the eternity of the Torah, and the supremacy of Moses as prophet, as well as the coming of the Messiah, only beliefs, contrary to Maimonides who considered them fundamental. Among the class of 'beliefs' Crescas also includes the efficacy of prayer and of penitence, probably in order to counter the claim to originality made by Christianity in regard to these beliefs.

Among the 'opinions' are included, on the intellectual level, the conception of (1) a prime mover and (2) the unknowability of the Divine essence; and, on the superstitious level, the belief in (1) the spatial location of Paradise and Hell, (2) demons, and (3) charms and amulets.

We cannot take leave of Crescas without referring to his doctrine of free will. His conception of the necessity of Divine Will carries with it a determinism which he extends to human actions. Nevertheless, Crescas insists on human free will, which he reckons among the 'fundamental principles'. Despite the fact that human actions are determined by a chain of causes over which man has no control, his own will is a vital link in that chain. As far as he is concerned, man feels himself free, and he must be rewarded or punished according to his decision to act in the right way or the wrong way.

Crescas's influence went beyond the restricted confines of Jewish religious thinking. His arguments against Aristotle have been used by Pico della Mirandola (1463–94) and Giordano Bruno (1548–1600). Crescas's basic teachings on the love of

God, creation, and free will had no little influence on Spinoza, while his conception of the infinite gave direction to the line of thought which led to the modern scientific conception of the Universe.

After Hisdai Crescas the period of independent thought in Jewish philosophy began to decline. All that subsequent generations brought forth were but summaries or reproductions of the thoughts and teachings of philosophers of preceding generations. Yet before Jewish philosophy was to make its bow, it was to offer a work which on account of its clarity of style and comprehensiveness of exposition became one of the most widely read of Jewish religious philosophical works. The name of this work is *Sefer ha-Ikkarim* (The Book of Fundamental Principles) composed by Joseph Albo (1380–1444) of Daroca (Spain), who was a disciple of Crescas. His main concern was with Jewish dogma, which he sought to clarify in the face of the onslaughts of the Church which was at that time threatening the Spanish Jews, and using every method of violence and persuasion to convert them. With this aim in view Albo takes constant issue in his work, both directly and indirectly, with Christianity, and it is in his vindication of the excellencies of Judaism that the originality and the vigour of the work is to be found. He it was who established the Hebrew term *Ikkar* (principle) in the technical sense of Dogma. Following in the footsteps of Crescas, he distinguished between fundamental principles and mere beliefs, which he termed *Shorashim* 'roots', though deviating from his master in the application of this distinction. He reduces the Maimonidean Thirteen Articles of the Creed to three 'Fundamental Principles': (1) God's Existence; (2) His Revelation; (3) Retribution. These three fundamental principles are not peculiar to Judaism but constitute the basis of all revealed religions. But to these belong, as of logical necessity, certain correlatives on which Judaism in particular lays stress. Thus, the existence of God has as its correlatives His Unity, Incorporeality, and Eternity; and so on. These correlatives are eight in number, making in all, with the 'fundamental principles', eleven dogmas, which are binding upon every Jew and cannot be denied without incurring the guilt of heresy. Besides these, there are also subsidiary beliefs, designated as *Anafim* (branches), the disavowal of which does not count as heresy, as they are not unconditional consequences of the fundamental principles. Among these latter beliefs are *Creatio ex nihilo*, the immutability of the Law, as well as the belief in the coming of the Messiah, which, Albo is at pains to point out, does not form an integral part of Judaism as it does of Christianity, which would be inconceivable without such a doctrine.[12] Of great significance is his inclusion of the belief human bliss may be attained by the fulfilment of one single command. This was evidently stressed by Albo in order to combat the Christian notion that the commandments were given as a mark of Divine wrath in order to increase the opportunity of sin, so as to make all the greater the need for Divine Mercy. His breadth of tolerance, at the same time, is unmistakeably reflected in his statement that only he is to be regarded as a heretic who deliberately and knowingly contradicts the Bible, but he who, misled by his speculation, denies a particular principle because he thinks that the Bible does not require him to believe it, is merely guilty of error and in need of Divine forgiveness, but is by no means to be branded as a heretic.[13]

As against the attitude of Albo and that of those of his predecessors, who sought to formulate dogmas, might be mentioned the disapproval of any formulation of creed by Isaac Abrabanel (1437–1508), the last in the line of distinguished Jewish statesmen in Spain. The Torah was divine and there was, accordingly, he maintained, no warrant for distinguishing between one set of Torah-doctrines and another, all being of equal fundamental importance.

With Joseph Albo the line of Jewish medieval philosophers, beginning with Saadya, came to an end. Following Albo, Jewish philosophy, in its medieval tradition, continued to be handed down as an intellectual and religious heritage to be cultivated, interpreted, and amplified, but no attempt was made to develop it further or to bring it into relation with the many and varied problems of contemporary philosophy. Henceforth there were a number of Jewish philosophers, the foremost among whom was Spinoza (1632–72), whose philosophy was rooted in his Jewish heritage; but there was, strictly speaking, until we come to the modern period, no new Jewish philosophy. The reason for the arrest in the development of Jewish philosophy was principally the bitter experiences of the Jews in Spain during the fifteenth century, which showed that whereas the simple, unsophisticated, folk defied to death the terrors of the Church, and remained steadfast in the faith, the devotees of philosophy were the first to yield, many of them abandoning Judaism. With philosophy thus discredited, the intellectual energies of the Jews turned more and more to the cultivation of their home-grown traditions centred on the Talmud and allied studies; whilst those who were attracted to speculative abstractions gave themselves over to the pursuit of the mystical lore, the *Kabbalah*, which came to play an ever-increasing part in the shaping of subsequent Jewish religious thought and practice.

NOTES

1. *Emunoth Wedeoth*, 3, 7.
2. op. cit., 10. 5.
3. Discovered by Solomon Munk in the *Bibliothèque Nationale*, Paris.
4. For the story of the Khazars and their medieval nomadic empire which for two centuries was ruled by kings and officials professing the Jewish religion, see D. M. Dunlop, *The History of the Jewish Khazars* (Princeton, N.J., 1954).
5. *Kuzari*, 4. 16.
6. op. cit., 2. 36. ff
7. See p. 208.
8. See p. 28.
9. See p. 138.
10. D. Yellin and I. Abrahams, *Maimonides* (London, 1935), p. 135.
11. *Light of the Lord*, 3. 1, 5.
12. *Sefer ha-Ikkarim*, 1. 1.
13. op. cit., 1, 2.

CHAPTER 19

JEWISH MYSTICISM: THE *KABBALAH*

KABBALAH, which means 'tradition', is the general term for a religious teaching which has originally been handed down orally from generation to generation. More specifically, it came to be used since the eleventh century, for that type of Jewish mystic thought which, claimed to have been received from the remote past, was first committed as secret doctrine to a privileged few only to become by the fourteenth century the manifest pursuit of the many.

Like all mystical systems, Jewish mysticism speaks of a supernatural world order to which man is linked, and on which he can call and transmit its infinite powers. As such, Jewish mysticism exhibits two types: (1) the speculative, which is concerned with the nature of the spiritual world and its connexion with this world and the place of man in both; and (2) the practical, which seeks to wrest energies from the spiritual world with psychological and wonder-working effects in the physical.

Characteristic of Jewish mysticism is its Messianic tendency. It sees the whole of creation – animate and inanimate – held in the throes of a universal struggle for redemption from the evil, which has somehow entered the world, and for the restoration of that harmony in which the whole will find salvation in the establishment of the universal kingdom of God, with the coming of Messianism.

Considered thus in its essence, the pivot round which Jewish mysticism revolves is none other than the very conception which, as we have seen throughout this work, Judaism with varying force and clearness has ever sought to affirm. It is the conception of man as a being created to be a co-worker with God and, as such, endowed with the capacity and power to control and influence things towards his own ends as well as towards the fulfilment of creation. What is distinctive in Jewish mysticism, as compared with other expressions of the Jewish spirit, is its claim to be in possession of the secrets of the *modus operandi* of this cooperative activity with the divine, and thereby able to make the human contribution all the more effective.

It would be impossible within the limited space of a chapter to give an account, however sketchy and fragmentary, of the involved and profound esoteric doctrines which constitute Jewish mysticism. All that is attempted here is to present a few of the leading ideas in Jewish mystic lore in their historical development and to indicate the extent of the influence they eventually came to exert in Jewish religious life.

Jewish mysticism has its roots in the Bible itself. On the practical side this is too obvious to need more than mere passing remark. The miracles performed by the prophets, such as Moses, Elijah, and Elisha, among others, involve an inter-relation between the phenomenal and supersensual world to which the name of practical mysticism may rightly be applied. But this is hardly less evident on the speculative side. The account of the creation in Genesis, Isaiah's vision in the Temple, and the descriptions of the divine chariot in the first chapter of Ezekiel, enshrine doctrines concerning the universe and the nature of the Godhead which formed the starting point of much of the mystical speculations in later Judaism. Similarly, the Apocalyptic visions in the Book of Daniel, with its portrayal of guardian angels, rivers of fire, and the 'Ancient of Days', as well as its Messianic calculation, are all charged with esoteric doctrines regarding the 'end of days' which in turn inspired a whole class of literature – the Apocalyptic – which includes such works as the 4 Ezra, Jubilees, and the earliest and far the most important of all, the Book of Enoch (approximately 200 B.C.), testifying to the existence of a mystical movement in Israel as early as the second century preceding the Common Era.

Evidences of mystical themes, both of a speculative and practical or theurgic character, are found in abundance in the Talmudic literature. The mystical speculations in the Talmud are centred in the main on the *Maaseh Bereshith* (The Work of Creation), described in the first chapter of Genesis, and the *Maaseh Merkabah* (The Divine Chariot), in the account of Ezekiel's vision. The former gave rise to cosmological or cosmogonic speculations, and the latter played a fruitful part in the speculations on the mysteries and attributes of the Godhead.

These mystical doctrines were, however, in Talmudic times, carefully guarded, and it was forbidden to expound them except to a few chosen disciples, for fear that their divulgence to the uninitiated might expose them to misunderstanding, resulting in the spread of scepticism and heresy.

The esoteric doctrines of *Maaseh Bereshith* and *Maaseh Merkabah* were claimed to have originated with certain mystics who, through the training of their ecstatic visionary faculties, were able to break through the barriers of the physical world and enter the celestial sphere where they learned the deepest mysteries of things.

Among the Tannatic teachers, Rabbi Jochanan ben Zakkai is mentioned as the father of *Merkabah* mysticism, while Rabbi Akiba is associated with the *Maaseh Bereshith* speculations.

In the Gaonic period, the schools of *Merkabah* and *Bereshith* mystics continued their speculations, the former chiefly in Palestine, the latter in Babylon.

A description of the experiences of the *Merkabah* mystics is given in that branch of mystic literature known as the *Hekaloth* ([Heavenly] Halls), which has come down to us though only in a fragmentary form from the Gaonic period. In order to prepare for their Heavenly ascensions, the *Merkabah* mystics, called *Yorede Merkabah* (Those who Descend to the Chariot), had to submit to a strict regimen of ascetic practices, including fastings and ablutions, invoke the secret names of God and those of His angels, and finally work themselves up into the ecstasy of a trance, culminating in a kind of a metamorphosis, wherein the flesh turned into fire. Having reached this stage, the mystic imagined himself admitted to the seven Heavenly Halls and, if worthy enough, rewarded by 'a vision of the divine chariot' and also, at the same time, initiated into secrets of the future or mysteries of the celestial world.

We are told little of the experiences of the mystics whose speculations were concerned with the mysteries of creation, and who in the Talmud are designated as 'Those who entered *Pardes*' (Paradise or Garden); but it is evident that entry into the 'Pardes' involved, like *Merkabah* mysticism, an ascension into the invisible world which brought the mystic into direct contact with the Divine.

What is most noteworthy in all the descriptions of the experiences of *Merkabah* mysticism was that the controlling conception of the mystic's relation to God, even at the height of his ecstatic passion, was not that of absorption into the Absolute, and loss of separate identity, as it is, say, in Hindu mysticism, but that of the relation between the subject and his King, into whose awesome and majestic Halls the mystic has been admitted.

Closely allied to the *Hekaloth* literature and belonging to the same period is the *Shiur Komah* (The Measures of the Divine Stature), an extraordinary treatise which purports to describe the bodily dimensions of the Godhead. This work was ascribed to the second century Talmudic teacher, Rabbi Ishmael (a martyr of the Hadrianic persecutions), and since Saadya was subject to allegorical interpretations; while Judah Halevi considered the work of value as a road along which the simple and devout mind can travel from superstition to religious devotion. Maimonides, on the other hand, condemned the work outright, declaring it to be a forgery and deserving to be destroyed because 'a substance which has physical stature is certainly a strange God.'[1] The impression gained, however, in reading the work is that the author, whoever he was, did not intend to describe an objective reality but merely a subjective feeling in the mind.

By far the most important mystical work of the period is the *Sefer Yetzirah* (Book of Creation) which, though ascribed to Abraham, seems to have originated in early Gaonic times in Babylon. A *Sefer Yetzirah* is mentioned in the Talmud as a kind of thaumaturgical work, the study of which conferred on the adept creative powers,[2] but that work does not seem to have been identical with our present *Sefer Yetzirah*. Historically the *Sefer Yetzirah* presents the oldest speculative work in Hebrew. In it there is a fusion of mysticism and philosophy which, as we shall see, form the constituent elements of the *Kabbalah*.

The *Sefer Yetzirah*, as indicated by its title, is concerned with the problems of cosmology and cosmogony. The keynote of the work is provided in its opening statement: 'By means of thirty-two mysterious paths did the Eternal, the Lord of Hosts, the Supreme God of Israel, etc. (here follow other attributes) engrave and establish His name and created His world.'

The thirty-two paths are then explained as the twenty-two letters of the Hebrew alphabet, together with what are designated as the ten *Sefiroth*. The term *Sefiroth* has given rise to considerable discussion. Generally it is derived from a Hebrew root meaning 'to number', and thus taken to mean numbered principles. There is, however, much to be said in favour of the view connecting it with the Hebrew *sappir* (sapphire) used in the description of the Divine throne both in Ex. 24. 10 and Ezek. 1. 26. The *Sefiroth* would, accordingly, owe their name to the conception of them as sapphire-like luminous rays which God poured forth at creation. The ten *Sefiroth* include three entities: (1) spirit-air, (2) water, and (3) fire. The six others are the six dimensions of space – the four cardinal points of the compass in addition to height and depth. These, together with the Spirit of God, constitute the ten *Sefiroth*, which are eternal.

The *Sefiroth* are described as 'without anything'. They are, that is to say, 'abstracts' or, in other words, non-material entities constituting, as it were, the moulds or forms into which all created things were originally cast. The letters, on the other hand, are the prime cause of matter which, by its union with the forms, gave rise to the world of corporeal beings.

The following will serve to illustrate the part which the letters of the Hebrew alphabet are conceived by the *Sefer Yetzirah* to have played in creation. All the letters of the alphabet are made to fall into three groups represented respectively by (1) the soft-breathing *alef* (a); (2) the mute *mem* (m); and (3) the hissing *shin* (sh). These three letters in turn symbolize the three primal *Sefiroth* (entities): the *alef* represents air; *mem*, water (fish in the water representing mute creation); and the *shin*, the hissing fire. In the beginning, these three entities had only a non-material existence; by the articulation of the letters they received a material substratum, which made creation possible when infinite space represented by the six other *Sefiroth* was produced.

The ascription of cosmic importance to letters is already mentioned in the Talmud, and the origin of this belief has been traced to various sources, Zoroasterian and Chaldean. But however that may be, the real clue to the teaching of the *Sefer Yetzirah* is to be found in the dictum of an early Mishnah (*Ethics of the Fathers*, 5. 1), declaring that the world was called into being by a series of ten Divine utterances – a dictum which, in turn, is but an exposition of the declaration of the Psalmist 'By the Word of the Lord were the Heavens made, and all the Hosts of them at the breath of His mouth' (33. 6). These Divine utterances are conceived in the *Sefer Yetzirah* as having included all the letters of the Hebrew alphabet which, in their various combinations, make up the Holy language (Hebrew), the language of creation, even as the series of numbers from one to ten provide for all possible combinations in numeration, even to infinity. Language and number, conjoined together, are thus declared to be the instruments whereby the cosmos in all its infinite variety of combinations and manifestations was called into existence by God.

Stripped of all its symbolism and mystical formulations, the underlying philosophy of the *Sefer Yetzirah* is the celebrated Theory of Ideas. This theory averring the existence of real incorporeal heavenly entities which served as patterns at creation for things on earth, has entered the history of philosophy through Plato, but it by no means originated with him. The Babylonians knew of an ideal celestial creation, according to the pattern of which the things on earth were brought into being. This theory is also vaguely intimated in the Scriptural doctrine of the heavenly pattern, shown to Moses on the Mount, of the Tabernacle and its Vessels which he was commanded to construct on earth (Ex. 25. 9, 40; 26. 30; Num. 8. 4). Definite traces of this doctrine are found in the Talmudic literature which speaks of the pre-existence of certain objects, persons as well as actions,[3] which were subsequently to play a part in Scriptural history. What was, however, perhaps original with Plato was that he conceived the Ideas not only as patterns, but also as active powers in the universe, bestowing upon all particular beings whatever qualities they are found to exhibit.

The Theory of Ideas became the starting point of Philo's philosophy, who gave it a Jewish interpretation by insisting that the Ideas were not eternal but created by God, and that it was from God that they derived their active powers.

In the *Sefer Yetzirah* we have the first finished Jewish product of the Theory of Ideas, both as patterns and active powers. Whether the author of the *Sefer Yetzirah* was in any way indebted to Philo is difficult to say. But however that may be, he goes beyond Philo in that he professes to describe the Divine 'techniques' whereby the world was constructed out of the primal substances, of which the *Sefiroth* were the Ideas, alike in the sense of patterns and powers.

In its account of the origin of the universe, it will be seen that the *Sefer Yetzirah* combines both the Ideas of emanation and creation. In this manner the *Sefer Yetzirah* attempts to harmonize the doctrines of Divine immanence and transcendence. God is immanent in so far as the *Sefiroth*, the forms, are an outpouring or emanation of His spirit; and He is transcendent in that the matter which was moulded into the forms and out of which the world was constructed, was the product of His creative activity.

The appearance of the *Sefer Yetzirah* proved a veritable landmark in the history of Jewish mysticism. Apart from its basic doctrine which leads us into the heart of Jewish mysticism, the striking symbolism and arresting expressions employed in the work set in motion a train of ideas that became most fruitful in the ramified literature of the *Kabbalah*.

From almost the beginning of its history, the *Kabbalah* developed along two distinct lines, the 'practical' and the 'theoretical' or 'speculative', giving rise respectively to the two great schools of *Kabbalah*, the German school and the Provence-Spanish school.

The 'practical' *Kabbalah* is a descendant of the Palestine-Babylonian mysticism of Gaonic times, and was first introduced into Europe by Aaron ben Samuel, a scholar from

Babylon, who, emigrating in the first half of the ninth century to Italy, imparted it to members of the Kalonymus family,[4] who, in turn, carried it with them about 917 to Germany, where it reached its highest stage of development in the thirteenth century.

The 'speculative' *Kabbalah* which also seems to have originated in Babylon, had its rise in Provence in the twelfth century, and attained its zenith in Spain in the fourteenth century.

The practical mysticism fostered by the German school was of the ecstatic type, centred principally on prayer, inner meditation, and contemplation. At the same time, it also expressed itself not infrequently in theurgical activities, in which alphabetical and numeral mysticism played an important part.

The first representative of the German school of *Kabbalah* was Judah ha-Chasid (the Pious d. 1217), himself a member of the Kalonymus family. He is the reputed author of the *Sefer Chasidim* (The Book of the Pious), one of the gems of Jewish medieval literature, combining the highest ethical ideals with the deepest native piety. His work was carried on by his disciple Eleazar of Worms (1176-1238), who introduced the esoteric doctrines of his school into larger circles.

The principal doctrines of the German school were concerned with the mystery of Divine unity. God Himself is too exalted to be comprehended by the human mind and all the anthropomorphic expressions in Scriptures refer to His 'glory' which is conceived as created by God out of Divine fire. This Divine Light, or 'Glory' – in Hebrew *kabod* – God has revealed to the prophets, and continued to reveal itself in various forms and modifications to the mystics of later ages, in accordance with the demands of the hour.

The vision of the *Kabod* was the express aim of German Jewish mystics. In order to attain this vision, the aspiring devotee had to cultivate the constant sense of God's presence and adopt a specific way of life, a life of *Chasiduth* (pietism). Such a life was to be characterized by prayer, devotions, contemplation, saintliness, and humility, as well as an indifference to derision, shame, and insults. In social relations, whether with Jews or non-Jews, *Chasiduth* demanded the most exacting standards, making self-abnegation and altruism the criteria of right conduct in everyday life. A life of *Chasiduth* was to lead eventually to the pure love of God, a love which had no other motive than the love of God itself and of the fulfilment of His Will.

In *Chasiduth* the love of God must not, however, shut out love for fellow man. The mystic, however much his gaze may be turned, so to speak, towards the vision of the *Kabod*, must not lose sight of the claims of his fellow men upon him, or of his duties to the community which, because of his spiritual attainments, turns to him as its master and guide.

It is from the mystics of the German school that there have come down the 'Unity Hymns', as well as the 'Hymn of Glory', which have been received in the synagogue liturgy and which, despite their mystic language, compel admiration for their emotional power and poetical beauty. To quote a few stanzas of the 'Hymn of Glory' recited daily at the conclusion of the Morning Service.

> Sweet hymns and songs will I indite
> To sing of Thee by day and night,
> Of Thee who art my soul's delight
>
> How doth my soul within me yearn
> Beneath Thy Shadow to return,
> Thy secret mysteries to learn.
>
> Thy glory shall my discourse be,
> In images I picture Thee,
> Although myself I cannot see.
>
> In mystic utterances alone,
> By prophet and by seer made known,
> Hast Thou Thy radiant glory shown.
>
> My meditation day and night,
> May it be pleasant in Thy sight,
> For Thou art all my soul's delight.[5]

.   .   .

The reason for the pursuit of the 'practical' *Kabbalah* by the Jews in Germany cannot be dissociated from the inferior social and political status to which they had been reduced in that country during the twelfth and thirteenth centuries. Oppressed and persecuted, and in constant fear for their lives, their families and possessions, they turned to the 'practical' *Kabbalah*, which, by virtue of its talismanic and ecstatic effects, provided them with a means of escape from the dangers and miseries that beset their existence. By contrast, the Jews of Provence and Spain were more fortunate in their external political and social relations; and, influenced in a large measure by the religious philosophy that was fully developed in their respective countries, they were attracted to the 'speculative' side of the *Kabbalah*.

The method of reasoning and technique of thought employed by the 'speculative' *Kabbalah* is not unlike that of Jewish philosophy which, in fact, in its deepest moods, has many points of contact with Kabbalistic doctrine. Nevertheless, there is a world of difference in the attitude of Jewish philosophy and that of 'speculative' *Kabbalah*. First, the categories within which the 'speculative' *Kabbalah* operates are traced back to a Divine source, in contradistinction to those employed by philosophy, which are fixed in man's inner consciousness. Second, whereas Jewish philosophy set itself the task of harmonizing the doctrines of the Bible with those of philosophy, the *Kabbalah*'s one and only aim, even when it strays into foreign fields for its views about God and the universe, is concerned with the discovery of the truth communicated through the Bible, and of the mysteries hidden in every single word or letter of the Holy Writ.

Among the earliest representatives of the 'speculative' *Kabbalah* in Provence was Jacob ha-Nazir (beginning of the twelfth century) who is the reputed author of *Masecheth Atziluth* (The Treatise on Emanation), which belongs to the classics of the *Kabbalah* literature. In this work there appears, for the first time, the doctrine of the four graduated worlds through which the Infinite made Himself manifest in the finite. These four worlds are: (1) the world of *Atziluth* (Emanation); (2) the world of *Beriah* (Creating); (3) the world of *Yetzirah* (Formation); and (4) the world of *Asiyah* (Doing).

These four worlds represent the four stages of the creative process as conceived by the *Kabbalah*. The first three are those already indicated in the account given of the *Sefer Yetzirah*, viz. (1) the emanation of the *Sefiroth* (Ideas) as patterns; (2) the investment of the *Sefiroth* with creative powers; and (3) the union of the *Sefiroth* with matter, to which is added here as fourth the world in which we live.

Another doctrine enunciated for the first time in this 'Treatise' is the one regarding the *Sefiroth*. Here the *Sefiroth* are not the three elements and points of space as in the *Sefer Yetzirah*, but hypostasized attributes and agencies of the Deity.

The credit, however, for establishing the Provençal school of *Kabbalah* is ascribed to Isaac the Blind of Posquières (Provence, middle of the twelfth century), who is said to have inaugurated the pursuit of the *Kabbalah* among a large number of adepts. His work was carried on by his leading disciple Azriel ben Menachem (*c.* 1160–1238), who is considered the foremost among the early exponents of the 'speculative' *Kabbalah*. Distinguished alike as a philosopher, Kabbalist and Talmudist, Azriel managed to clothe the doctrines of the *Kabbalah* in the language of logic, and to gather in his works the scattered elements of Kabbalistic ideas and concepts and combine them into an organic whole.

God, Azriel taught, is the *En Sof*, the Endless, the absolute Infinite. Being Infinite, nothing can exist outside Him. Hence the world, with all its manifold manifestations, was potentially contained in Him. But at the same time, since the world is finite and not perfect, it cannot proceed directly from the *En Sof*, and the *Sefiroth* – as interpreted by Azriel – constitute the medium by means of which God irradiates, so to speak, the elements of the universe without diminishing His power, even as the sun irradiates warmth and light without diminishing its bulk.

Azriel gathered round him many disciples who gave their master's message to the world. Foremost among them was Moses Nachmanides (*d.* 1270), the greatest Talmudic authority of his time, whose influence helped to spread Kabbalistic doctrines, though not precisely in the form taught by his master, throughout Spain. In enthusiastic letters to various communities in the country, Nachmanides averred that mysticism lay at the heart of Judaism. The Torah was, according to him, constituted of Divine names, every word in it containing a mystery, every letter being charged with spiritual power.

But what finally won for the *Kabbalah* its pre-eminent position in Jewish religious life was the appearance about 1300 of the Zohar (Splendour) which, written partly in Aramaic and partly in Hebrew, presents the very epitome of Jewish mysticism alike on the speculative and practical side. This work, said to have been compiled from heterogeneous sources by Moses de Leon of Granada (d. 1305), very soon became the textbook of Jewish mystics, and after the Talmud has exercised the profoundest influence in Judaism.

Moses de Leon himself ascribed the Zohar to the Talmudic teacher, Simeon ben Yochai (second century C.E.), who appears as the principal master in the work.[1] Rabbi Simeon ben Yochai lived, as previously mentioned, after the Bar Kocheba revolt. Having come into conflict with the Romans, the Rabbi fled with his son, and for thirteen years they both remained hidden in a cave where they are said to have been visited daily by the Prophet Elijah, who instructed them into the mysteries of the Torah; and it is these mysteries, asserted to have been communicated to Simeon ben Yochai, which form a large bulk of the doctrinal contents of the Zohar.

The central themes of the Zohar are the nature of the Deity, the way He made Himself known to the universe, the mysteries of the Divine names, the soul of man, its nature and destiny, the nature of good and evil, the importance of the Torah (written and oral), the Messiah, and redemption.

The Zohar takes the form of a commentary – a kind of Midrash – on the Pentateuch, and is intended to reveal hidden meaning of the Biblical narratives and the Divine commandments.

In its interpretation of Scripture, the Zohar employs the four methods which came to be known under the Hebrew term coined from their initial letters, *PaRDeS* (Paradise): *Peshat* (literal interpretation), *Remez* (allegorical), *Derush* (expository), and *Sod* (mystical). These four methods are not peculiar to the Zohar. They are all to be found already in the Talmud; but it was left to the Zohar to extol the mystical over all other methods of interpretation which it considers but the body of the Torah of which the hidden mysteries are said to constitute the soul (III, 152a).

The author of the Zohar has drawn largely on the Talmud and the Midrashim for many of his fundamental and his subsidiary teachings, not without, however, unfolding, broadening, and deepening the mystical content of his borrowed material.

The Zohar, as has already been indicated, sums up the Kabbalistic ideas that had been developed up to the time of its appearance. It accepts Azriel's concept of God as the *En Sof* as axiomatic. God is described as the most Hidden of all Hidden. At the same time, He is also called the All. 'For all things are in Him and He is in all things: He is both manifest and concealed: manifest in order to uphold the whole, and concealed for He is found nowhere' (III, 288a). Moreover, He is in a certain sense *Ayin* (non-existent), because as far as our minds are concerned, that which is incomprehensible does not exist (III, 283b). To make His existence perceptible and to render Himself comprehensible, He projected from the light of His Infinite self ten successive channels of light which served as media for His manifestations in the finite.

These ten successive 'channels of light' are the *Sefiroth*, called also 'grades' which, in the Zohar as in the 'Treatise on Emanation' and Azriel's works, are qualities and agencies of God. This idea in itself is already to be found in the Talmud which speaks of the 'Ten agencies through which God created the world, viz., wisdom, understanding, knowledge, strength, power, inexorableness, righteousness, justice, love, mercy.'¹ In the Zohar, however, the names vary somewhat, and as *Sefiroth* they are also classified according to a definite scheme and pattern. The *Sefiroth* are divided into three groups. The first of these form a triad constituting the world as a manifestation of Divine thought. The first of the *Sefiroth* is designated *Kether* (Crown), and is said to represent the same primary stage of the

Divine creative process as the *Will* in Gabirol. *Kether* gave rise
to two parallel *Sefiroth*, *Chochmah* (Wisdom) and *Binah* (Understanding). With these two, there enters the principle of
dualism which, according to the *Kabbalah*, runs through the
whole of the universe, and which it denominates by the sexual
terms of male and female. Applying this principle to the first
triad, *Chochmah* is the father, or the masculine, active principle
in that it contains in itself the plan of the universe in all its
infinite variety of forms and movements. *Binah* (Understanding), on the other hand, is the mother, the passive, receptive
principle, the principle of individuation and differentiation.
What was previously folded up and undifferentiated in *Chochmah* became as a result of its union with *Binah* unfolded and
differentiated. From the union of *Chochmah* and *Binah* proceeds *Daath* (Knowledge) which, however, for some reason is
not considered as a separate *Sefirah*.

Emanating from the first triad, which represents God as the
immanent *thinking* power of the universe, is the second triad
which interprets Him as the immanent *moral* power of the
universe.

Here, too, we have the application of the two opposing male
and female principles. The former is *Chesed* (Love) which is
the life-begetting and life-giving principle, whilst the latter is
Geburah (Might) which stands for justice, holding in check
what would otherwise prove the excesses of love. From the
union of the two comes *Tifereth* (Beauty), sometimes designated *Rachamim* (Mercy) for, as already stressed by the Talmud,[7] it is only by the combination of Love and Justice that
the moral order of the universe is assured.

The third triad represents the material universe in all its
physical and dynamic aspects and multiplicity and variety of
forces, changes, and movements. In this triad the male principle is denoted by *Netzach* (Victory), the lasting endurance of
God. *Hod* (Majesty) is the feminine, passive principle, whilst
the third, *Yesod* (Foundation) denotes the stability of the
universe as the effect of the union of the first two.

The last and tenth *Sefirah* is called *Malchuth* (Kingdom)
which represents the harmony of all the *Sefiroth* and denotes

the presence of God in the universe. This *Sefirah* is also named *Shechinah* (Indwelling), but whereas the former term refers to the fact of the ubiquitous Divine presence – Immanence – in the world, the latter signifies the special manifestation of God in the lives of individuals or communities as well as in hallowed spots and places.

The *Sefiroth* are visualized in arrangement under a human form, *Adam Kadmon* (Primordial Man), with the active qualities occupying the right side, and the passive the left, whilst the products of the union of any two of the *Sefiroth* have the position along the central meridian. Dominating the whole organism and at the head is the *Kether* (Crown), whilst the *Malchuth* (Kingdom) is situated at the feet.

The realm of the *Sefiroth* is the world of *Atziluth* (Emanation). Their influence, however, extends to the other three worlds where their real activity begins.

The *Sefiroth*, though ten in number, are interconnected with each other and form one unity. Furthermore, they all participate in each other's qualities and they are differentiated only by the predominance of the particular quality which gives each one its name. So do the four worlds in all their ramifications form one great unity with the *En Sof*, the primary source of them all, permeating them all and transcending them all, the *En Sof* and all the realms of His manifestations being linked together 'as the flame and the coal'.

This interconnexion of the *Sefiroth* and the worlds with one another means that they are all subjected to common influences; or, in other words, that the activity which affects the one cannot fail to affect all others. The means of conveyance of these influences from one *Sefirah* to another is called *Zinor* (Pipe). The general principle of the exertion of reciprocal influences of the *Sefiroth* on one another and on this world has been expressed by the Zohar in the dictum 'From an activity below there is stimulated a correponding activity on High. Come and see: a mist ascends from the earth and then a cloud is formed, one joining the other to form a whole.' (Zohar on Gen. 2. 6).

This doctrine is of far-reaching consequence in Kabbalistic

teaching as far as human conduct is concerned. Originally, the unity between God and His final manifestation in the world of human existence, or, to use the Kabbalistic terms, between the *En Sof* and the *Shechinah* was harmonious and complete. There was nothing to disturb the close relationship of God with the world of His creation, or to interfere with the steady and continuous outpouring of His love over the sons of man. But owing to the sinfulness of man, beginning with Adam's disobedience, man strayed from the primordial source of God. At once, the perfect unity was broken. This breach in the unity spelled *ipso facto* the appearance of evil in the universe. Thereupon harmony in creation gave way to discord, and the world order was turned into disorder. Since then the *Shechinah* is said to be in exile. Instead of pervading the whole universe with its immediately beneficent presence, it is to be found only here and there in isolated individuals or communities or special localities, whereas the rest of the world is bereft of the blessings of the *Shechinah*. With the result that the flow of the Divine Love became hampered and the severity of the judgement began to prevail.

To reunite the *Shechinah* to the *En Sof*, and thus restore the impaired original unity and renew thereby the unimpeded flow of Divine Love is the end to which man was created in the world (II, 161b). Nor is this task beyond man's capacity and power. Man, in the teaching of the Zohar, is an epitome of the cosmos. In him the 'upper' and 'lower' worlds have their meeting points. His body is a copy of the *Adam Kadmon* which, as we have seen, represents the world of *Sefiroth* in their totality and unity.

And as with the human body, so it is with the human soul. In it, too, there is reproduced 'a copy of what is above in the celestial world' (II, 142a). The soul, according to the Zohar, comprises three elements: (1) *Neshamah* (Super-soul), which is the most sublime and divine part of man and corresponds to the first of the three triads of the *Sefiroth*, representing intellectual world; (2) *Ruach* (Spirit), which is the seat of moral qualities, and corresponds to the second of the three triads representing the moral world; and (3) *Nefesh* (Vitality), which is immediately connected with physical life, and corresponds to the third triad representing the material world. These three elements of the soul are pre-existent in the World of Emanation, each having its source in one of the *Sefiroth* of its respective triad; and, working in unison, they enable man to fulfil his multifarious duties in life. All this means that the power of the *Sefiroth* exists and is active in man, linking him in body and soul to the *Sefiroth* and, at the same time, endowing him with a power to influence them and through them, for weal or woe, the whole order of creation.

The restoration of the unity, called in *Kabbalah Yichud*, is a constant process, in which every individual is bidden to participate, and is to be effected through communion with God and ethical and moral perfection. But the highest contribution towards this consummation must be made collectively by the Community of Israel. This is the charge laid upon them by virtue of their election. By this act the *Shechinah* attached itself to Israel and entered with it into a covenant relationship which received its closest intimacy at the building of the Temple. Since the destruction of the Temple, the *Shechinah*'s relations with Israel are not without strain and the blessings that emanate from this relationship are less constant and efficacious. Yet the *Shechinah* never deserted Israel. It accompanies them in exile, bestowing upon them the love and care that a parent would give to his beloved son; and on the advent of the Messiah, when Israel shall once more be rehabilitated securely in its Holy Land and the Temple rise on its former hallowed spot, the *Shechinah* will recover its former vigour and intensity, and be reunited to God, and all things shall be restored to the place they had in the original Divine scheme of creation. Then there shall be completeness above and completeness below, and all the world shall be united in one bond, as it is written (Zech. 14. 9), 'On that day the Lord shall be One and His name One' (III, 260b).

For achieving this unity Israel has been given the Torah; and it is by the study of the Torah and observance of its precepts that Israel can make effective their specific contribution towards this cosmic fulfilment.

This efficacy of the study of the Torah is derived from its correspondence with the world. The Torah is conceived by the Zohar as the 'blueprint' wherewith God provided Himself for the creation. 'When God resolved to create the world, He looked into the Torah, into its every creative word, and fashioned the world accordingly; for all the worlds and all the actions of the worlds are contained in the Torah' (II, 161a), every word presenting a symbol, every jot and tittle concealing a mystery.

The study of the Torah and the endeavour to discover its hidden meanings thus becomes one of the foremost duties of a son of Israel. 'For he who concentrates his mind on the Torah and penetrates into its inner mysteries sustains the world' (II, 61a). On the other hand, 'he who neglects the study of the Torah is as if he destroyed the world' (I, 184b).

Parallel with the correspondence which exists between the Torah itself and the world is the correspondence between the precepts of the Torah and the component parts of the human body.

The Torah, according to an early Talmudic enumeration, comprises 248 positive injunctions and 365 prohibitions, and these have their respective counterparts in the 248 limbs and 365 sinews of which the human organism is said to consist. In this way, every observance or breach of any of the commandments of the Torah produces through its corresponding counterpart in the human body, a reaction in the corresponding portion in the world of *Sefiroth*, with effects on the whole (I, 61b).

Similarly, the various 'appointed seasons' in the Jewish calendar – the Sabbath and Festivals – ordained by the Torah, derive their special mystical significance from their relation with the *Sefiroth*. In the Zoharitic teaching, every day comes under the specific influence of a particular *Sefirah*. The Sabbath comes immediately under the influence of *Malkuth* (*Shechinah*) which, as is seen, is the unifying *Sefirah*, harmonizing within itself the potencies of all the *Sefiroth*. The Sabbath is, therefore, a day of joyful reunion in the supernal worlds. On that day the rigours of Judgement are shut out and give way to the soothing and healing power of Love, enfolding with its blessings the whole of creation. Even the denizens of Hell find respite on that day from the expiating pangs of their sins.

The blessings of the Sabbath seep through to the other six days of the week. 'All the six days of the transcendent world derive blessing from the Sabbath day, and each supernal day sends forth nourishment to the world below from what it receives from the seventh day' (II, 88a). But the stream of the Sabbath blessing in the supernal world above is determined in its flow by the stimulus it receives from below. Herein lies the mystical significance of the Sabbath meals. They serve to set in motion from above the blessings of the day for the world below. 'For no blessing can alight upon an empty table' (II, 88a).

Herein, too, lies the significance of the joy that characterizes the Sabbath, as well as the special ceremonies in which this joy finds its expressions. The Sabbath is endowed with Divine beauty and becomes a bride, splendid and resplendent. Every Friday evening at sunset, *Israel*, the Lover, goes forth to meet *Sabbath*, the Bride, with songs of welcome and praise. This joy of *Israel* the Lover, with the Bride *Sabbath*, is the terrestrial stimulus for arousing the Love of God for his Beloved, celebrated in the Song of Songs – the Community of Israel.

The other important days in the Jewish calendar are also dealt with in the same mystical way. So are the ceremonial precepts, such as the 'frontlets' (phylacteries), the 'fringes', the eating of unleavened bread at Passover, the handling of the four plants on Tabernacles – in every case the Zohar seeks to describe the reaction set up in the worlds above as a result of the performance of these precepts by Israel on earth below. And not only the days, but also the various parts of the day are related to particular *Sefiroth*, and as such become propitious for the exercise of special religious duties. 'From sunrise until the sun declines westwards, it is called "day", and the attribute of Love is in the ascendant. After that it is called "evening", which is the time for the attribute of Judgement. It is for this reason that Isaac instituted the afternoon prayer

(*Minchah*), namely, to mitigate this ruling severity of Judgement, whereas Abraham instituted the morning prayer, corresponding to the attribute of Love' (ii, 21a-b).

Another important instrument for the restoration of the unity is prayer. Prayer is no magic device, as little as are the other commandments of the Torah. Prayer is described as a spiritual worship and its efficacy depends on the attendant devotion (*kawanah*). 'Prayer offered with concentrated devotion by a man who fears his Master produces great effects on High' (ii, 200b). These effects are described in terms of the unity of God and the *Shechinah*, with the result that the peace and joy engendered on High descends and envelops not only the prayerful soul but is distributed to all, thus making him 'a son through whose cooperation blessings are found on High' (ii, 62a).

In the last analysis the efficacy of all forms of cooperation with God, whether through the study of the Torah or the fulfilment of the commandments or prayer, is determined by Love. In Love, according to the Zohar, is to be found the secret of Divine Unity. He who worships God out of 'Love unites the highest and lowest stages and lifts everything to the stage where all must be one' (ii, 216a).

It is in proportion as man participates in this cooperative activity with the Divine and thereby contributes towards the restoration of the unity that his soul is rewarded or punished in the Hereafter. At the moment of death the three parts of the soul separate from one another, each entering upon the recompense awaiting it commensurate with its deserts. In the case of the just, *Neshamah* receives the 'kiss of Love' from the Infinite and immediately returns to the source whence it emanates, there to live for ever in the pure sparkling reflection of the Divine Light. The *Ruach* enters *Eden* where it dons the body it tenanted in the world, so that it may enjoy the lights of Paradise. *Nefesh* remains in the grave, where, after hovering for a time over the body until it is decomposed, it finally finds rest and peace on earth.

It is otherwise with those whose terrestrial lives were stained with sin. Their *Neshamah* encounters obstacles hindering its immediate ascent to its rightful place, and until it has reached its proper destination, the *Ruach* finds the door of *Eden* closed against it, whilst the *Nefesh* is doomed to wander hither and thither in the world.

The destiny of every soul is, however, to return to the source whence it emanated. Those who in their terrestrial existence failed to develop that purity and perfection necessary for gaining access to their source in the region above must 'experience' incarnation in another body, and even repeat that 'experience' over and over again until they have completed their task on earth and able to return to the heavenly region in a purified form.

These and similar teachings of the Zohar, which purported to disclose the supernal mysteries of existence in general and of Jewish religious life and observance in particular, and interwoven as these were with an elaborate angelology, rich imagery, and fascinating legendary, could not fail to make strong appeal to Jewish intellectuals as well as to the Jewish masses. In an incredibly short time the Zohar captured Jewish minds and hearts and became after the Bible and the Talmud the third sacred source of Jewish inspiration and guidance. The expulsion of the Jews from Spain in 1492 endeared the Zohar all the more to the Jewish world. The exiles from Spain found in the Zohar a fresh source of strength that saved them amid all their harrowing experiences from the pit of despair. More overpoweringly than any other book, more even than the Bible itself, did the Zohar fill them with a sense of spiritual power that enabled them to triumph over all their material ills and physical misfortunes. Through its teachings they learned to perceive in their own tragedies a reflection of the cosmic tragedy in which God Himself, so to speak, was involved, leaving them thus in no doubt as to the ultimate issue, and at the same time to apprehend the spiritual agencies they had at their command for resolving the tragedy, and securing healing and blessing both for themselves and the world.

The exiles from Spain carried with them their treasured Zohar to all countries that were open to them: Turkey, Palestine, and Egypt and later Italy, Germany, Holland, and England. Wherever they settled they continued to broaden and deepen its teachings. It was, however, at Safed in Palestine that Zoharic teaching reached its highest degree of development. Apart from its peculiarly clear and healthy air, which was believed to be more conducive than any other place to mystical pursuits, Safed had a special attraction for the mystics. It was close to the tomb of Rabbi Simeon ben Yochai, and to this town flocked accordingly the more renowned mystics from all parts of Europe, and established there what was to become the chief centre of Kabbalistic lore, both in its speculative and practical aspects.

Foremost among the speculative mystics of the Safed school was Moses Cordovero (1522–76), whose *Pardes* (Orchard) is the clearest and most rational exposition of the speculative *Kabbalah*. His work is essentially based on the Zohar and, clothed in the most beautiful Hebrew, reads like a poem. The problem to which he returns over and over again is the relation of the *En Sof* to the *Sefiroth*. He described the *Sefiroth* as *Kelim* (Vessels) in which the unchangeable light of the *En Sof* is present, and through which, by reason of the difference in their qualities, it is reflected in different forms, giving rise to all the changes that take place in the Universe. This is another way of saying that the Infinite is present in every part of the finite, which, in turn, is itself but a phase or 'mode' of the Infinite, and that, as Cordovero phrases it elsewhere, 'Nothing exists outside God'.[8] Here Cordovero gave expression to a view which appears surprisingly like the pantheism taught a century later by Spinoza who, in fact, is said to have avowed his indebtedness for his theory to Cordovero. Cordovero, however, safeguards the theistic position by defining his attitude in the formula: 'God is all reality, but not all reality *is* God[9]' – an attitude which came to be known in modern philosophy as 'panentheism'.

But overshadowing Cordovero in influence is the towering figure of Isaac Luria (1514–72), called the 'Ari' (the Lion), who elaborated both theoretically and practically Zoharic doctrines with surprising results. Central to Luria's system is the doctrine of *zimzum* (contraction), which conceives creation to have been preceded by a voluntary contraction or self-limitation of the Infinite (*En Sof*) in order to make room for the finite world of phenomena. Into the dark vacuum thus formed the Infinite projected His light, providing it at the same time with the 'vessels' which were to serve as media for its multifarious manifestations in creation. But some of the 'vessels', unable to endure the inrush of the light emitted from the *En Sof*, gave way and broke. The 'breaking of the vessels' (*Shebirath ha-kelim*) caused a deterioration in the worlds above and chaos and confusion in the world here below. Instead of its uniform diffusion throughout the universe, the light irradiating from the Infinite was broken up into sparks illumining only certain parts of physical creation, while other parts were left in darkness, a state which in itself is a type of negative evil. Thus did light and darkness, good and evil, begin to contend for the mastery of the world. The Divine harmony was disrupted and the *Shechinah* exiled. At the same time, scattered hither and thither, the sparks of Divine Light intersected everywhere the darkness, with the result that evil and good became so mixed that there is no evil that does not contain an element of good, nor is there a good entirely free from evil.

This state of confusion was aggravated through the sins of the first man. According to Luria, all souls destined for humanity were created with Adam. True, they were not all of the same quality, some being superior to others, but they all, in their own respective degree, were good, and complete harmony consequently prevailed among them. When Adam sinned, however, they all became tainted in varying degrees according to the power of resistance within them, leading to a rupture in their pre-existent harmony. Confusion thereupon ensued among the various classes of souls. The superior souls intermingled with the inferior, good with evil, so that the best soul received some admixture of the evil infesting the inferior souls, and the worst an admixture of good from the superior. This confusion among the souls gives a continued impulse to moral evil, but the malaise is not destined to last, but will come to an end with the advent of the Messiah who will be sent by God to restore the original harmony both to the souls of men and to the entire cosmos.

The initiative for the restoration of this original harmony must, however, come from man himself. Adopting the Zoharic doctrine of migration of souls, Luria developed it further by his theory of *Ibbur* (Impregnation). If a soul, that is to say, proves too weak for the task appointed for it on earth, it may have to return to this earthly life and become impregnated in the soul of another living person in order to receive support from it in its own endeavours to make good its deficiencies. Further, at times a stronger soul may be sent down again on earth to give aid to a weaker one, nursing it from its own substance as a mother does with a child in her womb.

Allied to Luria's theory of impregnation is his idea that the dispersion of the Jews has for its purpose the salvation of all human souls, the purified souls of the Israelites unifying with the souls of the men of other races in order to liberate them from the power of evil. With the complete separation of the good from the evil, both in individuals in particular and in the cosmos as a whole, the restoration of the original harmony (*tikkun*) will be effected and man and the world will find redemption.

For the separation of good from evil in the individual self, Luria advocated the practice of asceticism, self-mortification, fastings, and ablutions. These ascetic practices, however, were not intended to be other than mere aids to man in his spiritual strivings. They were neither regarded as charged with special merits for securing salvation or favour of God, nor conceived as punishments inflicted on a body contaminated with sin. Luria still insisted that the body was pure as much as the soul. The body was a sacred vessel comprehending the Divine spark, the soul and, as such, was holy and had to be kept in health and the utmost purity.

But this concern for the redemption of self must be considered only as part of the greater concern for the redemption of the whole of creation. In line with Zoharic doctrine Luria perceived in the precepts, and prayers, and the practice of kindly deeds instruments for accomplishing this universal redemption; but, going beyond the Zohar, he insisted on the need of bringing to the performance of every single devotional act special types of concentrated reflections (*Kawanoth*), which were to concern themselves with the mystical meanings he had ascribed to that particular act.

All these teachings of Luria were followed by the mystics of the Safed school, foremost among whom was his chief disciple, Hayyim Vittal Calabrese (1543–1620), whose works popularized the doctrines of his master throughout the world of Jewish mysticism.

If these ideas under the form in which they are presented may appear fantastic, there can be no mistake as to the profundity of thought they enshrine. In the idea of the *Zimzum*, with its correlative *Shebirath Ha-Kelim*, we have but an affirmation of the existence of tension between the Finite and the Infinite in the creative process, resulting in the intermingling of good and evil in physical creation; all good which created beings display being due to the activity of the Infinite, whilst all the evil is due to their nature as finite beings. Moral evil has, therefore, no independent being of its own. It is rather the negative of good, and hence to be overcome by the force of will. But because evil is universal it has to be overcome everywhere. This demands the merging of the smaller interests of self in the greater interests of the whole, and the narrow concern for the redemption of individual life in the wider concern for redemption of universal life.

It is within this universal context that the activities of the Safed mystics has to be viewed. Whilst seeking to attain self-perfection and to promote the salvation of their own individual souls, they never lost sight of the great universal tasks set before them; and to command, by means of study, prayer, and devotional exercises, such spiritual power as would enable them to speed on the Messianic redemption was, in the last analysis, the intense desire of the Safed mystics and the goal towards which they strove with mighty longing.

Nor did they for a moment doubt the worth of their ceaseless strivings. It was this certainty of the final redemption to come, coupled with the conviction of the effectiveness of their contribution, that filled the Safed mystics, notwithstanding their ascetic regimen, with a sense of joy. Joy was, in fact, one of the outstanding characteristics of the spiritual life of the Safed mystics. To this joy they gave expression in a number of in-spiriting practices as well as of liturgical compositions which, by virtue of their beauty and devotional power, rank among the most exquisite pieces of religious poetry in existence. Most celebrated among these compositions is the *Lechoh Dodi* (Come, O my Friend), a hymn with which its author, Solomon Alka-betz (1505–72), used to go forth with his friends to the fields on Friday at sunset to greet the Sabbath bride, and which occupies now an honoured place in almost all Synagogue rituals.

> Come forth my friend, the Bride to meet,
> Come, O my friend, the Sabbath greet.

Another hymn, though not so well known, but often sung by the devout, is the *Yedid Nefesh* (Beloved of the Soul) by Eleazar Askari (sixteenth century), a song breathing the spirit of passionate love for God, and of which the following are the first two stanzas:

> Beloved of the Soul, merciful Father,
> Draw Thy servant unto Thy will,
> That swift as a hart he may run
> To prostrate himself before Thy majesty,
> Finding Thy love sweeter than the honey-comb
> And every tempting savour.
>
> Exquisitely beautiful is the splendour of the world,
> My soul pineth for Thy love.
> O God heal it, I pray Thee, by showing unto it
> The delight of Thy splendour
> Then it will grow strong and be healed,
> And rejoice everlastingly.[10]

From the Safed school have also emanated most of the Table Songs (*Zemiroth*), chanted in Jewish households during meals on the Sabbath. Most popular among these is the one with the refrain: 'This day is for Israel a light and rejoicing'. Attributed to Isaac Luria, this song gives expression to the real joy of the Sabbath which brings with it the 'gift of a new soul' to the distressed and soothes the sighs of those imprisoned in spirit.

Another song which has gained widespread popularity, although written in Aramaic, is Israel Najara's (1550–c. 1620) *Yah Ribbon Olam* (O Lord, Sovereign of the World), which is both an ode to God, and a plea for redemption, and has been set to innumerable tunes. Very popular, too, is the 'Song of Peace', chanted in Jewish homes on Friday evenings before meals in greeting of the Sabbath angel which, according to a Talmudic notion, accompanies every man with blessings on his return from welcoming the Sabbath in the Synagogue.

From the Safed school is also derived the custom for the husband to recite in the home on Friday evenings the last chapter of the Book of Proverbs, eulogizing the *Esheth Hayil* (The Woman of Valour) – the ideal wife and mother.

In the Safed school there also originated a number of customs which tend to enrich Jewish religious and spiritual life and are conducive to inward devotion. Among these is the still fairly widespread custom of spending the whole night in the study of the Torah on the eve of the Festival of Revelation, in reminiscence of the preparation which the Israelites helped to make for receiving the Ten Commandments, as well as the vigil on the seventh day of the Festival of Tabernacles which, in Kabbalistic teachings, is a semi-day of judgement and thus an echo of the Day of Atonement.

Among other innovations of the Safed school are midnight prayers (*Tikkun Chazoth*) in lamentation of the destruction of the Temple and the exile of the *Shechinah*; and the fast on the eve of the New Moon – a fast instituted by Cordovero, under the name of *Yom Kippur Katon*, the minor Day of Atonement – the New Moon being conceived as an appropriate time for a monthly spiritual stocktaking.

The Safed mystics also prescribed the recital of special meditations before the performance of any religious devotion. Most of these meditations direct the mind of the worshipper to the mystical significance of the act he is about to perform as well as to its effects in the supernal world. Some of the meditations, however, are but self-exhortations to ethical conduct, and breathe the noblest humanism of the most universal sort. Nor is this surprising. It is but the inescapable sequel to the

Safed conception of the universe as a closely knit system in which all parts are sensitively interdependent upon each other, a deed, a word, and even a thought affecting the one not being without effect upon the other. Love for all human beings, including non-Jews, was thus one of the distinctive traits of the mystics of the Safed school and furthermore declared by them to be a prerequisite for acquiring the gifts of the Holy Spirit. To this all-embracing human love the Safed mystics made avowal in some of their meditations. Striking in this connexion is the meditation on retiring at night: 'Lord of the Universe, I forgive all who have made me angry, and harmed me, whether they hurt my body, my honour, or my property, whether wittingly or unwittingly, whether in deed or in thought. May no one be punished for my sake or because of me.' Of similar character is the meditation before prayer: 'I hereby take upon myself to observe the command: Thou shalt love thy neighbour as thyself.'[11]

From Safed the Kabbalistic doctrine spread to other Jewish centres in Palestine: Tiberias, Hebron, and Jerusalem, as well as to great Jewish centres in the Diaspora: Italy, Germany, and Holland. This mystic tide also swept into Poland, where among others, Isaiah Halevy Horowitz (c. 1570-1630) the author of what was to become the much admired and most widely read ethical-mystical work, *Shene Luchoth ha-Berith* (The Two Tables of the Covenant) contributed much to the dissemination of the Kabbalistic lore among Eastern European Jewry. The interest aroused throughout Israel for the new mystical learning led to the rapid adoption by Jews in many lands of most of the customs that had proceeded from Safed, not a few becoming accepted as norms of Jewish practice in every Jewish community. But, notwithstanding the widespread influence of Safed, the *Kabbalah* as a mystic lore was still restricted to the exclusive circles of the learned, and had yet to become the spiritual nutriment of the simple multitude. It was only in the eighteenth century, with the rise of Chassidism, which brought the masses under the direct influence of Lurianic doctrine, that *Kabbalah* entered upon a broader course which, notwithstanding the loss of its original impetus, has continued its steady and gentle flow with fructifying effects to the present generation.

This chapter cannot close without referring to the extraordinary influence of the *Kabbalah* on the non-Jewish world. The *Kabbalah* appealed greatly to the leaders of the Reformation who found in its mysticism a potent ally in their opposition to medieval scholastic theology. Christian mystical movements were particularly attracted to the *Kabbalah* because it furnished them with much valuable material for their esoteric pursuits; and it is to the *Kabbalah* that modern occultist movements turn in their efforts to place the whole of knowledge on a new basis.

NOTES

1 Maimonides, *Responsa* (Ed. Freimann), 373.
2. See T. Sanhedrin, 65b.
3. See T. Pesachim, 54a.
4. See p. 185.
5. Version of Mrs Alice Lucas, *The Jewish Year* (London, 1898), p. 111.
6. See pp. 177–8.
7. T. Hagigah, 12a. 7a. see Midrash Genesis Rabbah xii, 15.
8. Quoted in G. Scholem, *Major Trends in Jewish Mysticism* (rev. ed. New York, 1941), p. 253.
9. *loc. cit.*
10. Translated by Prof. S. S. Cohon, as quoted in A.Z. Idelsohn, *Jewish Liturgy* (New York, 1932), p. 52.
11. Luria's innovations and other customs that proceeded from the Safed school were collected and affixed to the Prayer Book of the Sephardi ritual under the name of *Siddur Ari*.

CHAPTER 20

THE CONTRIBUTION OF MEDIEVAL
RABBINISM

IT will have been seen in the two preceding chapters that
Jewish philosophy and the *Kabbalah* have each made their
specific contribution to Judaism, the former by clarifying its
teachings in the light of reason, the latter by probing its mysteries with the aid of mystical illuminations. Neither, however,
was without the dangers inherent in rationalism and mysticism,
respectively. Whilst rationalism is liable to become tainted
with scepticism, leading to the weakening and at times even
the destruction of religion, mysticism is apt to become wrapped
up in a subjectivity which makes for antinomianism and spiritual anarchy. It was the realization of these respective dangers
that, on the one hand, aroused the opposition, already noted,
to Jewish philosophy and, on the other, led many adepts in
Kabbalah to set their face against the popularization of its
teachings.

That Judaism, however, has been able, generally speaking, to
surmount these dangers, was due to the ascendancy of rabbinism
during the Middle Ages, which as far as Jews were concerned
lasted to the middle of the eighteenth century. Maintaining
and developing the Talmudic and Gaonic tradition to which it
was the direct heir, medieval rabbinism was able to provide
clear definitions of norms of action for every new situation
and circumstance, and thus to control and shape the existence
of the individual and the community from the most intimate
and sacred details to the wholly external and secular. In this
way, medieval rabbinism gave Jewish life an inner discipline
which, without curbing the mind or deadening the spirit, saved
Judaism from the excesses alike of rationalism and mysticism.

This unique contribution of medieval rabbinism, which
comes under the general classification of *Halachah* (Law), falls
into three principal divisions: (1) Talmudic commentaries;
(2) codes; and (3) responsa. Each of these has its antecedents

in the Gaonic age. But it was under medieval rabbinism that all these reached their highest development. The decline of the Gaonate in the eleventh century put an end to centralized authority. Henceforth, individual teachers with their written contributions took the place of the Geonim and their schools. A prince of commentators arose in France in the person of Rabbi Solomon ben Isaac of Troyes (1040–1105), affectionately called Rashi,[1] who has exerted a profound influence on Jewish thought and education. His running Commentary on practically the whole of the Talmud, in which hardly a term, idea, phrase, or concept is allowed to pass without interpretation or explanation, has almost from the time of its first appearance been the indispensable aid of Talmudic teachers and students alike.

Rashi's work was continued by a school of Talmudists known as Tosafists, from the *Tosafoth* (Additions), which they wrote to Rashi's Commentary on the Talmud. Theirs was the dialectical and critical method, and their aim was the closest logical analysis of Talmudic statements, enabling them to evolve new principles and to formulate the law and bring it up to date, and, on the whole, to lay Talmudic studies on a broader and deeper basis.

As the first Tosafists were the sons-in-law and grandsons of Rashi as well as his immediate disciples, most of the *Tosafoth* were the product of the French schools, but the Tosafists' method spread to Germany, Provence, and Spain, and reached even England, where it was represented by Jacob of Orleans as well as Yomtob of Joigny, both martyrs respectively of the massacres in London in 1189 and of those in York in 1190, and later by Elijah ben Menachem of London (*c*. 1220–*c*. 1284). The Commentary of Rashi and the 'Additions' of the Tosafists, whose activities extended to the end of the thirteenth century, appear in all the printed editions of the Talmud, Rashi occupying what is considered the more honourable place of the inner margin of the page, and the *Tosafoth* the outer margin.

Rashi and the early Tosafists lived during the Crusades (1096–1189), when the cup of suffering of the Jews in France and Germany was filled to overflowing. Fighting for their very survival, the Jews in these countries showed little inclination for alien philosophies and cultures, but instead turned for inspiration and strength to their own heritage, and, concentrating their intellectual energies mainly on the Talmudic sciences, many attained in them a profound and and an all-embracing mastery. Thus arose in France and Germany a considerable number of scholars who were competent to give to individuals and communities practical guidance in all requirements of Jewish life. Such, however, was not the case in Spain. Living at that time under more favourable conditions, the Spanish Jews were attracted to the claims of general culture, not without detriment to their Talmudic attainments, and except for a few encyclopedic and brilliant minds, the Spanish-Jewish scholars had to fall back on guides that had come down to them from the Gaonic period for regulating religious life and conduct. These compendia from a previous age were, however, too fragmentary and formal to satisfy the increased demand for learning which the rise of the schools in the West had brought in their wake. This led Isaac ben Jacob Alfasi of Lucena (1013–1103) to compose under the name of *Halachoth* (Laws) a code presented in the form of an abridged Talmud, in which he reproduced the practical contents which he extracted with considerable skill from the maze of Talmudic discussions, and summed up by a decision. Several other codes of larger and smaller compass followed; but the most systematic and comprehensive codification of the Law was made by Moses Maimonides in his *Mishneh Torah* (The Second Torah) called *Yad ha-Hazakah* (The Strong Hand), which he intended to serve both as a guide for his own times and as a basis for the Jewish state of the future. Instead of the dry Halachic compendia of the Gaonic schools, and the more discursive method of Alfasi's work, Maimonides employed the historical method, covering the whole ground of the *Halachah* from the Bible through all the phases of its development to his own days. His aim was, as he states in the Introduction, to present a work 'which everyone who will read it after the written Law will know from it the whole of the oral Law, and will not have to study any other intervening book'. He thus included in his Code also laws which were no longer in force, such as those relating to the Temple and the sacrifices, as well as theology and ethics.

Maimonides' Code is the supreme example of the power of the discipline of the *Halachah* on a rationalist mind such as Maimonides' undoubtedly was. With all his attempts to recon-cile Judaism with the thought and knowledge of his times, Maimonides did not allow his personal judgement to influence in the least his codification of Jewish laws and practices other-wise than in accordance with the strict application of well defined and recognized principles of the *Halachah*. He is thus found to include in his Code Talmudic rules which he himself contests in his philosophic *Guide for the Perplexed*. At the same time, under the influence of his rationalism, Maimonides omits from his Code all popular customs that had the force of law in Talmudic days, but which were essentially rooted in current superstitions, beliefs, and notions. There is thus, for example, no trace in his Code of those practices, common in Talmudic times, which caused people, because of their belief in the danger of even numbers – *zuggoth* – to abstain from, say, drinking two cups of any beverage or of eating two kinds of food.

Most distinctive in Maimonides' Code is his essentially humanistic approach in the formulation and application of the law. Whilst he is most rigorous in the laws of *meum* and *teum*, he is inclined to adopt a lenient view in ritual matters. His attitude may well be summarized in the words: 'The ritual law has been given to man and not man to the ritual law.' He therefore recognizes that at times it may be necessary for certain laws to be adapted, modified, and even abrogated 'in order' (as he states) 'to bring back the multitudes to religion and to save them from general religious laxity, even as the physician will amputate the hand or foot of a patient in order to save his life' (*Mamerim* II, 4).

His humanism is of a universal sweep, embracing all men and all peoples. This humanism finds its most striking expres-sion in the following paragraph occurring in his Code:

Not only the tribe of Levi (has been set aside to God), but whatever man among the denizens of the world who is moved, in spirit and in mind, to dedicate himself to the service and knowledge of God, and walks uprightly in the manner as God made man to walk, and rids himself from the yoke of 'the many inventions which men sought out', such a man becomes sanctified as most holy. The Lord will be his lot and portion for ever and ever and he will vouchsafe to him in this world, what will be deemed sufficient for his needs (*Shemittah*, 11. 13.)

Written in Cairo and completed in 1190, Maimonides' Code quickly spread throughout Israel and influenced the whole subsequent codification of Jewish Law. Even in a Jewry as far removed from Egypt as that of pre-expulsion England, Jacob ben Judah, the *Chazan*, or Reader of the synagogue in London (*c.* 1287) composed a work *Etz Chayyim* (The Tree of Life) quite in the manner of the *Mishneh Torah*, and for many centuries Maimonides' work remained for many communities the sole authoritative code for Jewish life, thought, and practice.

The centuries following the death of Maimonides saw a rapid development of Jewish law in all Western countries – Spain, France, Germany, and Italy – affecting all departments of life. The media of this development were the *Responsa*, a form of literature which, as we have seen, had played a most important part in the Gaonic period, and continued unbroken during the intervening centuries. Among the most famous Responsa of the post-Gaonic period were those of Rabbi Gershom of Mainz (b. *c.* 960) who laid the foundation of the system that helped to organize and strengthen French and German Jewries for half a millennium. He was a veritable support and comforter of his persecuted brethren on the Rhine, as well as a realistic reformer, adapting many Talmudic laws to the conditions of the Exile of which he was designated as 'the Beacon of Light'. A zealous defender of the rights of the wife, he forbade polygamy, and ordained that no divorce could be effected without the wife's consent. These rulings, although they involved a departure from Biblical and Talmudic law, were eventually accepted by all Jewries apart from a few in Mohammedan countries, and became generally speaking an integral part of Jewish law. Another famous ruling of his was the prohibition of reading another person's letters, a prohibition the purpose of which needs no remark. Responsa were also written by Rashi, who was a disciple of Rabbi Gershom. Many of Rashi's Responsa concerned themselves with interrelations of Jews and Christians. He ruled that Christianity was not to be classed as idolatry, and that therefore the laws set forth in the Talmud regulating the economic relations of Jews with idolaters did not apply to Christians. He thus permitted Jews to employ Christians in the production and distribution of wine, although idolaters could not by Talmudic law be so employed for fear they might, whilst at work, use the wine for idolatrous libations. He also insisted that forced converts to Christianity had to be treated with the utmost consideration, and once they returned to the Jewish faith must not be reproached for their lapse, and, moreover, if of priestly descent, were to be granted all the privileges they enjoyed before their conversion, such as the one to be 'called up' first to the Reading of the Law.[2]

With Jacob ben Meir (1100–71), commonly known as Rabbenu Tam (Perfect), a grandson of Rashi, and guiding spirit of the school of the Tosafists, the Responsa assumed a new form. Instead of the terse decisions of the Responsa writers of a former age, Rabbenu Tam introduced in his Responsa the dialectics of his school, and the Responsa henceforth became lengthy, learned disquisitions, discussions, and debates.

Rabbenu Tam's rulings include the prohibition of casting a slur on the validity of the bill of divorce after its delivery to the woman. He was also responsible for a regulation forbidding a Jew to drag a fellow Jew before a non-Jewish court, so as to avoid giving outside publicity to Jewish disputes; as well as for the law which requires the husband to return to the wife's family the dowry he has received should the wife die without issue within twelve months of the marriage.

But it was with the beginning of the thirteenth century that we enter upon the classical period of the Responsa literature. These Responsa arose from the peculiar needs of the times. Living amid a mixed population, and subject to the violent current of religious fanaticism and persecution, the Jews had to build up and maintain a religious, social, and juridical and fiscal empire within an empire. The Jewish authorities had no political force of their own on which they could rely. For what little power they needed they had to go to their overlords, but they had one great asset which made the orderliness of communal life within a communal life possible – the authority of the rabbis. Among the greatest rabbinical authorities of that period in Spain were Moses ben Nachman of Gerona (1194–c. 1270); Asher ben Yechiel of Toledo (1250–1328); Solomon Adret of Barcelona (1235–1310); and in Germany, there was Meir ben Baruch of Rothenburg (1220–93). Each one of these rabbis, wrote many long and elaborate responsa on heterogeneous new problems – religious, social, domestic, economic, moral, and political – which were thrown up by the conditions of their times. Whatever their responsa may have contained had formally no binding power, but their judgements and rulings set up judicial precedents that became part of the pattern of Jewish law in its application to the detail of life.

The manifold contributions made to the growth of the *Halachah* since the days of Maimonides called for a fresh digest presenting all the accumulated material and incorporating the different rulings which could serve as new precedents for adaptations of the law to new conditions. Furthermore, Maimonides gives neither sources nor proofs for his rulings, and whilst his Code is unsurpassable as a law-book, it is far too categorical in its pronouncements to leave any room for the further development of the Law. To remedy the situation, Asher ben Yechiel (1250–1327) wrote his famous Halachic Compendium known from his Hebrew initials as *RoSH* (*R*abbi *ASH*er). Born in Germany, he fled the country in 1303 owing to persecutions, and settled in Spain, where, establishing a school in Toledo, he introduced the dialectical method of the French and German Tosafists. His work is modelled after Alfasi's, but he goes beyond Alfasi in that he includes the rulings of Rashi and Maimonides, as well as the material drawn from the *Tosafoth*, which he amplifies by his own argumentations, serving to clarify and supply the reasons for his decisions, in which, often adopting an independent line, he disagrees with Maimonides, Alfasi, and even the Geonim.

The work of Asher was, however, too discursive and elaborate to serve the immediate needs of a practical guide. In order to meet this need, Asher's son, Jacob (1280–1340) compiled his *Sefer ha-Turim* (The Book of Rows), in which, taking Maimonides rather than Alfasi as his model, but omitting all those laws which had fallen into obsolescence since the destruction of the Temple, he systematizes the whole of Jewish Law in so far as it has bearing on practical life, bringing it up to date and also adding differences in practices and customs he had observed in various countries – France, Germany, and Spain.

Jacob's code, commonly called *Tur*, is distinguished for its lucidity and logical arrangement, and falls into four parts: (1) *Orach Chayyim* (The Way of Life), on the laws of the synagogue, prayers, sabbath, feasts, and fasts; (2) *Yoreh Deah* (Teacher of Knowledge), on the dietary laws, charity, respect to parents, mourning, etc. (3) *Eben ha-Ezer* (The Stone of Help), on laws of marriage and divorce, from their religious and civil aspects, etc.; (4) *Choshen ha-Mishpat* (The Breastplate of Judgement), on legal procedure and civil and criminal law.

Jacob's code is based essentially on the decisions of his father. He, however, quotes various other post-Talmudic authorities, particularly Alfasi and Maimonides, whose differences of opinion he records and contrasts, rounding off invariably a discussion by merely stating the view of his father, without however committing himself to a decision.

Within a few years after the death of Jacob ben Asher (1340) tragic changes affected the Jews not only of Germany and France but also of Spain. The fury of Jewish persecutions, which, let loose by the Crusades had gone on without intermission, reached its height at the time of the Black Death in 1348, when entire Jewish communities were wiped out in Germany as well as in France, whence the Jews were finally driven out in 1394. In Spain, where the Jews had had accorded to them better treatment than elsewhere in Europe, the year 1391 saw the bloody days of Seville in which thousands of Jews were massacred, and which were but the prelude to the very long tale of misery and woe that ended with the expulsion in in 1492, when about 300,000 Jews were forced to leave the country. Most of the Spanish exiles found refuge in the Mediterranean provinces of the Turkish Empire, including Palestine, leading to the revival of the land after the comparative sterility of centuries. Some Jews found their way to the New World, which had providentially been discovered by Columbus – said also to have been a Jew – in the very year of the expulsion. On the other hand, the exiles of France and Germany settled partly in Italy, but most of them in Poland, which had served as a haven of refuge since the beginning of the time of the Crusades. One of the effects of this new dispersion was to introduce much confusion in the whole range of Jewish ritual and legal practice. In many places there came into being mixed communities composed of Jews from different countries, with different usages and customs, leading to disputes as to which of these were to prevail. The times cried out for some authoritative word which would be accepted by all Israel. True, there was the *Tur*, which for almost two centuries had answered all the requirements of an authoritative code, but the fact that it studiously refrained, as has been noted, from giving decisions in matters where later authorities differed made the *Tur* more suitable as a source book for a few than as an everyday guide for the many. Besides, since the days of the *Tur* the *Halachah* had been far from dormant. Great authorities had arisen such as Nissim ben Reuben of Gerona (b. *c.* 1340), Yomtob ben Abraham Ishbili (d. 1360); Isaac ben Sheshet Barfat (1326–1408) – all in Spain; Simon Duran (1361–1444) in Algiers; and Joseph Colon (d. 1480) in Italy, in whose hands the *Halachah* had developed and established new precedents which could not be ignored in any code which was to win universal recognition. It was considerations such as these which led to the attempt made by Jacob Berab (1474–1546), an exiled Spanish scholar, to establish in Palestine, where he, together with many other Spanish exiles, had taken refuge, a Sanhedrin, which like its prototype in former times, was to wield supreme authority over all dispersed Jewries in various ways. For some reasons the attempt failed, but not before Berab had 'ordained' as members of his proposed Sanhedrin four scholars, among whom was Joseph Karo (1488–1575), another Spanish refugee, who was one of the foremost legists of his generation. The ordination of Karo was to prove of incalculable significance for the future of Judaism. It filled Karo with a sense of mission – that he was called upon to produce that instrument of unification which Berab's projected institution had failed to achieve. This instrument was to become none other than the *Shulchan Aruch* (Set Table). Taking Alfasi, Maimonides, and Asher as his three standard authorities, Karo decided to accept as authoritative the agreed opinion of any two of the three, except in cases where most of the ancient authorities were against them, and proceeded to fix the law accordingly. In this way Karo in his code, which followed exactly the plan and sequence of the *Tur*, achieved the unification of the Law.

If Maimonides, as previously indicated, exemplifies the power of the discipline of the *Halachah* over the mind of a rationalist, in Joseph Karo we have an exemplification of its power over the mind of a mystic. Karo was a leading light of the Safed school of mysticism and he was subject to mystical experiences. He claimed to have come under the direct guidance of a heavenly mentor (*Maggid*) from whom he received instruction on all sorts of personal matters. Nevertheless, in his legal activities and pursuits Karo remained the clear-brained, logical, and precise thinker, never allowing his occult illuminations to interfere with his exposition, interpretation, and application of the Law. In fact, it was precisely his mysticism that not only inspired his legal code, but also filled him with the courage to decide the law, even against the views of the most important and ancient authorities. His heavenly mentor was nothing less than the *Mishnah* personified, which revealed itself to him because he had devoted himself to its intensive study; and it was his *Mishnah* visions which moved him to do for his times what Rabbi Judah the Prince, the author of the *Mishnah*, had achieved for his own.

The *Shulchan Aruch* was first printed in Venice in 1565 and its appearance was generally hailed as an epoch-making event. Yet, notwithstanding its excellent qualities and extreme usefulness, it had to encounter much opposition, particularly in Poland, to which country the centre of gravity of Jewish life and learning had now shifted from Germany, and with which, in consequence, the recognition or denial of Karo's authority entirely rested.

Karo's code, as we have seen, was based in the main on the decisions of Alfasi, Maimonides, and Asher – all Spanish authorities, with little account being taken of the views of the Franco-German scholars, who also had contributed richly to the development of the *Halachah*. Neither were the decisions of the French Tosafists, except in so far as they had been embodied in those of Asher, considered by Karo. Nor did the great German teachers, such as Jacob Halevi Möllin, known as Maharil (d.1427), Israel Isserlein (d. 1460), and Israel Bruno (1410–80), all great masters of Rabbinic Law, exist as far as Karo's work was concerned. Particularly strong exception was taken to Karo's utter disregard of those local customs and usages which constitute the *Minhag* of the Ashkenazim (which by now included the Jews of Poland, Lithuania, Russia, and Wolhynia), as distinct from that of the Sephardim. This, indeed was a serious omission in a code which was intended to serve the needs of universal Jewry. *Minhag*, as expressive of the true sentiments of the people, has always assumed the character of binding law. The force of *Minhag* as creative of law is already recognized in the Talmud. Wherever codified usage and popular usage, whether in matters of ritual, marriage, and divorce, or civil law come into conflict, the Talmud ruling decides that 'All follows local custom.' Great importance was attached to local custom especially by the German Jews, and this led to the compilation among them of a series of works known as *Minhagim* (Custumals), wherein all the customs of the German Jewish communities were collected and given legal authority. Foremost among these works is Jacob Halevi Möllin's book on *Minhagim*, which is largely responsible for the synagogal ritual in use among the Ashkenazim to the present day. But of this and other similar works there is no trace in Karo's code.

Such were the defects in the *Shulchan Aruch*, which had to

be rectified before it could become generally acceptable. This work was undertaken by Moses Isserles of Cracow (*c.* 1520–72). Recognizing the exceptional merits of Karo's code, he sought to complete its usefulness by adding to it glosses, critical and supplementary, in which he set forth the views of the French and German authorities, wherever they differed from those codified by Karo, and also paid special attention to the *Minhag* that obtained among Ashkenazim.

The Glosses of Isserles have since 1578 invariably appeared within the text of the *Shulchan Aruch*, distinguished only by a smaller type and introduction of the word *Hagah* (Gloss). This composite work gained within half a century of its appearance universal acceptance and constitutes to the present day the most authoritative Code of Jewish Law and practice.

The *Shulchan Aruch*, although essentially a law book, is far from being a compendium of arid legalism, but is permeated with a deep spirit of piety and suffused with ethical wisdom. Its opening paragraph provides the keynote to the whole work:

A man should bestir himself with the strength of a lion to rise early in the morning for the service of his creator, so that he may awake the dawn.

A similar note of piety is struck in the introductory chapters to the laws of prayer:

He who prays must concentrate his mind on the words which he utters with his lips, bethink himself as if the Divine presence were before him, and remove all distracting thoughts until his thought, intention, and devotion remain pure in his prayer. And he should consider that if he were to speak before a king of flesh and blood he would have ordered well his words and enunciate them with precision so that he should not stumble, how much more so, before the King of Kings, the Holy One, Blessed be He, who examines all thoughts. . . Should a strange thought enter his mind during prayer, he should stop until the thought departs and, furthermore, it is necessary for him to reflect on thoughts which humble the heart and direct it towards his Father in Heaven. . .

The *Shulchan Aruch* had the effect of stereotyping in a large measure Jewish religious practice. Yet it did not put an end to the development of Jewish Law. This was due to the fact that in Rabbinism no code is considered final. Behind the codes stands the Talmud, and it is only because the *Shulchan Aruch* is deemed to be in accord with the most correct exposition of the Talmud that it enjoys its exceptional authority. But this very dependence of the *Shulchan Aruch* on the Talmud gives the right to every rabbinic scholar to decide, by reference to Talmudic sources, independently of the *Shulchan Aruch* and even against its rulings; and this right, theoretically recognized, though rarely exercised, has kept the Jewish Law, notwithstanding the acceptance of the *Shulchan Aruch*, in a state of fluidity. Ever since the *Shulchan Aruch* appeared many commentaries have been written on it, as well as numerous Responsa, in elucidation, extension, or adaptation of its rulings as demanded by circumstances, making it thus impossible for the law to stagnate.

Nor did the *Shulchan Aruch* displace the study of the Talmud, as had been feared by leading contemporaries of Karo and Isserles. That this fear was belied was largely the result of the endeavours of a number of outstanding scholars who flourished during the time when the *Shulchan Aruch* was fast winning its way to becoming the universal handbook of Jewish life. Chiefly under the inspiration of such men as Meir ben Gedalia of Lublin (1559–1610), Samuel Eliezer Edels (1565–1632), and Yomtov Lippman Heller (1579–1654), the study of the Talmud came to attract in Poland, where it had already reached great heights, larger multitudes than ever before. Talmudic centres (*Yeshivoth*), great and small, sprang up in all parts of Poland, Lithuania, and Wolhynia, and by the middle of the seventeenth century there was hardly a community in these lands in which a Talmudic school did not exist. In these schools new techniques of Talmudic studies were developed, involving the exercise of extreme mental ingenuity which held a special fascination for young minds, and which had considerable influence on the subsequent development of Talmudic studies – an influence which persists to the present day. From these schools, too, emanated most of the leading rabbis and scholars in the Ashkenazic communities throughout the world. The Sephardic communities, on the other hand, relied for their spiritual leaders and teachers on the products of the *Yeshivoth* in the Orient, particularly of those in the Holy Land – Jerusalem, Hebron, and Safed.

The *Shulchan Aruch* has certainly fulfilled all the expectations of its author. It has proved the greatest single cohesive force in Judaism, and imposed upon the Jews a uniformity of purpose and action which preserved them to the present day, amid all their diverse loyalties and conflicting interests, as one people on earth.

Standing in direct line of development of Talmudic teaching, Rabbinism in the middle ages did not concern itself merely with the ritual and the legal side of Judaism – the *Halachah*, but also showed the same wholehearted devotion to its complementary and ethical side – the *Aggadah*.

This devotion expressed itself in the form of an extensive ethical literature to which the greatest legists contributed. The aim of this class of literature was to cultivate inwardness of the precepts and duties, whether ritual or ethical, commanded by Judaism. It sought to inculcate piety and virtue of the highest order. Particular stress was laid on the fear and love of God, human love and human fellowship, purity of action, speech, and thought, meekness, truthfulness, and honesty in all relationships, Jewish and non-Jewish.

Reference has already been made in a previous chapter to the ethical work of Bachya ibn Pakuda, the philosopher, and that of Judah ha-Chasid, the mystic, both of which were widely read and studied. In this context attention is drawn to a few of the more important works of the later period which had exercised considerable influence on the Jews and Jewish ethical conduct.

The earliest among these works is the *Shaare Teshubah* (Gates of Repentance) by Jonah Girundi (d. 1263), who wrote copious commentaries on the Code of Alfasi. His ethical work, as indicated by its title, is devoted to the subject of penitence and self-improvement, religious and moral, and is studied by many devout Jews to the present day during the period between the New Year's Day and the Day of Atonement.

Modelled after Bachya's ethical work is the *Sefer ha-Yashar*

(Book of the Upright), by Zechariah ha-Yewani (the Greek), (d. *c.* 1394). In this work the author, who hailed from Greece, describes the inner obstacles that are a bar to a good and righteous life, such as indulgence and pleasure, anger, laziness, flattery, arrogance, etc. and offers advice how to overcome them.

Among the most esteemed and popular of medieval Hebrew ethical works is the *Menorath ha-Maor* (The Lamp of Light) by Isaac Abohab (*c.* 1492) who was one of the leading Talmudic scholars of his day, and an author of a number of legal works. The *Menorath ha-Maor* consists largely of religious and moral maxims which are derived from the Talmud and Midrash, but these are arranged skilfully under a variety of subjects, and interwoven with many beautiful parables and stories, and personal reflections of the author, which impart to the work its appealing charm that gained for it the greatest popularity among men as well as women, for whose benefit it was translated into Judaeo-German (Yiddish), the mother-tongue of the majority of the Jews in Eastern Europe.

Another very popular, though not original, compilation of ethical content is that of Jacob ben Chabib (beginning of the sixteenth century), in which are gathered all the Aggadic passages of the Babylonian Talmud presented in the sequence in which they appear in the original. Also widely read was Elijah di Vidas (d. 1518), *Reshith-Chochmah* (The Beginning of Wisdom), a work which, tinged with mysticism, deals with the fear and love of God, holiness, meekness, penitence, and personal and social morality.

Much in vogue, too, was the anonymous work *Orchoth Zadikkim* (The Ways of the Righteous), which has for its purpose to instruct man how to train the inner virtues, with which he is endowed, in the service of God and his fellowmen. At the basis of all right action is the fear of God, ' Fear of God is the bond which joins the virtues into one common whole and is like a thread which holds together a string of pearls. The moment you loosen the thread, the pearls scatter. Likewise, if you are lax in the matter of the fear of God, the virtues will become ineffective.'[3]

Serving to the present day as a textbook for those who aspire to moral and religious self-discipline is the *Mesillath Yesharim* (The Path of the Upright) by Moses Chaim Luzzatto (1707–47), which maps out the path of progress in saintliness.

Included in this class of literature are the Ethical Wills (*Zawwaoth*), composed by parents as a last testament to their children. Of these many are extant, but the best known example of this kind is the Testament by Asher ben Yechiel (the legist mentioned earlier in this chapter), which has found its way into a number of prayer books for the recital of a specific portion thereof on each day of the week.

In the presence of the superabundant wealth of ethical resources available in the Talmud and Midrash, Jewish medieval ethical literature was left little opportunity for independent creation. Yet, notwithstanding these limitations, it displays a purity and magnitude which is hard to match in any other ethical literature in the world. Impressive in this connexion is the testimony of a certain German university professor of the last century who, coming across the ethical Testament of Asher, was led to declare that 'nothing like it could have been expected, even from a Christian of his age.'[4]

A few examples cited from that Testament, where many could be adduced, should suffice to confirm this verdict:

Be not ready to quarrel; avoid oaths and passionate adjurations, excess of laughter and outbursts of wrath . . . Avoid all dealings wherein there is a lie. . . . Cut from under thee all mere human supports, and make not gold the foremost longing of your life; for that is the first step to idolatry. Rather give money than words; and as to ill words, see that thou place them in the scale of understanding before they leave thy lips. What has been uttered in thy presence, even though not told as secret, let it not pass from thee to others. And if one tell thee a tale, say not to him that thou hast heard it all before. Do not fix thine eyes too much on one who is far above thee in wealth, but on those who are behind thee in worldly fortune. . . . Do not struggle vaingloriously for the small triumph of showing thyself in the right and a wise man in the wrong; thou art not one whit the wiser therefor. . . . Be the first to extend courteous greeting to every one, whatever be his faith; provoke not to wrath one of another belief than thine.[5]

These, indeed, are fine thoughts, finely expressed, and are typical of the ethical gems that fill to the brim the medieval rabbinic Ethical writings.

To this class of Ethical writings belongs also the collections of religious and moral discourses (*Drush*) that began to make their appearance in the sixteenth century and have since grown to a voluminous literature. Originally delivered as messages to congregations, the object of these discourses, each of which unfolds some central theme, with logical sequence and linguistic precision, was to fortify and deepen the religious consciousness, ennoble the feelings, purify the impulses, and, at the same time, condemn prevalent religious and moral laxities and abuses, whether in individual or communal life. As such, these discourses may be said to have laid the foundation of the modern Jewish sermon.

The earliest of such collections is the *Nefuzoth Yehudah* (The Scattered of Judah) by Judah Moscato (first half of the sixteenth century), who is the most brilliant exponent and guide of this type of discourse. A younger contemporary of Moscato, and greatly influenced by him, was Azaria Figo (b. 1579), whose discourses are characterized by the social visions and spiritual intensity of the prophets. Both Moscato and Figo were Italians, but their method soon spread to Poland where, Solomon Ephraim Lunschitz (d. 1610), by virtue of the literary quality of his works and the spiritual depth of his thought, became its most prominent representative.

Medieval rabbinism was also responsible for the bulk of Hebrew devotional literature. Continuing on the lines of the early Palestinian *payyetanim*, its foremost representatives furnished much of the synagogue poetry in its different moods, joyous, solemn, and sad, for all holidays and fast days as well as special Sabbaths of the year. Some of the greatest liturgical poets, such as Meshullam ben Kalonymus (tenth century), and Simon ben Isaac ben Abun (eleventh century), were all renowned rabbis. Not a few of the liturgical poems were composed by Rabbenu Gershom and Rashi; so were many of the Tosafists liturgical poets; and one of the best known and beloved hymns sung on the eve of the Day of Atonement in the synagogue, was composed by the English Tosafist, Yomtob of York.[6]

It is also to medieval rabbinism that we owe those numerous Bible commentaries in which *Halachah* and *Aggadah* are linked together in perfect unity. Foremost among these commentaries is that of Rashi, which, distinguished by its clarity and its harmonious blending to a unique degree of the derived sense of the text with its simple, natural explanation, has made available an accumulated heritage of Biblical knowledge of some three thousand years not only to scholars but also to the masses. Not less prized among Jews than his commentary on the Talmud, Rashi's Commentary on the Bible also influenced greatly the Christian world. Nicholas de Lyra (1265–1349), who is an important link between the Middle Ages and the Reformation, quotes Rashi constantly in his *Commentaries*, which, in turn, was one of the main sources Luther used in his translation; and many of Rashi's interpretations entered in the King James' version of the Bible.

Rashi, had no capable imitators, but following him there arose a succession of Biblical commentators, each of whom had a distinctive approach in his exposition of Scripture. Abraham Ibn Ezra, born in Cordova or Toledo (1092–1167), combined in his Bible commentary the scientific method with due regard for traditional authority. The Tosafist, Samuel ben Meir (1085–1175), a grandson of Rashi, laid in his commentary on the Pentateuch great emphasis on the *Peshat* (literal meaning). The great Talmudist and Kabbalist, Moses ben Nachman of Gerona (1194–c. 1270),[7] in his great commentary on the Pentateuch, besides giving a simple explanation of the text, based on true philology, combines a purely rationalistic approach to the Bible with a search for its hidden meanings. David Kimchi of Narbonne (1160–1235), developed the strictly grammatical method, and by his lucidity and thoroughness established for his commentaries supremacy in the field of Biblical exegesis. His works exercised considerable influence on Christian Hebraists at the time of the Reformation, and the translators of the English Authorized Version owed so much to him that they are said as it were to 'have sat at the feet of Kimchi'.

An entirely new method in Biblical exposition was introduced by Don Isaac Abrabanel (1437–1508) – the consideration of the historical factor in scriptural narratives. He accordingly cites historical and political parallels in illustration of the events described in the Hebrew scriptures; whilst Moses ben Hayyim Alshech of Safed (1508–1600), a disciple of Karo, endeavoured in his commentary, usually cited under the title 'The Holy Alshech', to strike the happy medium between the rationalistic and mystical exposition of the Biblical texts.

The unity of *Halachah* and *Aggadah*, external observance and inward piety, which medieval rabbinism strove to maintain and foster, prepared the ground for the rise of that extraordinary religious movement – Chassidism, which, starting in the middle of the eighteenth century in some remote corner in the Ukraine, spread like wildfire over surrounding countries and within a few decades embraced almost half of world Jewry.

Contrary to what is often asserted, Chassidism was no revolutionary movement. It neither wished to free the people from the legalistic bonds of rabbinism, which in fact it sought to enforce with even greater rigour, nor did it introduce any new fundamental ideas into Judaism. Its twin parents were Rabbinism and *Kabbalah*, and it is in these progenitors that is to be found all that Chassidism thought and taught.

The important contribution of Chassidism lay rather in the strong emphasis it gave to certain ideas, whilst relegating others to the background. By these means Chassidism injected a new and vital power into Jewish religious life, with transforming effect upon those men and women who came under its spell and influence.

Fastening upon the Talmudic principle that 'the Holy one, blessed be He, requires the heart' (T. Sanhedrin, 106b), Chassidism directed its appeal to the feelings and emotions rather than the mind and intellect. This appeal was especially adapted to the needs of the times in which Chassidism took rise. The Cossack persecutions in 1648 under Chmielnicki, in which about a quarter of a million Jews are said to have perished, brought about social and economic stagnation for the Jews of Poland. The people perceived in their sufferings the 'birth pangs' of Messianism, and with this their mind became receptive to the Shabbethai Zvi (1626–1716) Messianic movement, which swept masses into a frenzy with false hopes of redemption and speedy release from all their trials and tribulations. The collapse of this movement wrought even greater moral and spiritual havoc among the people. But whereas the learned could fall back on the study of the Torah to sustain them in their disillusionment, there was no such resource for the uneducated and untutored. It was to these simple, ignorant folk, who formed the bulk of the Jewish masses, particularly in the Ukraine, that Chassidism, of which Israel Baal Shemtob Besht (1700–60) was the founder, offered a way of escape from the degeneracy and despair to which they had succumbed.

Central to the teachings of Besht was the love and concern for the uneducated man, commonly described as *Am-haaretz* (people of the soil). Characteristic of this, his attitude, is his declaration:

Like the soil, everyone treads upon the Jew, but God had in this very soil put the power to bring forth all kinds of plants and fruits wherewith to sustain all His creatures. In the soil are also to be found all such treasures as gold, silver, diamonds and all other precious and important metals and minerals So too are the Jewish folks: they are full of the finest and most precious qualities that man can possess, even the most ordinary among them. As our Sages said: 'Even the unworthy among you are full of virtue as a pomegranate is full of seeds!'[8]

Theoretically considered, the teachings of Besht were based on the Kabbalistic doctrines of Luria. Affirming the Lurianic doctrine of *Tikkun*, Chassidism stressed the need for the restoration of harmonies in order to effect the redemption of Israel, the *Shechinah*, and the whole of creation. But instead of the Lurianic appeal to Apocalyptic visions of Messianic deliverance in the future, Chassidism directs the mind to the redemptive power of God in the present and in the context of everyday life. Without weakening the hope in the Messianic redemption, Chassidism taught that every present moment was a moment of redemption for the individual, leading to the ultimate consummation for the whole. With this message, Chassidism sought to lift the masses out of the slough of despondency into which they had fallen. Their Messianic expectations had surely been falsified, but there still was going on *here* and *now* a process of blissful redemption in which every individual could participate. For this purpose no special qualifications were necessary. Every individual, whatever his status or capacity, could be caught up in this redemptive process. All that he needs is a heart willing to cleave to God and to enter into communion with Him. Let him but follow these divine volitions of the heart and he will help to bring about the restoration of harmonies on earth as in Heaven, and thereby secure a healing, both for his ailing body and ailing soul. The ideal means of communion with God is prayer – prayer recited with exalted joy and in a state of ecstatic fervour (*hithlahabuth*) in which man forgets self and all his surroundings and concentrates all his thoughts and feelings on union with God. Such a state of ecstasy is of incalculable consequence, as it is capable of breaking through and over-ruling the normal laws of the universe with wonder-working effects in the world of everyday existence.

To attain this state of ecstasy, Chassidism resorts to artificial stimuli, such as strong bodily motions, loud chantings, and even dancing. And what applies to prayer, applies equally to the precepts which form also an ideal ladder of communion. In all religious acts, the chief thing is the ecstatic fervour in which they are performed, rather than the acts themselves.

This emphasis laid by Chassidism on the fulfilment of the present involved of necessity a break with asceticism of the Lurianic *Kabbalah*, as no fulfilment in the present, at least as far as the masses are concerned, is possible without satisfaction of the claims of daily existence. Thus it is that Chassidism ascribed a positive virtue to physical enjoyments of life. Man, it urged, must eat, drink, and at all times be joyful, cheerful, happy, and merry. Sadness in any form was to be eschewed; even if man had committed a sin he must not give himself over to sadness. He should rather forget about it and resume his rejoicing in God.

The joy of life in Chassidic teaching is grounded on its peculiar doctrine of Divine omnipresence. Taking over the

Lurianic doctrine of *Zimzum*, Chassidism modified it to denote not a withdrawal of God into Himself, in order to make room for His creation, but rather an adaptation of the power of His Infinite Light to the capacity of endurance in His creatures, in the same way as 'a loving father adapts his words to the understanding of his small child whom through his love he wishes to instruct.'[9] On this interpretation, the initial act of Creation did not involve, as in the Lurianic system, the formation of a dark vacuum, but merely a diminution in the intensity of the Divine Light. There is thus no place in Creation which is not illumined to a great or lesser degree by the Divine. The sparks of divinity permeate everything in nature, organic or inorganic, and inheres in all creatures, good or bad. But if there be sparks of the Divine everywhere and in everything, matter as such cannot be hostile or opposed to God, but, on the contrary, must be something of great worth and value to be embraced and enjoyed. All that man needs is to enjoy the pleasures of life in all purity and sanctity as manifestations of the divine, and thereby help to transform the material into the spiritual or, in the Kabbalistic phrase, 'cause the sparks to ascend' and become united to the Infinite Light. 'Only ordinary people think that they can serve God solely by prayers and Torah. In reality it is not so, for His dominion ruleth over all, and even gross matter can serve as a vehicle of Divine worship. Just as there is a significance in spiritual matters – in the Torah, prayers and the performance of precepts – in that they serve to elevate the fallen sparks, so there is the same significance in earthly things – eating, drinking, and all kinds of work.'[10]

Moreover, there is greater merit in serving God also by means of earthly things and the functions and appetites of the senses than solely by things spiritual; for, by the former method, the earthly is sublimated into the heavenly, and the 'evil impulse' is redeemed and transformed into the good.

The Chassidic doctrine of *Zimzum* also determined its attitude to evil. Evil in Chassidic teaching is merely relative, not absolute. It is not the negative of good, having its source in darkness, as in the Lurianic *Kabbalah*, but a lower grade of the good, owing to the diminution of the Divine Light illumining

It. Without this Divine Light, evil could not exist. But if, in the last analysis, it is God that gives evil its vitality, surely there are extenuating circumstances for man's weakness in falling into sin. No longer, therefore, need the sinner despair of forgiveness. Even though he sinned grievously, God who, as it were, aided him, will still be with him and pardon his transgression. By these and similar teachings Chassidism brought to the simple folk a consciousness of the nearness of God and of His redemptive activity that served to uplift their spirit and raise their self-esteem, and at the same time, to inspire in them all the religious virtues that spring from such a consciousness – the fear and love of God, trust in His goodness, self-surrender to His will, as well as that inner contentment which remains unshaken amid all the griefs and tragedies of life.

The message of Chassidism, however, was as much social-ethical as it was religious. Its doctrines, particularly the one relating to the Omnipresence of God, formed the basis of some of the distinguishing features of Chassidism in social ethics. Great stress is particularly laid on the love of man. All men, irrespective of their merits and qualities, must be loved. Even sinners and evil-doers must be loved; for they too have in them sparks of divinity; so must a personal enemy be loved, yea, as much as the dearest friend. Love, however, can fulfil itself only through humility, 'for only the truly humble man in heart will not feel it a hardship to love one of the wicked, thinking: for all his wickedness, he is better than I am; nor will he be able to disregard a request when he is in a position to grant it.'[11] From these virtues flow all other social virtues which Chassidism seeks to instil: unselfishness, industry in doing good, peaceableness, charity in judgement, truthfulness in speech, integrity, honesty, and sincerity in all dealings with fellow-man.

Thus did Chassidism proclaim an affirmative philosophy of life which, though warmly emotional and intensely mystical, was yet highly ethical, and rich in the joys of life.

Notwithstanding the power of its appeal, Chassidism would not have spread with such rapidity nor attained such dimensions but for the extraordinary galaxy of saint-mystics, veritable human dynamos, it produced during the first fifty years of its existence. Apart from its founder, Besht, there was first and foremost his disciple and successor Dov Baer of Meseritz (1710–72), who was commonly known as the Great Maggid (Preacher). Possessed of a powerful gift of oratory and talent for organization, he sent out 'missionaries' to all parts of the Ukraine, and thus won numerous souls for Chassidism, making it a real mass movement. Dov Baer introduced the concept of the *Zaddik*, the perfectly righteous, which came to occupy a central position in the subsequent history of Chassidism. Besht had taught that prayer was possible for all and that its efficacy was not conditioned by any special qualifications. Dov Baer, on the other hand, did not believe that the average man, engulfed in the cares and distractions of daily life, could attain the height of ecstatic fervour which close communion with God demanded. Only the perfectly righteous, the *Zaddik*, who can free his mind from all distracting thoughts and earthly things, could concentrate upon God and offer effective prayer and supplication. The duty, therefore, of ordinary mortals is to attach themselves to the *Zaddik*. By the force of his example the *Zaddik* can help and develop the spiritual faculties of his adherents, whilst at the same time, through the mediation of his communion with God, he can secure favours for them in both earthly and heavenly matters.

The concept of the *Zaddik* was further developed by a younger disciple of Besht, Jacob Joseph of Polonnoye (d. *c.* 1775), who was the first literary exponent of Chassidism. The *Zaddik*, whose main task it was to redeem evil, had, Jacob Joseph maintained, to come at times into contact with evil-doers and even descend to their level in order to raise them to a higher state. This idea served to raise the *Zaddik* above all criticism, any action of his, however strange and startling, being imputed to a holy and mystical motive. Thus arose the *Zaddik* cult to which Chassidism owed some of its most original fruits. Unlike the rabbi, the *Zaddik* was distinguished not by his intellectual attainments and knowledge, but by his charismatic gifts that stamped themselves over his whole personality. Crediting him with supernatural powers, the followers of the *Zaddik* turned to him at all times for help and counsel, and the *Zaddik*, taking upon himself the whole weight of their sorrows and anxieties, would pray for them, strengthen them, and fill them with new faith, fresh courage, and assured hope.

Characteristic of the *Zaddikim* is that they each made a speciality of a particular quality or activity. Some of the *Zaddikim* were distinguished for their fervent devotions, some for their ecstatic visions, some for their psychic powers, some for their heavenly purity, some for their miraculous works; others for their intense humility; others for their resolute trust in God, others for their boundless charity, others for their compassion for sinners, whilst others again for their self-effacing love. In illustration, mention might be made of Pinchas of Koritz (d. 1791) as exemplar of compassion for sinners. He it was who declared that we should love the evil-doer more in order to compensate for the lack of the power of love he himself has caused in his place in the world;[12] whilst Moses Leib of Sassow (d. 1807) may be taken as a veritable exemplar of self-effacing love. Sitting beside all the sick boys of his city, nursing and tending them, he once said: 'He who cannot suck the matter from the boils of a child sick with the plague has not yet gone half-way up the height of love for his fellow men.'[13]

What is regarded as the greatest originality in Zaddikism is the intimate communal life centring round the personality of the *Zaddik*. Even to the present day the house of the *Zaddik*, more often called the *Rebbe* (Teacher, Leader), is the meeting-place of the Chassidim. On Sabbath and Festivals, many of his Chassidim join the *Zaddik* at his table for meals, during which he expounds the ideals of Chassidic life. Of particular solemnity is the 'third meal' of the Sabbath Day, which is marked by special songs in which the *Zaddik*, leading in a melancholy voice, recites some mystic hymns, verse by verse, which the Chassidim repeat after him. On the High Holidays, particularly, the Chassid even from afar will make pilgrimage to the *Zaddik*, often taking with him his wife and children. On these Holy Days, the prayers of the *Zaddik* and the unity among his Chassidim reach the highest pitch of fervour. This community in worship expresses itself in a fellow-feeling of common helpfulness and concern. The Chassidim feel as one family, ever ready to assist each other in their need, and sharing each others' sorrow no less than their joys.

Dov Baer gathered a large number of disciples, according to tradition as many as three hundred, most of whom played an important part in the spread of Chassidism, either in the role of *Zaddikim* or by means of their writings.

Mendel of Vitebsk (d. 1788), one of the oldest disciples of Dov Baer, occupies a unique place in the history of Chassidism in that he transplanted the movement to Palestine, when in 1777 he went up with a contingent of three hundred Chassidim and settled in Safed and Tiberias, to be followed by numerous other Chassidim from Eastern Europe, thus laying the foundation of what was to become the Zionist movement, culminating in the rise of the Jewish State

Levi Isaac of Berditchev (d. 1809), another disciple of Dov Baer, is distinguished for his all-consuming love for Israel. He is known as the Intercessor of Israel before their Father in Heaven, and his communions with God were characterized by a daring intimacy. His following communion-piece may serve as an example:

Good morning to Thee, Lord of the Universe!
I, Levi-Yitzchok, son of Sarah, of Berditchev
Have come to Thee in a law-suit
On behalf of Thy people Israel.
What has Thou against Thy people Israel?
No matter what happens, it is,
  'Command the Children of Israel!'
No matter what happens, it is:
  'Say to the Children of Israel!'
No matter what happens, it is:
  'Speak to the Children of Israel!'
Father dear! How many other people are there in the world?
Babylonians, Persians, and Edomites!
The Germans - what do they say?
'Our King is a King!'
The English - what do they say?
'Our Sovereign is a Sovereign!'
And I, Levi-Yitzchok, son of Sarah, of Berditchev, say:
Hallowed and magnified be Thy name, O God!

Unique as a master of tales and fantasies in the whole of Jewish literature is Nachman of Bratzslav (1772–1811), a great-grandson of Besht. His tales full of rich and wild imagination are still the most popular of their kind. They are all charged with a deep spiritual and ethical content, although their significance may not be always evident. One of the most famous of the shorter fantasies is 'The Stone on the Mountain':

At one end of the world there stands a mountain. The mountain crest is crowned by a Stone. From the Stone these gushes forth a Fountain. Now, everything is dowered with a heart. So has the world a Heart. The World-Heart stands pulsating at the other end, pining and longing continually with mighty longing to get to the Fountain. The Fountain, too, in response, yearns for the World-Heart. But neither can the World-Heart get nearer the Fountain, nor the Fountain nearer to the World-Heart. Were they but to draw closer to one another, the Mountain crest would soon be obscured from the sight of the World-Heart. And no longer being able to behold the crest and the Fountain, the World-Heart would cease to beat, and would expire. With the World-Heart stilled, the whole World would be undone. The Heart is the life of the World, and all that it contains: and thus the World-Heart dare not approach the Fountain, but must for ever stand at a distance, and strain itself with mighty longing.

Shneur Zalman of Ladi (1746–1813), another disciple of Dov Baer, was the philosopher of Chassidism. Born in Lozna, a town in Lithuania which was a veritable stronghold of Jewish learning, Shneur Zalman, after obtaining complete mastery in Talmudic lore, made for Meseritz and, coming under the influence of the Great Maggid, embraced Chassidism which he resolved to introduce into his native Lithuania. But the Chassidism that proceeded from Meseritz was all emotion and feeling. Even the theoretical doctrines on which it was based had little of the speculative element in them. Everything was taken for granted. Nothing was questioned, much less critically investigated or analysed. All that mattered, to give an example, was the belief that there were sparks of divinity everywhere and in everything, in good as well as in bad. How precisely such a notion could be reconciled with the fundamental tenet of divine holiness was of no concern to the Chassidim. Whilst such an attitude was well suited to the mentality of the uneducated Ukrainians, it could by no means commend itself to the intellectually-minded Lithuanians. This led Shneur Zalman to form a new type of Chassidism in which theoretical doctrine was presented in a clear understandable system of thought, and emotion, controlled by the powers of reason. This was the Chassidism of Chabad, a term derived from the Hebrew initials of the three highest *Sefiroth*: *Chochmah* (Wisdom), *Binah* (Understanding), and *Daath* (Knowledge) – wisdom denoting the formation of an idea; understanding, the working out of its details; knowledge, its full comprehension by the mind. Such are the thought-forms of the Chabad, which, applied to the Chassidic doctrines concerning God, the soul, and man's duties in life, Shneur Zalman set forth with considerable acumen and depth of thought in his *Sefer Tanya* (Book of Teaching), which became the textbook of the Chabad Chassidim, as well as in several of his other writings.

In consonance with its intellectual approach, Chabad attaches great importance to the study of the Talmud; and the *Zaddik*, instead of being regarded in Chabad as quasi-mediator between man and God and a worker of miracles, is simply the venerated teacher – venerated because of his great scholarship and knowledge of the Torah. The full glow of ecstatic attitude towards prayer is nevertheless maintained, as is the intimacy of Chassidic communal life in which the *Rebbe* forms the living centre. As in all other Chassidic groups, song plays an important part in the religious life of the Chabad. Shneur Zalman himself had composed a number of religious songs, some of them revolving round the word '*Tatenyu*' (Darling Father) – a term by which God is often addressed in Chabad. Most popular among the Chabad is Shneur Zalman's song of the Torah, of trust in God, and of the longing and love for Him – a song without words which came to be known as the Rebbe's *Niggun* (Melody). Shneur Zalman also indited a number of meditations; and in moments of spiritual awakening, he was wont to cry out 'Master of the Universe! I desire neither Paradise nor Thy bliss in the world to come. I desire Thee and Thee alone'.[14]

As a product of Rabbinism, Chassidism, despite the anti-nomian tendencies which are the characteristic of all mysticism, stood firmly rooted in the *Shulchan Aruch*, even going so far as to add to the minutiae of ritual and ceremonial beyond the requirements of the Code. It nevertheless effected a number of changes in the Liturgy. Although originating with the Ashkenazim, Chassidism adopted the Luria Prayer Book which in essence follows the Sephardic ritual,[15] because it was considered of greater efficacy for bringing about the restoration – *Tikkun*. Prayers began with them when they had brought themselves, by means of introspective meditations, into a proper devotional frame of mind. They consequently paid little regard to the prescribed hours for prayers, maintaining that you cannot order a child when to speak with its father, such restraints being fit only for slaves. They also inserted new prayers and new hymns of their own, and did away with the salaried Reader, the prayers being recited either by the *Zaddik* himself, or by one of the distinguished laymen of their group. They also performed frequent ablutions, many of them being particular in doing so before morning prayers.

As long as Chassidism was content to restrict its activities among the uneducated Ukrainians, it was allowed to unfold itself without let or hindrance. But no sooner did it attempt to conquer the Lithuanian strongholds of Torah, than it had to encounter the bitterest opposition. The opponents of Chassidism, who came to be known as *Mithnaggedim*, perceived in Chassidism a threat to organized Jewish life, and its intellectual discipline, as maintained and fostered by the study of Torah. What particularly drew the fire of the *Mithnaggedim* was the cult of Zaddikism in which the religious leader (*Zaddik*, or *Rebbe*), by virtue of his very personality, and irrespective of his knowledge, came to be considered as authoritative a source of inspiration as the Torah itself; and with the rise in the multiplicity of *Zaddikim*, each one claiming and receiving the exclusive allegiance of his group of followers, there was a real danger that Chassidism would lead to the atomization of the Jewish entity into tribal sects.

A leader in the opposition to Chassidism was Elijah ben

Solomon, known as the Gaon of Vilna (1720–97). Although himself a past master in Kabbalistic lore, he was nevertheless uncompromising in his hostility to Chassidism, and it was mainly due to his resolute stand and his tremendous influence that Chassidism was led to shed its extravagances and to accord to the knowledge of Torah its proper and rightful place. In this way, Chassidism, without losing any of its peculiar warmth and enthusiasm, became one of the major pillars of support of Rabbinism and, at the same time, one of its finest and richest products. Notable indeed are the gifts which Chassidism has made not only to the religious and spiritual life of the Jew, but also to his general cultural life. It has enriched the Hebrew language with a new and varied terminology for the dissemination of its concepts among the people. It has created a rich treasury of wonderful tales which have won the greatest admiration of poets and writers of fiction. It has brought into being a new ethic which has attracted the attention of scholars and thinkers; and today Chassidism has gained recognition as an important factor making for the rejuvenation of contemporary Jewish life.

In this connexion, mention should be made of the extraordinary influence exercised by the Chassidism of the Chabad School known as Lubavicher[16] which, from its present quarters (since 1940) in New York under the direction of Rabbi Menachem Mendel of the Shneurson family, forms one of the most intense religious brotherhoods in the modern world. With a particular flair for organization, they have established their own schools and publishing houses, and train missionary-minded mystics, whom they send out all over the world, and who are particularly successful in North Africa and Israel, where they bring back many of the secular nationalists among the youth to religious life and practice.

The Gaon of Vilna was the greatest intellectual and spiritual force in Rabbinic Judaism since Maimonides. His very existence raised the whole intellectual and spiritual level of Lithuanian Jewry, and exercised an elevating influence far beyond the boundaries of the country in which he lived. He was wholly a native and authentic product of Rabbinism, and least influenced by foreign thought. His all-controlling passion was the Torah, in which he saw the source of all self-perfection. Yet he demanded the widest secular education, declaring that 'If a man be ignorant of the secular sciences, he will be a hundredfold more ignorant of the Torah, for both Torah and science go together.'[17] He wrote over seventy works, covering practically the whole spiritual heritage of Judaism, Bible, Talmud, Mishnah, Tosefta, Midrashim – Halachic and Aggadic – *Kabbalah*, and, what is perhaps his most important work, a commentary on the *Shulchan Aruch*. He was also the first to introduce the critical study of Talmudic and kindred texts, and many of his emendations, which have indeed unsealed a great part of the earlier Talmudic literature, have been confirmed by subsequently discovered manuscripts. Nor did he hesitate to interpret pre-Talmudic texts, independently of the Talmud, or to disregard a rule of the *Shulchan Aruch* when he thought it was not in agreement with the proper Talmudic interpretation. He also wrote books on astronomy, trigonometry, algebra, and grammar. His educational methods gained wide application throughout the Lithuanian schools and left an unmistakable stamp and character on the intellectual standing of Russian Jewry.

Hand in hand with his gigantic intellect went a great heart. His charity knew no bounds, and often he sold all his furniture to assist the poor, or gave away his last meal. He was also possessed of a rich inner life. An ascetic by nature, he was always in a joyful mood and in a state of spiritual exaltation. The service of God expressed through study and worship was for him life's fulfilment, and in the joy he experienced in this service he found the greatest recompense for his exertions, requiring no other. 'Elijah,' he used to say, 'can serve God without a reward.' If there is any doubt about the vitality of rabbinism, its inwardness, and its humanism (in the best sense of the word), the Gaon of Vilna is the most complete answer.

A more direct consequence of the Chmielnicki atrocities was the reversal in the current of Jewish immigration which henceforth flowed from East to the West. Many of the exiles from Poland settled in Germany where, from the time of John

Reuchlin (1455–1527) and his fellow-humanists, the Jews though still confined to their ghettos were treated less ferociously. Some were received in France, many more in Moravia and Bohemia; not a few in Holland, which had been a haven of refuge for the Jews from Spain and Portugal, who fled from the fires of the Inquisition. The influx into Western Europe of large masses of penniless Jewish fugitives from the East made the need for the search of a new land of refuge more desperately urgent than ever. Moved by the plight of his brethren, Menasseh ben Israel (1604–57), a leading Rabbi of Amsterdam, scholar, physician, and mystic, turned his eyes towards the neighbouring 'Land of the Isle', whence the Jews had been expelled in 1290, and thanks to his persuasive eloquence and tireless efforts a handful of Jews were permitted by Cromwell in 1656 to settle in England. The earliest settlers were Sephardi Jews who hailed directly and indirectly from the Iberian Peninsula. They soon organized themselves into a community and within less than ten years of the Resettlement, invited Jacob Sasportas of Amsterdam (1610–98), a Talmudist of great repute, to become their spiritual head Haham (Sage). Sasportas was the author of a most important volume of Responsa, which deals, *inter alia*, with the question of the personal and religious status of the Marranos (forced converts), with which were often mixed up intricate problems of inheritance, marriage, and divorce. But it was as a relentless opponent of the Shabbethai Zvi movement, the pretensions of which he more than anyone else succeeded in exposing, that he has carved out for himself a niche in Jewish history.

Sasportas, who took up his position in 1664, remained in England only for one year, having left it for Amsterdam on the outbreak of the Great Plague; yet the impression he made on contemporary London Jewry was indelible. By far the most eminent of the spiritual heads the Sephardi ever had was David Nieto (1664–1738), one of the most accomplished Jews of his age, distinguished equally as Talmudist, philosopher, poet, and mathematician. A voluminous author, his most enduring work is the *Kuzari ha-Sheni* (Second Kuzari), a work modelled after Judah Halevi's classic,[18] and written in defence of the Oral

Law. Nieto was also the first to fix the beginning of the Sabbath Eve for the latitude of England. On the Continent the leading Talmudic authority of that period was Zvi Hirsch Ashkenazi (1660–1718), who, born in Vilna, was at various times the spiritual head respectively of Altona, Amsterdam, and finally Lemberg. His Responsa are considered among the classics of this class of literature, and in one of them he defended Nieto against the charge of Spinozistic tendencies. Ashkenazi, from his seat in Altona, exercised great influence over English Jewry and was equally revered by the Sephardi as well as by the Ashkenazi who, hailing from Germany and Poland, followed at their heels and set up the first Ashkenazi congregation in London in 1690.

The eighteenth century witnessed in Western countries a whole galaxy of Rabbinic giants who have left their mark on subsequent generations. Among these might be mentioned the towering figure of Ezekiel Landau (1713–73) of Prague, whose work *Noda bi-Yehudah* occupies one of the highest pinnacles in the entire range of the later medieval Responsa literature. Another famous Talmudist was Jacob Emden (1697–1776), of Altona. A veritable genius, he was the author of many works of a wide variety of interests, including Responsa and a Commentary on the Prayer Book, in which he incorporated *inter alia* Kabbalistic notes. His Kabbalism notwithstanding, he did not hesitate to denounce the Zohar as being for the most part the work of an impostor. In his attack on the Zohar, Emden was actuated by the desire to bring into disrepute a work on which the Shabbatheans had largely based their claims. The countless tragedies which Shabbatheanism had caused to Jewish moral and spiritual life filled Emden's soul with hatred for the movement, and for whatever was, however remotely, connected therewith. This hatred, which became with him a veritable obsession, involved him in a bitter feud with Jonathan Eybeschütz (1690–1761), one of the wisest and most brilliant Talmudists of his time, whom he suspected of the Shabbathean heresy. Both Emden and Eybeschütz had the most cordial relations with Moses Mendelssohn (1728–86), the most famous Jew of the eighteenth century, whom they both greatly admired for his wisdom and general culture. We now come to the dawn of the modern age which saw the gradual unfolding of the as yet not ended drama of the emancipation of the Jews from the many civil disabilities, which centuries of oppression in Christian and Moslem lands had forged against them, and of their admission to full rights of citizenship. With the enfranchisement of the Jews, however, the autonomy of the Jewish communities and their power to enforce the discipline of Rabbinism among their members ceased. Henceforth Rabbinism, whilst continuing unabated with its many and varied contributions, enjoyed no longer its former almost undisputed ascendancy, but was obliged to yield ground before the pressure of new movements with which it had to contend for the mastery of the Jewish soul; and it is to the consideration of these movements that our attention is next directed.

NOTES

1. From the Hebrew initials *Rabbi SHelomo Itzchaki*.
2. See p. 164.
3. Introduction.
4. See Leopold Zunz, *Zur Geschichte und Literatur*, p. 123.
5. See Israel Abrahams, *Jewish Quarterly Review*, 1891, p. 475-6.
6. See p. 253.
7. See p. 233.
8. Quoted in *Lubavitscher Rabbi's Memoirs* (Eng. trans. by N. Mindel, Brooklyn, 1949), pp. 40 f.
9. Quoted in S. A. Horodetsky, *ha-Chasidim We-ha Chasiduth*, 1, 88.
10. op. cit. 1, p. 120.
11. Quoted L. I. Newman, *Chasidic Anthology* (New York, 1944), p. 186.
12. Quoted in Martin Buber, *Tales of the Chasidim*, 1, The Early Masters (London, 1956), p. 19.
13. Quoted in S. H. Spiegel, *Hebrew Reborn* (London, 1931), p. 197.
14. Quoted in A. Z. Idelsohn, *Jewish Liturgy*, (New York, 1932), p. 262.

15. See p. 251, n. 11.
16. Derived from the name of a town in North-West Russia, where the descendants of Shneur Zalman, who adopted the name of Shneersohn, lived and made the centre of the *Chabad* activities from 1813 until 1916.
17. Reported by Baruch of Shklow (1752–1810) in his Introduction to the Hebrew translation of the *Six Books of Euclid's Geometry* which he did at the request of the Gaon of Vilna.
18. See p. 205.

CHAPTER 21

MODERN MOVEMENTS IN JUDAISM

ALL modern movements in Judaism stem directly or indirectly from the Enlightenment – the movement which characterized the general atmosphere of the eighteenth century and represents the efforts of Western mankind to apply the rule of reason to all phases of human life.

In the domain of religion the autonomy of reason involved the rejection of all dogma, authority, and tradition, every individual being declared to be sole judge of his beliefs; whilst in the sphere of political and social relations it opposed every form of intolerance and absolutism, and demanded freedom and equality for all men.

Arising at first in the Netherlands and England, the Enlightenment reached France where, assuming eventually a violent form, it culminated in the Revolution which, with its declaration of the Rights of Man, broke down the barriers whereby Church and State kept the Jews apart from their neighbours. From France the movement spread to Germany and other countries in Europe up to the Volga.

To the penetration of the Enlightenment among the Jews no small share was contributed by Moses Mendelssohn. While under the influence of Leibnitz he made clear the relation of reason to religion, he transformed the conception of Judaism in that he refused to admit to it any single article of faith save such as unaided reason could discover. 'I recognize no eternal verities' (he declared in his *Jerusalem*) 'except those which can not only be conceived but also be established and verified by human reason.'[1] All that Judaism insists on, in his view, in matters of religious truth, is the acceptance of three articles: (1) the existence of God; (2) Providence; and (3) the Immortality of the Soul. But these articles admit of the same sort of direct proof as do the postulates of mathematics and, as such, are essentially founded on pure reason.

These three articles, furthermore, because of their basic

rationality, constitute the common truths of all persuasions; but whereas other religions have superimposed upon the body of the common truths a system of creeds and dogmas indispensable to individual salvation, Judaism, Mendelssohn asserts, boasts of no exclusive revelation of immutable truths. 'Judaism is not revealed religion, but revealed legislation.' The Divine Voice at Sinai issued forth commands which consisted only of deeds, not beliefs, such commands having as their purpose the preservation of the Jewish ethnic group, so that it might be able to fulfil its priestly mission to the nations of the world.

It is hardly necessary to emphasize that the 'reason' enthroned by Mendelssohn as mistress to religion is a totally different thing from that employed by Maimonides, and other Jewish religious philosophers, as its handmaid. Nor is there need to point out that in reducing Judaism to a narrow code of legislative observances, Mendelssohn ran counter to the whole trend of the history of Jewish religious life and experience. Therein, indeed, lay the fundamental weaknesses in Mendelssohn's philosophy which soon made themselves felt among the men and women affected by it. Many came to discard all positive religion because reason, which their master had taught them to follow wherever it might lead, had so dictated; whilst others, including most of his children, went further, and for the sake of social advancement did not hesitate to embrace the dominant faith.

Mendelssohn himself, however, was far too staunch in his Judaism to have intended in the least to wean away his brethren from their ancestral faith. But Mendelssohn was something beside a rationalist philosopher. He was a man of good practical sense, who, concerned with the plight of his brethren, laboured zealously for their civil emancipation; and it was his belief that the best way he could achieve this end was by showing that Judaism was essentially in harmony with the rationalism of the age: hence the rationalistic position adopted by him in his *Jerusalem*. With the same end in view, he worked also for their educational emancipation – an emancipation which, by enlarging their intellectual horizon beyond the confines of the Talmud and its allied disciplines, and introducing them into the broader fields of general European culture, would, he believed, make them acceptable to their non-Jewish fellow-men.

His first step in this direction was his translation of the Pentateuch into German, whereby he encouraged the German Jews to replace their Judaeo-German vernacular by the language of the land, and thus prepared them for participation in the march of Western civilization.

Accompanying this translation was the Hebrew commentary (*Biur*) which he sponsored and which, interpreting Scripture in the light of contemporary thought, served to stimulate among the Jews of his generation an interest in the general culture of the outside world.

Mendelssohn's educational efforts aroused considerable opposition within the Jewish camp. Many there were who feared, not without good reason, the effect of the sudden impact of foreign cultures upon Jewish religious loyalty and devotion; but Mendelssohn was not alone in the struggle on behalf of educational emancipation. Round him there clustered a band of devoted disciples who assisted him in his labours. Making *Haskalah* (Enlightenment) their watchword, they called themselves *Maskilim*, and started to publish a literary periodical entitled *Hameasef* (The Collector), to which they owe also their name as *Measefim*. The language of this periodical, which appeared at irregular intervals between 1784 and 1811, was Hebrew, which the *Maskilim*, disdaining the Judaeo-German vernacular (Yiddish), considered to be the best medium for the spread of their ideas. Furthermore, anxious to break down the onesidedness of an exclusive Talmudic education, they cultivated in their writings on general subjects the pure and beautiful language of the Bible. But with all that, the real goal of the *Maskilim* was general culture, Hebrew being used by them merely as the means to pave the way for the assimilation by the Jews of the cultural values of the West.

Most distinguished among Mendelssohn's supporters was Naphtali Herz Wesseley (1725–1805). A poet of considerable merit, his fame rests on the zeal with which he championed the cause of general culture in his *Divre Shalom We-Emeth* (Words of Peace and Truth), in which he urged Jews of Austria and Hungary to answer the call made to them by the Emperor Joseph II (1741–90) in his 'Edict of Toleration', issued in 1782, to adopt the German language and establish modern schools for giving instruction in secular subjects.

Mendelssohn lived to see the first-fruits of his educational work in the opening in 1778 of the Jewish Free School (*Freischule*) in Berlin, the first modern Jewish school where all subjects, secular as well as religious, were taught in German.

Mendelssohn's efforts, however, on behalf of Jewish civil emancipation showed little result in his lifetime. The old prejudices against the Jews and Judaism died hard. Frederick the Great of Prussia (1712–86) well might have proclaimed in the true spirit of the Enlightenment: 'In my states everyone may be saved after his own fashion'; yet the Jews remained beyond the pale of the law.

The beginning of the emancipation of the Jews came in sight only five years after Mendelssohn's death, that is in 1791, when the French National Assembly, consequent on the French Revolution, established the principle of religious toleration by bestowing full citizen rights upon Jewish subjects. This new status accorded to the Jews in France was imposed by Napoleon, the legatee of the French Revolution, in practically every land he conquered, including Western Germany. Soon, one by one, Jewish disabilities in one country after another disappeared. By the nineteenth century Jewish emancipation in most countries of Western Europe, as well as in America, was complete. Wherever the Jews were given civic equality, they threw themselves heart and soul into the service of the state, contributing richly to political, social, cultural, and economic life. In all but religion the emancipated Jews identified themselves with the destiny, interests, and endeavours of their fellow citizens. But within this vortex of social and economic change the Jews were caught unawares. A crisis of the first magnitude thereupon ensued for the Jewish people, which for the first time in its exile, seemed unable to adapt itself to changed conditions. Unaccustomed as they were after centuries of seclusion to the idea of a full Jewish citizenship in a non-Jewish national state, the problem of adjusting completely their religious loyalty to the new political and social status which they had won appeared to them formidable. A large number solved the problem for themselves by deserting to the dominant faith. Many others, on the other hand, saw a solution in a process of assimilation which, conceiving Judaism as a merely abstract creed based on the three Mendelssohnian postulates, allowed for attachment to the Jewish religion and the Jewish religious community while, at the same time, carrying with it a denial of all distinctive national elements in Judaism. Even the name 'Jew' was to be rejected. They were no longer Jews as such but merely 'Germans, Frenchmen, Englishmen, etc., of the Mosaic persuasion'. Assimilatory tendencies involving the renunciation of religious and national traditions thus developed with great rapidity and took hold of those elements of the Jewish people which came into professional and social contact with the cultured circles of the host-people. The result was the Reform Movement, which, originating in Germany and spreading from there to America and England,[2] aimed at adjusting the old forms of Jewish life and practice to the spirit and culture of the peoples into whose history the Jews were being drawn.

The real originator of the Reform Movement in Judaism was David Friedländer (1756–1834), one of the best-known of Moses Mendelssohn's disciples. He it was who laid down the basic principles of Reform, from which the movement never departed. Although designed to stop the drift from Judaism, the real motive which lay at the bottom of the movement, and determined its course, was a desire for assimilation. Its far-off look was directed to the effect which loyalty to Jewish life and practice would have on the relations of the Jew with the outside world. Friedländer himself went so far in his assimilatory zeal as to petition in 1799 the Lutheran authorities in Berlin to admit him and his associates to the Church, on the condition that they be excused from believing in the divinity of Jesus and from practising the distinctive rites of Christianity. This offer of conditional conversion was naturally rejected. Forced to bear the burden of Judaism, Friedländer sought to reform the

Jewish religion in such a way as to eliminate from it whatever might hamper the intimate relations of Jews with their neighbours and tend to call in question their loyalty to the state. He accordingly urged the abolition of all prayers with a Jewish national colouring, and the substitution of German for Hebrew as the language of prayer and public worship.

Friedländer had not a few sympathizers, but none dared at the time translate his principles into action; and the story of Reform as an organized movement begins mainly with the attempt to model the externalities of Jewish religious services after the pattern of the services of the Church, without, however, tampering with the actual contents of the prayers.

The story centres round the name of Israel Jacobson (1768–1828). He it was who founded in 1810 the first Jewish Reform Temple which he built at Seesen, Brunswick, at his own expense, and wherein he instituted services which embodied features adapted from the Church. This was the first time that a Jewish house of worship was called a 'temple', a name reserved hitherto for the Temple in Jerusalem, and its adoption by Reform to denote their places of worship betrayed their attitude to the hope of the restoration of Israel's ancient national shrine.

Apart from a few minor changes in the liturgy, the innovations introduced by Jacobson consisted of German sermons, German chorals, some German prayers, and the use of the organ.[3] Jacobson was also the first to institute the confirmation of boys on the Feast of Pentecost instead of on their respective attainment of the age of thirteen, as prescribed by tradition,[4] and to abolish the chanting of Scriptural reading at congregational services.

Growing bolder with the years, the Reformers proceeded, though cautiously at first, to adopt in practice the principles laid down by Friedländer, and in 1818 a Reform Temple was established in Hamburg after the pattern of the Temple in Seesen, but going beyond it in that the traditional prayers for national restoration were re-phrased to mean the general restoration of mankind, and the traditional conception of a Messiah was changed to one of a Messianic era for all mankind. In this

Reform Temple at Hamburg there was also introduced the confirmation of girls, a practice which has no roots in Judaism.[5]

With Samuel Holdheim (1806–60) and Abraham Geiger (1830–74) Reform entered upon a more radical phase. These Reform leaders asserted unequivocally that Judaism was wholly religious and had nothing national about it, and accordingly proceeded to advocate the abolition of all laws and ceremonies which tended to make the Jews distinct from their neighbours. Samuel Holdheim of the Berlin Reform Temple in 1849 replaced the Sabbath services by Sunday services, and also abolished the observance of the second day of festivals.[6] Other reforms instituted in the Berlin congregation were the non-segregation of the sexes, prayers without head cover,[7] or praying shawl (*tallith*), the elimination of Hebrew in the service, the abolition of the blowing of the *Shofar* (Ram's Horn) on New Year, as well as of the blessings by those of priestly descent (cf. Num. 7. 23–27), because this rite was reminiscent of Temple times.

Less radical than Holdheim in practice, though no less in theory, was Abraham Geiger, who believed that Reform should move slowly so as to maintain as much as possible its connexion with the whole House of Israel. He therefore, despite his own personal predilection for prayers in German, demanded the retention of Hebrew as the principal medium of public worship. He, however, sought to educate the people in the ways of Reform by means of his writings, in which he denied the divine origin of the Pentateuch, ridiculed the dietary laws, and advocated the abolition of circumcision.

Strictly adhering to the view that the Jews were only a religious sect and not a nation, he insisted on a purely universal conception of Judaism, any nationalistic interpretation being considered by him as a misrepresentation of the purpose of God. In accordance with this standpoint, he expurgated from the Prayer Book he edited in 1854 all prayers for the restoration of the Jewish State in Palestine and the rebuilding of the Temple as a centre for Israel, as well as all references to the Messianic hope of the ingathering of the exiled – all such ideas being extinct, he maintained, in the Jewish consciousness.

Geiger claimed to base his views on an historical and scientific examination of the Biblical documents which, studied in the light and conditions of the times in which they were written, justified the changes he favoured. He furthermore professed to follow in the line of Talmudic tradition which was one of continuous development, keeping pace with the needs of the times. In reality, however, Geiger cared little either for the Talmudic tradition or even for the Bible itself, neither of which was considered by him any longer authoritative and binding. All that mattered was the 'spirit of the age' which for him, as for his fellow reformers, was also a revelation of God, supplanting the revelation of previous ages which the Bible and the Talmud embody.

This denial of the authority of the Bible and Talmud by Reform Judaism made for individualism and gave rise to a divergency of views in the ranks of Reform as to what constituted Judaism and the Jewish way of life. To bring about some uniformity in belief and practice and to obviate confusion resulting from the conflicting individual opinions, efforts were made to establish a Synod that should exercise some degree of authority over those who had enlisted under the banner of Reform. Several such synods were held. But each time the members of the respective synods met, they were too hopelessly divided alike on questions of principle, aim, and purpose to achieve any positive result. The most important among the synods, historically considered, was that held in Frankfurt in 1845, at which the question of changes in the liturgy was discussed for the first time. Many delegates advocated the entire abolition of Hebrew, because its retention would imply that Judaism was a national religion. The majority, however, decided that Hebrew must be kept, but only out of consideration for the feelings of the older generation. This readiness to surrender Hebrew led to the secession of Zechariah Frankel (1801–75), who founded the 'positive-historical' school of Judaism, which divorces belief and practice, and combines full freedom of inquiry relating to Israel's creed and Israel's past, with an observance of Jewish law and national traditions as the product of the collective experience of the Jewish people.

Both Reform, and to a lesser extent the positive-historical school, met with opposition alike within and without Germany on the part of the traditionalists, whom the Reform dubbed as 'Orthodox'. Most bitter in his denunciations of Reform was Rabbi Moses Sofer of Pressburg (1763–1839). A towering Rabbinic figure and an author of voluminous Responsa, which to the present day are considered highly authoritative, Moses Sofer set his face against all modernity in Jewish religious life, and it was mainly owing to the energetic activity with which he threw himself into the struggle against Reform that the movement was never able to make any headway in Hungary, notwithstanding its enthusiastic champions in that country.

In Germany the traditional type of Judaism found its most valiant and vigorous defender in the person of Samson Raphael Hirsch (1808–88) who, opposing both Reform and the positive-historical school, founded what came to be described, as Neo-Orthodoxy, which, with variations determined by local conditions, is the present orthodoxy of the Western world. In reality it is not a new Orthodoxy, but a revival of the Judaism of the Arabic-Spanish period which presented a blending of the old with the new, and of the strictest adherence to traditional beliefs and observances with a full participation in the science and culture of the age.

As Rabbi of an Orthodox group at Frankfort-on-the-Main, Hirsch proclaimed the principle of *Austritt* (Separatism), maintaining that observant Jews had to leave communities in which Reform tendencies prevailed, and form communities of their own. Although few congregations followed his appeal, he succeeded in building up his community in Frankfort into a powerful religious organization with its own modern schools and subsidiary institutions, which formed the model for similar bodies elsewhere in Germany and in other countries beyond.

The progress of the Reform Movement in Germany was brought to a halt with the Breslau Conference in 1846, which broke down on the question of the transference of the Saturday observance to Sunday. Henceforth the centre of Reform activity shifted to the United States whither the movement was transplanted by ardent Reform leaders who had joined the stream of Jewish immigration from Germany and other countries in Europe, which, beginning in 1830, reached its highest point in 1848–50 in consequence of the reaction that followed the failure of the 1848 Revolution. In this new world, with little organized opposition, the Movement under the energetic leadership of such men as Isaac Wise (1819–1900), David Einhorn (1809–99), and others, was able to make rapid strides and to develop without hindrance on radical lines. In 1885 the American Reform Movement at a conference in Pittsburgh formulated its principles, which called, *inter alia*, for the rejection of the whole of the Mosaic and rabbinic legislation, including the dietary laws and other similar institutions, the inauguration of Sunday services, and the repudiation of Jewish nationalism. A direct sequel of this 1885 conference was the Central Conference held in 1892, at which the requirements of circumcision was officially dropped for proselytes. As a protest against the acceptance of the 'Pittsburgh Platform', an influential group of moderates led by Sabato Morais (1823–1901) formed themselves into what came to be known as the Conservative movement. Adopting the position of Zechariah Frankel's positive-historical school, the Conservative movement, thanks to the energetic and spirited leadership of Solomon Schechter (1830–1915), at one time Reader in Rabbinics at Cambridge University, and famous for his Genizah discoveries,[8] grew in influence and in numbers to become a major force in the religious, intellectual, and social life of American Jewry today.

Occupying a position midway between Orthodoxy and Reform, Conservatism has on the one hand taken over a number of the externalities of worship of the Reform. With rare exceptions the segregation of the sexes at worship, which is the undeviating practice of the Orthodox synagogue, is not observed; prayers in English are included in the service; and many synagogues employ the organ. On the other hand, Conservatism claims to accept the entire structure of rabbinic tradition, although it does permit itself to interpret the Law in accordance with modern needs and convictions. Conservatism accordingly, to give an example, permits, contrary to rabbinic law, riding to the synagogue on the Sabbath. Conservatism has still to define its principles in applying in practice the implications of its attitude to rabbinic law. In matters of belief, Conservatism accepts the specific revelation of God to Israel, adopts a positive attitude to Jewish national aspirations and hopes for the restoration of Israel's ancient homeland, and attaches great importance for national historic reasons to the retention of Hebrew in the service. As against Orthodoxy but like Reform, Conservatism rejects the doctrine of the resurrection, though upholding the belief in immortality.

The three principal objectives of Conservative Judaism are: (1) the fostering of the unity of what Schechter called 'Catholic (that is, Universal) Israel'; (2) the perpetuation of Jewish tradition; and (3) the cultivation of Jewish scholarship. Given agreement on these three objectives, the rest can take care of itself. Thus it is that Conservatism refuses to commit itself to a definite platform of principles and dogmas, and allows considerable latitude in matters of practice and belief among its constituent groups. This made possible the rise within Conservatism of the Reconstructionist movement. Inaugurated by Mordecai Kaplan (b. 1881) Reconstructionism is based on the proposition that the Jewish religion exists for the Jewish people and not the Jewish people for the Jewish religion. In the light of this proposition, Judaism is conceived merely as a civilization in which religion, though occupying an important place, is but one of the many forms in which a civilization expresses itself, like language, law, literature, and art. As such the Jewish religion is but a folk-religion, in the same way as Communism has become the folk-religion of Russia, and the Jewish religious practices are but folk-ways, in the same manner as the observance of Trafalgar Day is a folk-way for the British, the 14th July for the French, and Independence Day for the Americans. Even God is no longer conceived as the Supreme Being who created and controls the Universe, but a kind of cosmic process to be identified 'with that aspect of reality which elicits the most serviceable traits, the traits that enhance individual human worth and further social unity'.[9] It goes without saying that this God-idea leaves no room for the conception of the personal relationship between God and man which constitutes the core of all living religion, much less for the doctrine of Israel's election or for God's purposeful activity in creation and in history. Reconstructionism, in brief, is Conservatism minus its religious affirmations, and as such, notwithstanding its synagogues, ministers, prayers, and sermons, can hardly be considered a religion in the commonly understood sense of the word.

With all the idealism that inspired the Reform leaders, Reform Judaism, in dissociating itself from the Jewish national entity to which the Jewish religion belongs, brought Judaism perilously near to Christianity, which many in consequence did not hesitate to embrace. It was this realization of the danger of Reform that led Leopold Zunz (1794–1886) to break with the movement and to seek to achieve the aims, which had motivated the Reformers, by founding the *Wissenschaft des Judentums* (The Science of Judaism) which concerns itself with a scientific evaluation of the history and achievements of the Jewish people.

The movement started by Zunz entered immediately upon its golden era which saw the production of some of its basic works. With this era is connected a whole band of outstanding figures. Occupying the highest pinnacle is Leopold Zunz himself, who for the range of his writings and epoch-making character of his major works has no peer in this field. His *Gottesdienstlichen Vorträge der Juden* (Sermons of the Jews) presents the greatest effort in tracing the development of the Aggadic (Homiletical) literature and its evolutionary character. His *Zur Geschichte und Literatur* (On History and Literature) blazed a new path in the history and literature of the Jews in Germany and France during the Middle Ages. His *Synagogale Poesie des Mittelalters* (The Synagogal Poetry of the Middle Ages) systematizes the vast mass of the religious poetry of the Jewish people over a period of a thousand years; while his *Ritus des Synagogalen Gottesdienstes* (Ritual of the Synagogue Service) describes the growth of two thousand years of Jewish liturgical literature.

Although Zunz is commonly denominated the founder of the

Science of Judaism, he himself owed much to the works of a Galician savant, Solomon Judah Rapoport (1790–1867) who, in his biographical and other historical studies, evolved the critical method in the investigation of Jewish history and literature. Rapoport, in turn, was greatly indebted to his fellow-countryman, Nachman Krochmal (1785–1840) who, tracing in his *Moreh Nebuche ha-Zeman* (Guide for the Perplexed of the Times) with profound insight the genesis of Jewish traditions, showed how to utilize Talmudic records for the purpose of history.

Krochmal and Rapoport were the earliest representatives of the Galician *Haskalah*. Influenced by the German *Haskalah*, the *Maskilim* in Galicia fought with as much zeal for the secularization of Jewish education as did their German compeers. But the course of the development of the *Haskalah* in Galicia was on more wholesome lines than in Germany. In Germany, as we have seen, the aim of the *Haskalah* was general culture. Once the German Jew had learned enough of the language of the country to enable him to drink of the general culture from the original sources, he had little use for the Hebraic compositions of the *Maskilim*. Thus did the *Haskalah* in Germany, notwithstanding its contributions to Biblical scholarship, and Hebrew philology and grammar, become before long associated, and ultimately amalgamated, with the forces of assimilation. It was otherwise in Galicia, where the far greater concentration of Jewish masses, combined with the high standards of Rabbinic learning, prevented the *Haskalah* from going the way of its German counterpart. Although the Galician *Maskilim* did not hesitate to undermine the authority of Rabbinism, yet they were, on the whole, constructive and bent on preserving and perpetuating the ethnical and cultural distinctiveness of Jewish life.

Thus it is that whereas the German *Haskalah* was doomed to be short-lived, the Galician remained alive and continued fruitful in its many and varied contributions, written in Hebrew, to the knowledge of the Jewish past.

To the same group of scholars as Krochmal and Rapoport, who wrote in Hebrew, belonged also the Italian, Samuel David

Luzzatto (1800–60). A man of encyclopedic learning, Luzzatto was the greatest Jewish Biblical scholar and most brilliant exponent of Hebrew poetry of his age and, in his numerous writings in Hebrew and Italian, played a conspicuous part in the creation of the Science of Judaism.

Although the scientific interests of Krochmal and Luzzatto lay, as indicated, in separate fields, the former in Talmudics, the latter in Bible and poetry, they both had in their studies a common practical aim which distinguished them from all the other *Maskilim* of their generation. Whereas all these others explored the Jewish heritage merely as a relic of the past with little relevance to the present, Krochmal and Luzzatto investigated it as a guide to contemporary Jewish life as well as to the future. Thus it is that Krochmal and Luzzatto, apart from their share in the creation of the Science of Judaism, also made some original contributions to religious thought, which proved of great significance for Jewish life of recent times.

Krochmal was the first to attempt to meet the crisis in Judaism created by the Enlightenment by his very use of the philosophic thought-forms of his age. Operating with ideas he borrowed from Hegel, he showed that the conflict between historic Judaism and contemporary rationalism was more apparent than real. Each nation had its own spirit – or, in the language of Krochmal, its own god – which is the originator of all its national attributes. The Greeks, for example, had the spirit of science, philosophy, art; the Romans had law and physical courage. All these attributes of the various nations were but different manifestations of the all-embracing thought, the 'Absolute Spirit', which unfolds itself in the tortuous march of history, and is the sum and source of all spiritual existence. This 'Absolute Spirit' is none other than the God of Israel, with whom the Jewish people is linked in an indissoluble bond, and the realization of whose Will in the world is the ideal and destiny of the Jewish people. Judaism consequently can no longer be considered an isolated cultural entity, apart from all other national cultures. On the contrary, it is closely related to them all, embracing them all in harmonious unity.

As against Krochmal, Luzzatto sought to relieve the crisis

in Judaism by dethroning the rationalism of the Enlightenment from the high position it came to occupy. Following the line of Judah Halevi, Luzzatto emphasizes the supremacy of religion over philosophy. In this connexion, he contrasts the legacy of Greece, which he designates Atticism, with the spiritual heritage of Israel, which, maintaining that it began with Abraham, he often calls Abrahamism. The former seeks to improve the intellect, the latter the heart. The former develops a calculating mind, which is apt to give preferences to self-interest; the latter demands the performance of good deeds even if they are opposed to all utilitarian reckoning.

Expounding his thesis, Luzzatto writes:

The civilization of the world is the product of two dissimilar elements: Atticism and Judaism. To Athens we owe philosophy, the arts, the sciences, the development of the intellect, order, love of beauty and grandeur, intellectual and studied morality. To Judaism we owe religion, the morality which springs from the heart and from selflessness, and the love of good. . . . Beauty and grandeur cannot take the place of good. Society needs emotion; but intellect and Atticism, far from inspiring emotion, weaken it and snuff it out. This is why human nature reacts – and always will react – in favour of the heart, of good, of Judaism.[10]

Among the contemporaries of Zunz in Germany who made highly significant contributions to the Science of Judaism were Abraham Geiger, who, however, as already indicated, utilized his researches in the history of the Bible and Jewish tradition to justify his radical Reform views; and Zechariah Frankel, whose work in the Talmudic and allied literature raised him to the rank of the first historian and expounder of the *Halachah* in a scientific manner and spirit. Both Geiger and Frankel edited scientific journals, the *Monatsschrift für Geschichte und Wissenschaft des Judentums*, begun by the latter in 1851, having had an almost consecutive run until the beginning of the Second World War.

Other famous names connected with the golden era of the Science of Judaism were those of Heinrich Graetz (1817–91), the greatest Jewish historian, whose *History of the Jews* in eleven volumes, written in a grand and sweeping style, and translated from the original German into many languages, has served more than any other work to bring the knowledge of the history of the Jewish people to the rank and file of the Jews, and remains to the present day a standard work; and Moritz Steinschneider (1816–1907), the greatest Jewish bibliographer of all times and the compiler of the famous Catalogue of the Hebrew Books at the Bodleian (Oxford).

As a result of the labours of these devotees of the science of Judaism and other kindred spirits, an entirely new and hitherto unsuspected world of history, literature, and culture was disclosed which not only helped to stem partly the flight from Judaism in Germany during the nineteenth century, but has also profoundly affected Jewish life and thought in every part of the world to this day.

The growing recognition of the necessity of preaching in the vernacular and of explaining and defending Judaism in modern and scientific terms led to the establishment of Rabbinical seminaries for the training of spiritual leaders combining a knowledge of Judaism with a good university education. The first of all modern seminaries for the training of Jewish spiritual leaders was the Collegio Rabbinico which was opened in Padua in 1829 and where Samuel David Luzzatto became the ruling spirit. A year later there was founded the Séminaire Israélite de France in Metz, whence it was transferred to Paris in 1859. The first of the Rabbinical seminaries that sprung up in Germany was the one in Breslau which was opened in 1854 under the direction of Zechariah Frankel. In 1872 there followed the Reform seminary in Berlin, with Geiger as its head. A year later an Orthodox Rabbinical seminary under the leadership of Israel Hildesheimer (1820–99) was founded in the same city, and a seminary more or less on the lines of the one in Breslau was established in Budapest in 1877. In England, as early as 1855, Jews' College was founded by Chief Rabbi Nathan Marcus Adler (1803–90), Sir Moses Montefiore (1784–1885), and others.

Designed originally to serve the parochial needs of the 40,000 Jewish souls which constituted at that time the Anglo-

Jewish community, Jews' College has grown into a great English institution of Hebraic and Semitic learning associated with the University of London, and occupies today a unique position in the religious and spiritual life of the 750,000 Jews in the British Commonwealth of Nations.

Following the pattern of its sister communities in Europe, American Jewry saw in 1874 the opening of the Hebrew Union College, Cincinnatti, for the training of Reform rabbis, and in 1886 of the Jewish Theological Seminary, New York for the training of Conservative rabbis. In 1896 was opened the Rabbi Isaac Elchanan Yeshivah[11] for the modern training not only of Orthodox rabbis and teachers but also of laymen.

The combined efforts of all the constructive forces in Judaism, notwithstanding, the inroads of conversions and assimilations in the West continued at such a rate as to make to all appearance the complete disintegration of organized Jewish life in that part of the world only a matter of time. The Science of Judaism was too critical, too objective, and too cold to impart warmth of the spirit to Jewish life. Besides, the Science of Judaism was far too specialized to make any appreciable impact on the masses. Nor was modern Orthodoxy, despite its achievements, able to do much to stem the flight from Judaism. Concentrating on practice rather than on higher Jewish learning, it did little to cultivate among young and old the Talmudic discipline from which the Jews have at all times drawn the spiritual sustenance and moral fortitude which enabled them to triumph over all subversive trends and influences.

What saved West European Jewries from the quasi-extinction that seemed to threaten them was the constant influx of Jews from Russia and Poland, as well as Hungary, during the nineteenth century who, owing to their superior standards of religious scholarship and traditional Jewish piety, served not only to revitalize but also to enrich more and more the content of Jewish life in the lands in which they found their new homes.

These superior standards of the Jews of Russia, Poland, and Hungary were due to the vast network in their native lands of Rabbinic schools (*Yeshivoth*) which brought forth through a succession of generations thousands of students filled with the knowledge of the Torah and fortified in the fear of God.

The most celebrated *Yeshivah* of the nineteenth century was that of Voloshin, Lithuania, founded in 1802 by Hayyim ben Isaac (1749–1822), the foremost disciple of the Gaon of Vilna. In this academy in which the Gaon's educational methods gained practical application, the most outstanding talents in Russian Jewry received their Jewish education and lifelong inspiration. About the same year Moses Sofer[12] established in Pressburg a *Yeshivah* for five hundred students, which has been functioning without interruption until the beginning of the Second World War, and which has furnished numerous spiritual leaders and scholars to many Jewish communities in all parts of the world. Another famous *Yeshivah* in Lithuania was that of Slabodka, near Kovno, which was founded in 1882, and included in its curriculum the daily study of ethical and other devotional works such as those of Bachya ibn Pakuda's *Duties of the Heart*;[13] and Moses Hayyim Luzzatto's *Path of the Righteous*.[14] The aim of these studies, known as *Musar*, was the development of great spiritual personalities capable of influencing others to walk in the way of piety and righteous conduct. The example of Slabodka was soon adopted by other *Yeshivoth* in Eastern Europe, and is being followed by most of the Talmudic schools that have within recent years arisen in the West.

The originator of the study of *Musar* in the *Yeshivoth* was Israel Salanter (1810–83) who, alarmed at the inroads which the *Haskalah*, travelling from Germany, was beginning to make in Russia in his days, organized in Vilna in 1842 a conventicle (*Stiebel*) at which members of all classes of society – students, professional and businessmen, artisans and labourers – met daily at twilight, when the melancholy atmosphere of falling darkness was apt to stir the emotions, for the study under his guidance of religio-ethical works. This idea caught on, and thus was born the *Musar* Movement, which has exercised considerable influence upon orthodox Jewish life. The keynote of this movement is the improvement of moral character through a process of self-education. This process consists of three stages: (1) the subjugation of all evil desires and impulses through the constant discipline of the will-power; (2) the recognition of one's own faults and failings as a result of honest self-analysis and self-criticism; and (3) the conscious effort at the improvement of character, making of virtue a second nature. This self-education, according to *Musar* teaching, can be achieved through the study of religio-ethical works, which was to be followed by quiet meditation and reflection. 'Not one day,' declared one of the leaders of the movement, Simcha Zissel Ziv of Khelm, 'should be allowed to pass without habituation in the practice of reflection, for it is the key to wisdom, the focus of all the faculties leading to the attainment of the whole man.'[15]

Meantime, in the West, there was little to arrest the disintegration of Jewish life. Surveying the situation, Moses Hess (1812–75) came to the conclusion that the only salvation for Judaism was Jewish nationalism: 'It is only with a national rebirth,' he declared in his *Rome and Jerusalem* (1862) 'that the religious genius of the Jews, like the giant of the legend touching Mother Earth, will be endowed with new strength and again be inspired with the prophetic spirit. No aspirant for Enlightenment, not even a Mendelssohn, has so far succeeded in crushing the hard shell within which Rabbinism has encrusted Judaism, without at the same time destroying the national ideal in its innermost essence.'[16] 'What we have to do at present for the regeneration of the Jewish nation', he continues, 'is first to keep alive the hope of the political rebirth of our people and next to re-awaken the hope where it slumbers.'[17]

The problem of reconciling the idea of Jewish citizenship in a non-Jewish national state with loyalty to the Jewish nation – a problem which exercised so much the mind of his contemporaries, particularly in Germany – presented to him no problem. 'The Judaeo-Spanish cultural epoch,' he declares 'succeeded in solving the problem, namely, how it is possible to be a good patriotic national Jew in the full sense of the word, and at the same time participate in the culture and political life of the country of residence to such a degree that the country will become a second fatherland.'[18]

Hess had no illusions as to the hostility his views were to

arouse among the Jews in the West enmeshed in the phantas-
magoria of emancipation. It was therefore to the millions of his
faithful brethren in the east saturated with learning and piety
that he looked for that mighty impulse towards the Jewish rebirth on its ancestral soil.

Hess's nationalism was moulded by the universal ideals of
Hebrew Messianism. The Jews were the Messianic people: on
them was laid the task to work for the realization of the principles of social justice, human cooperation, and permanent
peace in an organized and united humanity; and only the
return to their ancestral homeland would give the Jews the
possibility of discharging properly their divinely assigned task
and help to bring about in the social sphere what Hess describes as 'the historical Sabbath' of mankind.

Hess's call to the Jews in Russia and Poland was no voice in
the wilderness. At that time there was in Russia a national
revival which, strange as it may appear, was inspired by the
emancipation. The full rights accorded to Jews in many lands
and the consequent rise of a number of them to high positions
in the councils of States and the world of commerce were interpreted by many Jews in Eastern Europe as signs of the approach
of Messianic redemption. This served to displace gradually
the belief of centuries that the restoration to Palestine would
be brought about suddenly amid miracles and wonders through
the direct intervention of God, and to give rise to the idea that
the Redemption would come gradually through the instrumen-
tality of human resources, God Himself manifesting His redemptive powers in consummation of the Redemption after
man has done his share. The first exponent of this idea was
Rabbi Zvi Hirsh Kalisher of Thorn (1785–1877), who in his
Derishath Zion (1862) propounded his theory, by reference to
Scriptural and Talmudic sources, that the Messianic era must
be preceded by the establishment of Jewish colonies in Palestine, through the cooperation of willing governments and the
benevolence of wealthy Jews. He accordingly outlined a plan
of colonization in which he secured the interest of Sir Moses
Montefiore (1784–1885) and Lawrence Oliphant (1829–88), as
well as the Earl of Shaftesbury (1801–85), leading to the estab-

lishment in 1870 of the agricultural school, Mikweh Israel, near Jaffa, and of the first Jewish colony, Petah Tikwah, in 1878.

The national feelings of the Jews in Russia were fed by the *Haskalah* which, as already mentioned, had reached the country from the West. Although under the liberalizing policy of Alexander II (1818–81) the *Haskalah* displayed assimilatory tendencies, the great forces of Rabbinic tradition and learning which confronted the movement in Russia turned it into an instrument of Jewish national revival and Hebraic renaissance, which gave rise to a rich new type of literature in books and periodicals – modern Hebrew literature.

Foremost among the early pioneers of the modern Hebrew literature in Russia were Isaac Baer Levinson (1788 – 1860), commonly known as the 'Russian Mendelssohn' because of his advocacy of reforms in educational methods and defence of Judaism; Abraham Mapu (1808–67), the father of the Hebrew novel; Abraham Lebensohn (1789–1878), the first to introduce Hebrew poetry in Lithuania, and his son Michael Joseph (1838–52) who, judging from the two volumes of his poems, would but for his early death have become the greatest lyric poet of the Russian Haskalah; and Judah Leib Gordon (1831–92), the greatest Jewish poet of his time.

These early Hebrew *Haskalah* writers, however, had too much faith in emancipation, in which they saw the panacea of all Jewish miseries, to be attracted to the idea of Jewish nationalism. It was only with Peretz Smolenski (1842–85), a romantic novelist and editor of a Hebrew journal, that the *Haskalah* took on a definite nationalistic complexion. He it was who was the first to awaken the idea of Jewish nationalism among the Jewish intellectuals in Russia. He castigated mercilessly the conception that the Jews were merely a religious community and maintained that the Jews must proclaim to the whole world that they were one united people, although they had no kingdom, no country, no territory of their own. At the same time he insisted that the Jews must consider themselves citizens of their respective countries, their unity as a nation being only one in spirit.

Smolenski's nationalism was thus a nationalism without Palestine – a spiritual nationalism in the Diaspora. The first apostle of Jewish restoration to Palestine to arise in Russia was Eliezer ben Yehuda (1858–1922). In an article entitled 'The Burning Question' which he contributed in 1881 to Smolenski's journal *Hashahar* which appeared in Vienna, he pointed to the national movements in Europe whereby young, small peoples were achieving political independence, and maintained that what was possible for other nations was also possible for the Jewish people. In this article he also demanded the restoration of the Hebrew language as a spoken tongue, so that it might become the daily vernacular of the Jewish people. This idea became the consuming passion of his life. Settling later in Palestine, he realized that the language lacked the necessary words. He thereupon set himself the task of supplying this deficiency, and started on the compilation of a Lexicon (*Millon*), which became the greatest and most comprehensive work of its kind, for which he drew from all sources of Hebrew literature – Biblical, Talmudic, and medieval, and to which he added his own neologisms, contributing thereby to the considerable enrichment of the Hebrew language. By his fanatical persistence and refusal to converse in any other language than Hebrew, he proved that Hebrew could be a language of everyday life and daily needs, and thereby made the Hebrew Palestine possible.

At that time there also arose in Russia one of the brightest stars in this firmament of Hebrew poetry in the person of Nachman Bialik (1873–1934), whose unusual artistry, rich imagery, and prophetic fire served, more than any other work of poetry, to arouse the dormant spirit of nationalism among the Jewish masses.

The violent reaction that set in with the accession in 1881 of Alexander III, culminating in the notorious May Laws of 1882 forbidding Jews to settle or acquire property outside of towns or to move from place to place, apart from many other disabilities imposed upon them, imparted a tremendous impulse to Hebrew nationalism in Russia, making that country the home of the Jewish national movement. The first clarion call of the movement was made in 1882 by Leo Pinsker (1821-91) of Odessa, in his famous pamphlet 'Auto-Emancipation', in which he described anti-Semitism as an incurably social-path-ological disease, which he called 'Judeophobia' and which sprang from the homelessness of the Jew who, 'for the living is dead, for the native-born a stranger; for the long-settled a vagabond, for the wealthy a beggar; for the poor a millionaire and an exploiter, for citizens a man without a country, for all classes a hated competitor. The Jews must, therefore, become once more a nation, a people with a territory of their own.'[19] This call rang in the birth of the Choveve Zion[20] Movement, which Pinsker headed up to the day of his death. Founded at the Conference of Kattowitz in 1884, the movement spread to Rumania, Germany, Austria, America, and also to England. Its most practical result was to give an impetus to the creation of Jewish agricultural villages in Palestine and to large-scale settlement. In the same year as Pinsker's pamphlet appeared, a group of Jewish Youth was organized in Kharkov under the name of *Bilu*, formed from the initial letters of the Hebrew *Beth Jacob Lechu Wenelchah* (O, House of Jacob, come let us go up).[21] Consisting for the most part of students, the *Bilu* set themselves the aim of becoming the prototype for pioneer colonization of Israel's ancient homeland, and thus became the fathers of the new Jewish settlement in Palestine.

In 1883 Baron Edmond de Rothschild of Paris (1845-1934) took the struggling settlements in Palestine under his care and contributed much towards their development. It was, how-ever, under the leadership of Theodore Herzl (1860-1904) that Jewish nationalism ceased to be a philanthropic religious move-ment and was transformed into an organized world movement with political aspirations. The outbreak at the time of the Dreyfus case of violent anti-Semitism in France, considered hitherto the most civilized country of the world, drove Herzl to the conclusion that the only solution of the Jewish problem lay in the establishment of a Jewish State.

Herzl's thoughts ran more or less on the lines of Hess and Pinsker, whose work incidentally he had not yet read. But Herzl was the first not only to bring the Jewish problem into the arena of international politics, but also to be possessed of the conviction which he expressed in the plain, simple words: 'The Jews shall have their own State.'[22] He developed his ideas in his *Judenstaat* (The Jewish State) published in 1895, which became the classic of the movement he inaugurated and which assumed the name of Zionism – a name coined in 1892 by one of his early supporters, Nathan Birnbaum (1864–1937). Although Herzl was in his youth removed from Jews and Judaism, he could not fail to be inspired in his ideas by the Messianic tradition, and the State which he envisaged was to be one which would serve as a blessing not only for the Jewish people but for all the nations of the world. 'The world,' he wrote, 'will be liberated through our freedom, enriched by our wealth, and enlarged through our own greatness. What we shall attempt over there for our benefit will help all mankind.'[22] In pursuance of his ideas, Herzl convened in Basle in the year 1897 the first Zionist Congress at which the programme of political Zionism was formulated in the words: 'Zionism aims to establish a publicly and legally assured home for the Jewish people in Palestine.'

No sooner was the movement launched upon its career than it encountered much opposition from both the Orthodox and the Reform. Among the Orthodox there were some who perceived in Zionism an attempt to 'fly in the face of heaven', whilst others there were who, in view of the secular outlook of most of the Zionist leaders, feared the effects of the movement upon Jewish religious life and practice. At the same time, there was a large section of Orthodox Jews, including such a distinguished Rabbinical figure as Samuel Mohilever (1824–98) who, adopting the attitude of Kalisher, joined the movement from the very outset, and under the leadership of Rabbi Isaac Jacob Reines (1834–1915) formed themselves into a party within the Zionist movement under the name of *Mizrachi*, adopting as its motto, 'The land of Israel for the people of Israel, according to the Law of Israel.'[23] On the other hand, within the Reform camp, the attitude to Zionism was one of uncompromising hostility in that the Reformers saw in the movement a public challenge in the eyes of the world to their basic conception of the Jews as a mere religious community. Then again, alike among the Orthodox and Reform, there were many who considered political Zionism to be in conflict with political loyalty to the country with which they had become identified.

Among the Rabbinic authorities who, more than any other, influenced Orthodox Jews in support of Zionism was Abraham Isaac Kook (1868–1935), the first Chief Rabbi of the Holy Land, who was indubitably the most gigantic spirit of religious Judaism in his generation. He held fast to the conviction that the national movement, notwithstanding the secular tendencies it exhibited, was, in the final analysis, religious at heart and sprang from the peculiar gift for godliness with which the Jewish people were endowed. In his view, there were two factors which conduced to the holiness of the Jewish people and their attachment to the idea of godliness. One factor was their heritage, the inner spirituality which was transmitted to them by heredity from their ancestors, and which could never disappear entirely. The second factor was the good deeds of the individual. The Messianic fervour with which the national movement was charged and the universal ideals of justice and righteousness which animated it, could only be accounted for by the spirit of the heritage of the nation which informed the Jewish masses. This made the national movement one of redemption, notwithstanding the fact that the religious conduct of the individuals was not much in evidence.

The prevalent religion among the young *Chalutzim* (pioneers) in particular, was in his opinion, not to be compared with the infidelities of the past. The young today were singularly free from all superstitions and idolatrous cults which are the real enemies of godliness and spirituality. Theirs was but a loss of sensitiveness to things divine through a lack of understanding and perception. Their estrangement from Judaism, he furthermore declared, was motivated in most cases by ideals of social justice, which they were led to imagine found no response among their elders, in view of their failure to participate in the socialist revolutionary movements that were astir in Eastern Europe. But this very quest for social righteousness was in itself the 'Way of the Lord' which Abraham the Patriarch commanded his children and his household to keep – the way of 'righteousness and justice' (Gen. 18. 19).

It was this belief which determined Rabbi Kook's relations with the non-observant Jews in Palestine. He continuously preached and practised tolerance towards them and showed them every friendship. He firmly believed that the Holy Land, as the scene of the highest manifestations of divine holiness, could not fail to exert its spiritual influence even over transgressors and sinners and that, moreover, out of these transgressors and sinners in Israel there would one day arise a movement for the return to God which was destined to embrace the whole world. In the light of these tremendous implications, Israel's restoration became a necessity for the world no less than for the Jewish people themselves. 'Israel,' he used to say, 'exerts holy influences by her very existence. Many hate her, many persecute her, but none can deny her existence, and her existence will never cease influencing human thought and cleansing humanity from its dross.' But this influence Israel can make most effective only from the Holy Land. Indeed, the fact that many ideas of Judaism have already become part of the culture of humanity should make it much easier for the Jews, once they return to the Holy Land, to exert spiritual influences upon other nations.[24]

Notwithstanding his pre-eminence and enormous influence, Rabbi Kook did not carry all the Orthodox forces with him. Fiercely opposing Zionism because it conceived the Jewish nation as a secular nation and not as 'God's Messianic people', a number of Orthodox Rabbinical and lay leaders met in Kattowitz under the Presidency of Jacob Rosenheim (b. 1871) and founded the *Agudas Israel*, with the aim of uniting the Jewish people on the basis of Torah and of solving all problems in Eretz (the land of) Israel and in the Diaspora in the spirit of the Torah.

The opponents of political Zionism, on the other hand, included also one whose entire philosophy of Judaism was based on Jewish nationalism – Asher Ginzberg (1886–1927), commonly known by his pseudonym Ahad Ha-am (One of the

People), and as the founder of 'Cultural Zionism'. For him the Jewish problem was not so much economic and political as cultural and spiritual – the progressive disintegration and dissolution of Jewish spiritual life through the increased pressure of a non-Jewish social and cultural environment. As a majority of Jews would, in any event, have to remain in the Diaspora, the establishment of a Jewish State in itself would still leave the Jewish problem unsolved. Instead, therefore, of Herzl's idea of a Jewish State where Jews of different, and unrelated, cultures and civilizations would be transferred from all parts of the world, he called for the establishment in Palestine of an autonomous Jewish community built up gradually by the devotion of an intellectual *élite* of Jews imbued with the historic culture of their people and who, freed as they would be from the necessity of conforming to alien patterns, would be able to give full play to the Jewish genius with its characteristic persistence on the primacy of absolute ethics, based on ethical equality of men and spiritual unity of mankind, as proclaimed by the Jewish prophets. Such a community situated in Israel's ancient home-land would serve as a 'spiritual centre' for all the scattered Jewries of the world, radiating to them spiritual influences and unifying them all into one new national bond. In this way the Jewish people would become equipped spiritually and culturally for the building of the ideal Jewish State in the future.

Ahad Ha-am dissociated the ethical ideas of Judaism from the theological structure of Judaism. He fixed the unique ethical bent of the Jewish mind in some unconscious force deep down in the Jewish soul. Nevertheless, true to Jewish tradition, he upheld the belief of the mission of Israel and regarded the State of the future as a necessary condition for the fulfilment of Israel's Messianic hope for the universality of mankind.

A living proponent of cultural Zionism is Martin Buber (b. 1878). In contrast, however, to Ahad Ha-am's approach which, as seen, was essentially rationalistic and secular, Buber's is mystical and religious, having its roots in Chassidism which he discovered and interpreted for the West. His attitude to Zionism is in line with the Biblical tradition that the Jewish people had from the very first laid upon them the task of building a universal Kingdom of God through the realization of righteousness and justice in the totality of the nation's communal existence. The faith in this task imparts significance to every present moment in the individual and corporate life of the Jew, giving rise to a new type of Jewish personality in which the ideals of the nation and the interests of humanity are made its own. In the light of this conception the deepest motive of Jewish nationalism is the religious-social idea, involving the cooperation of all men and nations on the basis of equality and brotherhood.

Buber's nationalism is directly related to his famous *I-thou* philosophy which conceives the nature of reality as fundamentally *social*, consisting of inter-personal relations 'between man and man', a relation expressed in moral action and in the recognition of other men as persons. This, in turn, carries with it a feeling of an 'I-thou' relation with the 'Eternal Thou', that is with God. The aim of Zionism must, therefore, be the building up of a social life directly related to God and realized in the mutual perfection of society.

Whilst all this is but a philosophic formulation of sound Jewish doctrine, Buber ignores Talmudic teaching and, in fact, does not consider the observances of Jewish practices as essential to the ideal of society which he advocates. Nor does he attempt to formulate a programme indicating how these ideas are to be realized, which accounts for the limited influence of Buber on Jewish practical life.

Whilst both Ahad Ha-am and Buber held that the realization of the Messianic ideal, in whatever form it may be conceived, required the restoration of Israel to the Land of Israel, the famous German-Jewish neo-Kantian philosopher, Hermann Cohen (1842–1918) took up a diametrically opposite position. Unlike the Reformers he recognized that the Jews were not merely a religious community, but also a nation; but he drew a sharp distinction between the concept of 'nationality' and that of 'nationhood', the former having reference to a biological and historical unity, the latter to a political unity. As the bearers of the Messianic ideal, the fulfilment of which was bound up with their continued existence, the Jewish people must preserve their coherent nationality. This nationality could be maintained within the framework of existing political states, which particularly with the broadening of the idea of the state, allow for diversity in the cultures of the people they embrace. But at the same time the quintessence of Jewish nationality must be recognized in the Messianic ideal which makes Israel a living emblem of the unity of mankind. As such, the Jewish people cannot be confined to a distinct territory nor form themselves into a separate state; and Zionism, whether in the Herzleian or the Ahad Ha-am version, in so far as it aims at the restoration of a Jewish State, stands in Cohen's view, in opposition to Jewish Messianic religion.

These controversies, centring round the idea of the Jewish State, continued in an atmosphere of growing enthusiasm among the oppressed masses in Eastern Europe, who saw in the restoration of the Jewish State the only way of escape from their miseries, and in a large measure of indifference among their more comfortable brethren in the West, who treated the whole idea as a visionaries' dream. And a dream it might well have remained but for the issuance in 1917 at the initiative of Chaim Weizmann (1874–1952) of the Balfour Declaration, in which Great Britain, acknowledging historic rights of the Jews to Palestine, pledged itself to facilitate the creation of a 'National Home' for the Jews in their ancestral land, and the international endorsement of this Declaration three years later, when the League of Nations assigned the Mandate for Palestine to Great Britain in order that she might carry out her promise.

A wave of enthusiasm sweeping through the entire Jewish world greeted the Declaration. Thousands of Jews were drawn to Palestine, bringing in their wake prosperity to that almost derelict country. They drained swamps, irrigated desert lands, fertilized the exhausted soil, set up industries, equipped Palestine with the apparatus of modern civilization. They revived the Hebrew language, built up a comprehensive educational system in the Hebrew language, and finally founded a University on Mount Scopus, a symbol of their resolve that the

National Home be built upon spiritual foundations. Yet, notwithstanding these achievements, opposition to the idea of the Jewish State still persisted in certain not uninfluential sections of Diaspora Jewry. But the dynamic of tragic events set in motion by Hitler's persecution of the Jews, and culminating, in the course of the Second World War he unleashed, in the 'liquidation', alas, of about six million Jews in Europe, a third of the entire Jewish population of the world, was stronger than all fears, theories, and philosophies, and many of the earlier fiercest opponents of the idea of the Jewish State came to be reckoned among its staunchest supporters.

The denial of immigration and settlement by Great Britain after the War to the remnants of the death-camps and gaschambers in Europe led to an acute conflict between Palestine Jewry and the Mandatory Power, which resulted in a resolution of the United Nations adopted at a session held on 29 November 1947, to terminate the Mandate of Britain and to establish in Palestine two independent states, the one Arab, the other Jewish.

Things were now moving to a climax. On the day after the First Zionist Congress in 1897, Herzl made an entry in his diary in which he foretold the rise of the Jewish State fifty years hence as a certainty.[25] On Friday afternoon, 14 May 1948, almost exactly fifty years later, Ben Gurion, the Zionist leader, called together a meeting of one hundred notables and correspondents in the Tel Aviv Museum, and declared, 'We hereby proclaim the establishment of the Jewish State in Palestine, to be called Israel.' It was 4.38 on that afternoon when the Jewish State was born.

Thus did the dream of Herzl become a reality, and Israel's hope of two thousand years enter upon its fulfilment.

NOTES

1. *Jerusalem* (Eng. trans. by M. Samuels London, 1838) II, p. 98.
2. The first Reform Congregation was established in England under the designation 'Western London Synagogue of

British Jews' in 1842. Its first Minister, David W. Marks (1811–1909), in outlining the programme of his congregation declared that while denying the authority of the Talmud, it accepted the Bible as authoritative. This proved too moderate for some of the members who, in consequence, under the leadership of Claude G. Montefiore (1858–1938) seceded to form in 1902 what came to be known as the 'Liberal movement'. Whilst the Reform and Liberal movements have since been increasing in numbers, they together form a mere minority in Anglo-Jewry which overwhelmingly belongs to the Orthodox.

3. Orthodox practice does not permit the use of musical instruments in divine service in token of the destruction of the Temple at which instruments of music formed a distinctive feature of the worship (cf. Psalm 137. 5).

4. See p. 168.

5. See p. 169.

6. See p. 120 n. 4.

7. See p. 165.

8. See p. 109 n. 8.

9. M. Kaplan, *Judaism as a Civilization* (New York, 1934), p. 397.

10. See Sholem Spiegel, op. cit., p. 57.

11. Named in memory of Rabbi Isaac Elchanan Spektor of Kovno (1817–96), one of the foremost Rabbinical figures of his generation and an authority of world-wide repute, famous for his *Responsa* in which he evolved new principles of law.

12. See p. 295.

13. See p. 204.

14. See p. 267.

15. Quoted by Jacob B. Agus, *Guideposts in Modern Judaism* (New York, 1954), p. 26.

16. *Rome and Jerusalem* (Engl. Trans. by M. Waxman, New York, 1943), p. 77.

17. op. cit., p. 146.

18. op. cit. p. 108.

19. Quoted by Sh. Spiegel, *op. cit.*, p. 216.

20. Lit., 'Lovers of Zion.'

21. See Isaiah 2. 5.

22. Quoted by J. Fraenkel, *Theodore Herzl*, London, 1946, p. 60.

23. Mizrachi is an abbreviation of *Merkaz Ruchani* (Spiritual

Centre), an idea which underlies the spiritual religious aim of religious Zionism, and at the same time is derived from *Mizrach* (East), symbolizing the origin of Jewish tradition and the faithful love of the Holy Land.

24. See I. Epstein, *Abraham Yitzhak Hacohen Kook* (1951) p. 19.
25. 'If I were to sum up the Basle Congress in a single phrase – what I would not dare to make public – I would say: In Basle I created the Jewish State. Were I to say this aloud, I would be greeted by universal laughter, but perhaps five years hence, in any case, certainly fifty years hence, everyone will perceive it.' – Quoted by A. Bein, *Theodore Herzl* (Eng. trans. by Maurice Samuel, Philadelphia, 1945) p. 243.

CHAPTER 22

THE JEWISH STATE AND JUDAISM

THE rebirth of the Jewish State after a submergence of about two thousand years is one of the great miracles of the ages. The success that has crowned Israel's struggle for national independence and the amazing sequence of events that led to this consummation will remain to the unbiased historian one of the inexplicable episodes in the annals of mankind. Miraculous, too, must be accounted the ingathering, in the course of the first decade of the State's existence, of one million destitute exiles from about sixty different countries, and their integration into the economic, social, and cultural structure of the country. No less astonishing and unprecedented is the rapid development of the new State, the expansion of its agricultural settlements and industries, the exploitation of its resources, and the creation, out of what was once a wilderness, of a modern welfare state with a rich social and cultural life, with schools, universities, research institutes, social services, labour organizations, hospitals, libraries, museums.

On the cultural side, the creative activity of the State is evident in the growth of its fine arts, music, poetry, drama, but particularly in the great revival of the Hebrew language and literature. In the religious sphere, too, though Israel is a democracy where religion is a matter of choice, and though indeed widespread non-observance is noticeable, there has been notable progress. Evidence of this is the fact that much of what constitutes the Jewish way of life has found and is finding its way more and more into the fabric of the Jewish State. Saturday is the national day of rest. On this day all government offices are closed, no ship loads or unloads at Israeli ports; no aircraft lands or takes off; no train runs. Shops and cinemas are closed; public bus services are suspended. What applies to the Sabbath applies equally, *mutatis mutandis*, to the religious festivals. The dietary laws, Biblical and Rabbinic, are strictly observed in the Army, as well as in other public institutions and services under government control, such as the police, schools, hospitals, and prisons. The law of personal status (marriage and divorce) conforms to traditional Jewish law and is under the exclusive jurisdiction of the Rabbinical Courts, except for the non-Jewish population who have recourse to their respective religious tribunals.

State religious schools cater for the wishes of observant parents. A new religious University, named after the late Mizrachi leader Meir Bar Ilan (1880–1949) has been established in Ramat Gan near Tel-Aviv. Nor has there been since the destruction of the Temple such a large concentration of Torah and Jewish learning in Israel as there is today. There are as many as 160 Talmudical colleges (*Yeshivoth*) with over seven thousand students, apart from many other religious schools and seats of Jewish learning. Many leading Rabbinic sages from all parts of the world have taken up residence in the State of Israel, all contributing to the enrichment of spiritual life and to the fostering of religious knowledge throughout the length and breadth of the country. There is also a very significant literary production in the religious field. Books and publications on every aspect of Jewish thought and teaching are appearing in quick succession, transmitting the wisdom of the ages to the sons and daughters of the new Israel.

At the same time it should be noted that there is no interference whatsoever in the private life, beliefs, and practices of the individual, and that the link between 'Religion and State' in Israel is no greater than it is in most Western countries, including Great Britain. Israel has as yet no constitution, but in its proclamation of Statehood, full religious freedom is guaranteed to all citizens of whatever creed. In Israel there is no State Religion. Yet despite the religious freedom obtaining in the country, the majority even of the non-observant elements, which number about fifty per cent of the population, are not unaware of the fact that, in view of Jewish history and the spiritual ties between Israel and the Jews in the Diaspora, such public association with Jewish tradition is an indispensable requisite for the maintenance of world Jewish unity.

Attachment to Israel's ancient religious heritage is particularly fostered by the general study of the Bible. Speaking what is basically the language of the Bible, and living and moving in an atmosphere saturated with Biblical associations, the men and women in Israel find the study of the Bible natural and easy. Children from a tender age are steeped in the Biblical lore, and whatever methods may be employed in teaching them, such a knowledge cannot fail to make an indelible impression on their minds.

Ethically speaking, the State of Israel has already shown qualities of the highest order not only in its readiness to make the greatest sacrifices in order to absorb in its midst hundreds of thousands of Jews and Jewesses from various continents, but also in the large measure of good-will and brotherly feelings it exhibits towards its Arab citizens, notwithstanding the continued strains and hazards to which it is being subjected in consequence of the implacable hostility of its Arab neighbours.

While the physical suffering of the Jews and their miserable plight in Central and Eastern Europe as well as other lands have driven the Jews to these achievements, there is no denying that the basic urge behind this transformation of the people and the land has been of the spiritual order which, as indicated in this work, has its roots in the divine promise to the patriarch Abraham at the beginning of Jewish history, and has always been central to Jewish existence and being. Eloquent expression to this truth was given by Ben Gurion, the Prime Minister of Israel, when, in addressing the meeting of the Zionist General Council held in Jerusalem in July 1957, he declared: 'The suffering of the Jewish people in the Diaspora, whether economic, political, or cultural, has been a powerful factor in bringing about the immigrations to the Land of Israel. But it was only the Messianic vision which made that factor fruitful and guided it towards the creation of the State. Suffering alone is degrading, oppression destructive; and if we had not inherited from the prophets the Messianic vision of redemption, the suffering of the Jewish people in the Diaspora would have led to their extinction. The ingathering of the exiles, that is the return of the Jewish people to its land, is the beginning of the realization of the Messianic vision.'

What is meant by this Messianic vision is that just as Abraham's deliverance from Ur of the Chaldees and the exodus from Egypt, were identified respectively in the mind of Abraham and Israel with divine purposes and ends,[1] so the restoration of the Jewish people as a unified political group after a dispersion of 2,000 years, marked by unparalleled persecutions and sufferings, is identified in the mind of the Jew of today with the purposes of God for Israel, and through Israel for the whole of humanity. Down all the ages the Jew has felt deeply his integral relationship with mankind as a whole. In the self-same spirit the new-born Jewish State feels that the vindication of the Jewish faith and hope of thousands of years is destined to prove of extreme significance for all nations in a world torn by crises, tensions, and the fear of wholesale destruction.

Only time can tell whether the rebirth of the State signifies the beginning of the realization of this Messianic vision. There is, however, no question that the influence of the Jewish state on world Jewry has been profound. It has not only imparted to many Jewries a new dignity, and a sense of moral and physical security, such as they had hitherto not possessed, but has also inspired a renaissance of Hebrew culture, given rise to a deeper appreciation of Jewish values, stimulated Jewish studies, and intensified Jewish spiritual loyalties. Among the Reform it has led to a restoration of many Jewish national traditions and religious practices which they had discarded, and among the Orthodox it has inspired a greater confidence in promoting their principles. Everywhere it has tended to secure Jewish solidarity and to foster among Jews a sense of unity based on their common historical and cultural traditions and their common spiritual aspirations for the future. It is thus not fantastic to expect that sooner or later even those children of the House of Israel who are still estranged from their people will come to draw fresh inspiration from Zion and Jerusalem whence the Torah and the word of the Lord will go forth, as foretold by the prophets of old.

There are many, indeed, who profoundly believe that after a period of adjustment, consolidation, and peace the Jewish people will recover in their ancient land those creative spiritual energies which marked the grand epochs in their earlier history. At all times the noblest Jewish minds have seen Jewish nationalism not as an end in itself, but as a means for the maintenance of Judaism and its glorious Messianic ideals of perfection for the benefit of the whole human race. To the fulfilment of these ideals the Jewish people, by their unquenchable faith and their strong fidelity to the Torah and its teachings, have made a unique contribution – made it through trials and sufferings which have no parallel in human history; and they hope the day will come when these ideals will become a reality and be accepted universally. This hope is cherished by all Jews, from the most secular nationalists to the adherents of extreme Reform. Though differing in approach and method, they all, influenced and sustained by the loyalty and example of the followers of four thousand years' revelation and tradition, are united in seeking to advance towards that same divinely assigned national goal – the establishment of the Messianic kingdom, which is none other than the Kingdom of God, among the sons of men.

NOTE

1. See pp. 13 and 21.

BIBLIOGRAPHY

This bibliography which supplements that covered already in the notes as well as in the main body of the text is limited to books available in English. It is far from being exhaustive, but is intended for those who wish to pursue further the study of the individual subjects discussed in the work chapter by chapter, and as such also includes works which represent points of view different to those adopted in this book. For fuller information the following works are recommended:

[Abbreviations: J.P.S.A. – Jewish Publication Society of America (Philadelphia); J.T.S.A. – Jewish Theological Seminary of America (New York); and J.C.P. – Jews' College Publications (London).]

Baeck, L. *Essence of Judaism*. New York (Schocken Books), 1948.

Baron, S. W. *A Social and Religious History of the Jews*. Columbia University, revised ed., 1952–7, vols. I-V.

Bevan, E. R. and Ch. Singer. *The Legacy of Israel*. Oxford University Press, 1928.

Finkelstein, L. *The Jews: their History, Culture and Religion*, 4 vols. New York (Harper), 2nd ed., 1955.

Goldstein, M. *The Religion Grows*. New York (Longmans, Green), 1936.

Grayzel, S. *History of the Jews*. Philadelphia (P.S.A.), 1952.

Hertz, J. H. *A Book of Jewish Thoughts*. Oxford University Press (many editions).

Hertz, J. H. *The Pentateuch and Haftorahs*. London (Soncino Press), 1947.

Joseph, M. *Judaism as Creed and Life*. London (Routledge), 1958.

Josephus, *Works*. 4 vols. London (Loeb Classical Library), 1925–30.

Kastein, A. M. *History and Destiny of the Jews*. London (Lane), 1933.

Margolis, M. L. and Marx, A. *A History of the Jewish People*. Philadelphia (J.P.S.A.), 1927.

Roth, C. *A Short History of the Jewish People*. London (Illustrated ed., East & West Library), 1953.

Schechter, S. *Studies in Judaism*. Philadelphia (J.P.S.A.), 3 series, 1896, 1908, 1924.

BIBLIOGRAPHY

For the Hebrew Scriptures students should consult:

(a) *The Holy Scriptures according to the Masoretic Text.* Philadelphia (J.P.S.A.), 1947, and Cambridge University Press, 1958.
(b) *Soncino Books of the Bible*, ed. by A. Cohen. London (Soncino Press), 1949 etc.

For reference works on all subjects appertaining to Judaism the following are most useful:

Encyclopaedia Britannica, articles on 'Judaism', 'Jews', 'Jewish Philosophy' etc., 12 vols. London Printing 1958.
Encyclopedia of Jewish Knowledge. 1 vol., New York, 1934.
Jewish Encyclopedia. 12 vols., New York (Funk & Wagnalls), 1916.
Universal Jewish Encyclopedia. 10 vols., New York, 1948.
Vallentine's Jewish Encyclopaedia. London (Shapiro, Vallentine), 1938.

CHAPTER I

Albright, W. F. *Archaeology and the Religion of Israel.* Baltimore (Johns Hopkins), 1953.
Jack, J. W. *The Date of the Exodus.* Edinburgh (T. & T. Clark), 1925.
Woolley, C. L. *Ur of the Chaldees.* Pelican Books, 1938.
Yahuda, A. S. *The Accuracy of the Bible.* London (Heinemann), 1934.

CHAPTERS 2–3

Epstein, I. *The Faith of Judaism.* London (Soncino Press), 1954, Ch. 14.
Epstein, I. *Judaism.* London (Epworth Press), revised ed., 1945.
Snaith, N. H. *The Distinctive Ideas of the Old Testament.* London (Epworth Press), 1944.
Wright, G. Ernest. *The Old Testament Attitude toward Civilization*, in *Theology Today.* Princeton, 1948, Vol. v, pp. 3–7 ff.

CHAPTERS 4–7

Albright, W. F. *From the Stone Age to Christianity.* New York (Doubleday). Second ed. with a new Introduction, 1957.
Caiger, S. L. *Lives of the Prophets.* London (S.P.C.K.), 1949.
Garstang, J. *The Foundations of Bible History.* New York (R. R. Smith), 1931.

BIBLIOGRAPHY

Lods, A. *Israel from its Beginnings to the Middle of the Eighth Century*. London (Kegan Paul), 1932.

Orlinsky, Harry M. *Ancient Israel*, Ithaca, New York (Cornell University Press), 1954.

Oesterley, W. O. E. & T. H. Robinson. *A History of Israel*. Oxford (Clarendon Press), Vol. 1, 1932.

Robertson, E. *The Old Testament Problem*. Manchester University Press, 1950.

Wiener, Harold M. *Early Hebrew History*. London (Robert Scott), 1924.

CHAPTERS 8–9

Buttenwieser, M. *The Prophets of Israel*. New York (Macmillan), 1914.

Epstein, I. *Bible Teachings in our Times*. London (Jewish Educational Publications), 1944.

Hoschander, J. *Priests and Prophets*. New York (J.T.S.A.), 1938.

Lods, A. *The Prophets and the Rise of Judaism*. London (Kegan Paul), 1937.

Mattuck, I. *The Thoughts of the Prophets*. London (Allen & Unwin), 1953.

Oesterley, W.O.E. *The Psalms*, 2 vols. London (S.P.C.K.), 1939.

Rankin, O. S. *Israel's Wisdom Literature*. Edinburgh (T. & T. Clark), 1936.

Wiener, Harold M. *The Prophets of Israel in History and Criticism*. London (Robert Scott), 1923.

CHAPTERS 10–11

Bentwich, N. *Hellenism*. Philadelphia (J.P.S.A.), 1919.

Bevan, E. R. *Jerusalem under the High Priests*. London (Arnold), 1924.

Box, G. H. *Judaism in the Greek Period* (Clarendon Bible V). Oxford, 1932.

Buechler, A. *Types of Jewish Palestinian Piety from 70 B.C.E.– 70 C.E.* J.C.P., Oxford University Press, 1926.

Oesterley, W. O. E. *An Introduction to the Apocrypha*. London (S.P.C.K.), 1935.

Herford, Travers T. *The Pharisees*. London (Allen & Unwin), 1924.

Herford, Travers T. *Talmud and Apocrypha*. London (Soncino Press), 1933.

Parkes, James. *Judaism and Christianity*. London (Gollancz), 1948.

Radin, M. *The Jews among the Greeks and Romans*. Philadelphia (J.P.S.A.), 1915.

Zeitlin, S. *The History of the Second Jewish Commonwealth*. Philadelphia (Dropsie College), 1933.

DEAD SEA SCROLLS

Allegro, J. M. *The Dead Sea Scrolls*. Pelican Books, 1956.

Burrows, M. *The Dead Sea Scrolls*. New York (Viking Press), 1955.

Burrows, M. *More Light on the Dead Sea Scrolls*. New York (Viking Press), 1958.

Gaster, Theodor H. *The Scriptures of the Dead Sea Sect in English Translation*. London (Secker & Warburg), 1957.

Yadin, Yigael. *Message of the Dead Sea Scrolls*. Weidenfeld & Nicolson, 1957.

CHAPTER 12

Bokser, Ben Zion. *Pharisaic Judaism in Transition*. New York (Bloch), 1935.

Finkelstein, L. *The Pharisees*, 2 vols. Philadelphia (J.P.S.A.), 1938.

Finkelstein, L. *Akiba: Scholar, Saint and Martyr*. New York (Covici Friede), 1936.

Roberts, B. J. *Old Testament Text and Versions*. Cardiff University, 1951.

Wüerthwein, Ernst. *The Text of Old Testament* (translated from the German by Peter R. Ackroyd). Oxford (Blackwell), 1957.

Zeitlin, S. *A Historical Study of the Canonization of the Hebrew Scriptures*, in *Proceedings of the American Academy for Jewish Research*. Philadelphia (J.P.S.A.), 1931–2, pp. 121–58.

CHAPTER 13

Danby, H. *The Mishnah*, translated from the Hebrew with introduction and brief explanatory notes. Oxford University Press, 1933.

Epstein, I. (editor). *The Babylonian Talmud in English*, with Introductions, Translation and Commentary, Vols. I–XXXVI. London (Soncino Press), 1935–53.

Freedman, H., & Simon, M. (editors). *Midrash Rabbah*, translation with brief notes, Vols. I–X. London (Soncino Press), 1939.

Ginzberg, L. *On Jewish Law and Lore*, (Essay: 'Introduction to the Babylonian Talmud'). Philadelphia (J.P.S.A.), 1955.

Lauterbach, J. Z. *Midrash and Mishnah*. Philadelphia (J.P.S.A.), 1941.

Strack, H. L. *Introduction to the Talmud and Midrash*. Philadelphia (J.P.S.A.), 1931.

CHAPTERS 14–16

Abrahams, Israel. *Studies in Pharisaism and the Gospels*, 2 Vols. Cambridge University Press, 1st Series 1917; 2nd Series 1924.

Cohen, A. *Everyman's Talmud*. London (Dent), 1932.

Epstein, I. *The Faith of Judaism*. London (Soncino Press), 1954.

Epstein, I. *The Jewish Way of Life*. London (Goldston), 1947.

Epstein, I. *Judaism*. London (Epworth Press), revised ed., 1945

Friedländer, M. *The Jewish Religion*. London (Shapiro, Vallentine), 1953.

Hertz, J. H. *The Authorised Daily Prayer Book, with Commentary*. London (Soncino Press), 1947.

Kaddushin, M. *The Rabbinic Mind*. New York (J.T.S.A.), 1952.

Lazarus, M. *Ethics of Judaism*, translated from the German by Henrietta Szold. Philadelphia (J.P.S.A.), 1901.

Lehrman, S. M. *The Jewish Festivals*. London (Shapiro, Vallentine), 1953.

Marmorstein, A. *The Old Rabbinic Doctrine of God*. J.C.P., Oxford University Press, Vol. I, 1927; Vol. II, 1931.

Montefiore, C. G. and Loewe, Herbert J. *A Rabbinic Anthology, Selected and arranged wih Comments and Introduction*. London (Macmillan), 1938.

Moore, G. F. *Judaism in the First Centuries of the Christian Era*. 3 Vols. Harvard University Press, 1930–2.

Singer, S. (editor and translator). *Authorised Daily Prayer Book* (many editions).

   A Companion to (Singer's edition of) the Authorised Daily Prayer Book, by Israel Abrahams. London (Eyre & Spottiswoode), revised ed., 1922.

CHAPTER 17

Abrahams, I. *Short History of Jewish Literature*. London (Unwin), 1906, chs. v–xii.

Ginzberg, L. *Geonica I: The Geonim and their Halakic Writings*. New York (J.T.S.A.), 1902.

Idelsohn, A. Z. *Jewish Liturgy and its Development*. New York (Henry Holt), 1932.

Malter, H. *Saadya Gaon: his Life and Works*. Philadelphia (J.P.S.A.), 1927.

Mann, J. *The Jews in Egypt and in Palestine under the Fatimid Caliphs*, 2 vols. Oxford, 1920–2.

Nemoy, Leon. *Karaite Anthology*. Yale University Press, 1952.

Winton, Thomas D. 'The Textual Criticism of the Old Testament' in *The Old Testament and Modern Study* (editor H. H. Rowley). Oxford, 1951.

Waxman, M. *A History of Jewish Literature*, Vol. I, New York (Bloch), 1930.

Zimmels, H. J. *Ashkenazim and Sephardim*. J.C.P., Oxford University Press, 1958.

CHAPTER 18

Cohen, A. *The Teaching of Maimonides*. London (Routledge), 1919.

Epstein, I. (editor). *Maimonides VIII Centenary Memorial Volume*. London (Soncino Press), 1935.

Husik, I. *A History of Medieval Jewish Philosophy*. Philadelphia (J.P.S.A.), revised ed. 1946.

Roth, L. *Moses Maimonides: The Guide for the Perplexed*. London (Hutchinson), 1948.

Waxman, M. *A History of Jewish Literature*. Vols. I–II. New York (Bloch), 1930–3.

TRANSLATIONS

Albo, Joseph. *Sefer ha-Ikkarim*, edited and translated by I. Husik, 5 vols. Philadelphia (J.P.S.A.), 1929–35.

Bachya Ibn Pakuda. *Duties of the Heart*, by M. Hyamson (5 vols.). New York (Bloch), 1925–45.

Yehudah ha-Levi. 'Kitab al Khazari' (*Kuzari*), translated by H. Hirschfeld. Cailingold, 1931.

Maimonides, Moses. *Guide for the Perplexed*, translation and comprehensive introduction by M. Friedländer, London (Routledge), 1919.

Saadya Gaon. *The Book of Doctrines and Opinions*, by S. Rosenblatt. Yale University Press, 1948.

ABRIDGED TRANSLATIONS WITH INTRODUCTION
AND COMMENTS

Judah ha-Levi. *The Kuzari*, by I. Heinemann. London (East & West Library), 1947

Moses Maimonides. *The Guide for the Perplexed*, by C. Rabin. London (East & West Library), 1952.

Saadya Gaon. *The Book of Doctrines and Beliefs*, by A. Altmann. London (East & West Library), 1946.

CHAPTER 19

Abelson, J. *Jewish Mysticism*, London (Bell), 1913.

Ginsburg, Ch. D. *The Kabbalah*. London (Longmans, Green), 1865.

Ginzberg, L. 'Cabala' in *Jewish Encyclopedia*. Vol. III.

Müller, E. *History of Jewish Mysticism*. London (East & West Library), 1946.

Waxman, M. *History of Jewish Literature*, Vol. II. New York (Bloch), 1933.

TRANSLATION

The Zohar, translated by H. Sperling, M. Simon and P. Levertoff. London (Soncino Press), 1931–4.

CHAPTER 20

Abrahams, I. *Hebrew Ethical Wills*, 2 vols. Philadelphia (J.P.S.A.), 1920.

Bettan, Israel. *Studies in Jewish Preaching*. Cincinnatti (Hebrew Union College), 1931.

Buber, M. *Tales of the Hasidim*, London (Thames & Hudson), 1956.

Buber, M. *Jewish Mysticism and the Legends of the Baal Shem*, translated from the German by Lucy Cohen. London (Dent), 1931.

Epstein, I. 'The Rabbinic Tradition' in *The Jewish Heritage*, edited by E. Levine. London (Vallentine, Mitchell). 1955.

Ginzberg, L. 'Codification of the Law' in *Jewish Encyclopedia*, Vol. VII, *s.v.* Law.

Ginzberg, L. *Students, Scholars and Saints*. Philadelphia (J.S.P.A.) 1928.

Horodezky, S. A. *Leaders of Hassidism*. London (Hasefer), 1930.

Waxman, M. *A History of Jewish Literature*. Vols. II–III. New York (Bloch), 1933–6.

CHAPTER 21

Cohen, I. *A Short History of Zionism*. London (F. Muller), 1951.

Friedman, M. *Martin Buber*. London (Routledge), 1955.

BIBLIOGRAPHY

Greenstone, Julius H. *The Messiah Idea in Jewish History.* Philadelphia (J.P.S.A.), 1943.

Grunfeld, I. *Eternal Judaism,* 2 vols. Selected Essays from writings of S. R. Hirsch. London (Soncino Press), 1957.

Halkin, S. *Modern Hebrew Literature.* New York (Schocken Books), 1950.

Heller, J. *The Zionist Idea.* London (Joint Zionist Publications Committee), 1947, and revised ed. New York (Schocken), 1949.

Hirsch, S. R. *The Nineteen Letters of Ben Uziel,* translated from the German by B. Drachman, New York (Funk, & Wagnalls), 1899.

Klausner, J. *A History of Modern Hebrew Literature,* translated by H. Danby. London (Cailingold), 1932.

Mattuck, I. *The Essentials of Liberal Judaism.* London (Routledge), 1947.

Philipson, David. *The Reform Movement in Judaism.* London (Macmillan), 1907.

Raisin, M. *The Haskalah Movement in Russia.* Philadelphia (J.P.S.A.), 1913.

Reitlinger, Gerald. *The Final Solution.* London (Vallentine, Mitchell), 1953.

Rosemarin, T. W. *Religion of Reason: Hermann Cohen's System of Religious Philosophy.* New York (Bloch), 1936.

Simon, L. *Ahad Ha-Am: Essays, Letters and Memoirs.* London (East & West Library), 1946.

Sokolow, N. *History of Zionism,* 2 vols. London (Longmans, Green), 1919.

Waxman, M. *A History of Jewish Literature,* Vol. III.

CHAPTER 22

Cohen, I. *The Rebirth of Israel.* London (Goldston), 1952.

Parkes, J. *End of an Exile.* London (Vallentine, Mitchell), 1954.

Patai, R. *Israel between East & West.* Philadelphia (J.P.S.A.), 1953.

Sacher, H. *Israel: Establishment of a State.* London (Weidenfeld & Nicolson), 1952.

Rushbrook, William L. F. *The State of Israel.* London (Faber & Faber), 1957.

Waxman, M. *A History of Jewish Literature,* Vol. IV (revised ed.). New York (Bloch), 1947.

INDEX

INDEX

334

FOR THE BEST IN PAPERBACKS, LOOK FOR THE 🐧

In every corner of the world, on every subject under the sun, Penguin represents quality and variety – the very best in publishing today.

For complete information about books available from Penguin – including Pelicans, Puffins, Peregrines and Penguin Classics – and how to order them, write to us at the appropriate address below. Please note that for copyright reasons the selection of books varies from country to country.

In the United Kingdom: Please write to *Dept E.P., Penguin Books Ltd, Harmondsworth, Middlesex, UB7 0DA*

In the United States: Please write to *Dept BA, Penguin, 299 Murray Hill Parkway, East Rutherford, New Jersey 07073*

In Canada: Please write to *Penguin Books Canada Ltd, 2801 John Street, Markham, Ontario L3R 1B4*

In Australia: Please write to the *Marketing Department, Penguin Books Australia Ltd, P.O. Box 257, Ringwood, Victoria 3134*

In New Zealand: Please write to the *Marketing Department, Penguin Books (NZ) Ltd, Private Bag, Takapuna, Auckland 9*

In India: Please write to *Penguin Overseas Ltd, 706 Eros Apartments, 56 Nehru Place, New Delhi, 110019*

In Holland: Please write to *Penguin Books Nederland B.V., Postbus 195, NL–1380AD Weesp, Netherlands*

In Germany: Please write to *Penguin Books Ltd, Friedrichstrasse 10–12, D–6000 Frankfurt Main 1, Federal Republic of Germany*

In Spain: Please write to *Longman Penguin España, Calle San Nicolas 15, E–28013 Madrid, Spain*

In France: Please write to *Penguin Books Ltd, 39 Rue de Montmorency, F-75003, Paris, France*

In Japan: Please write to *Longman Penguin Japan Co Ltd, Yamaguchi Building, 2–12–9 Kanda Jimbocho, Chiyoda-Ku, Tokyo 101, Japan*